$78.50

Literary Celebrity, Gender, and Victorian Authorship, 1850–1914

Literary Celebrity, Gender, and Victorian Authorship, 1850–1914

Alexis Easley

UNIVERSITY OF DELAWARE PRESS
Newark

Published by University of Delaware Press
Co-published with The Rowman & Littlefield Publishing Group, Inc.
4501 Forbes Boulevard, Suite 200, Lanham, Maryland 20706
www.rlpgbooks.com

Estover Road, Plymouth PL6 7PY, United Kingdom

British Library Cataloguing in Publication Information Available

Library of Congress Cataloging-in-Publication Data
Library of Congress Cataloguing-in-Publication Data on file under LC#2010020827
ISBN: 978-1-61149-016-9 (cl. : alk. paper)
eISBN: 978-1-61149-017-6

♾™ The paper used in this publication meets the minimum requirements of American National Standard for Information Sciences—Permanence of Paper for Printed Library Materials, ANSI/NISO Z39.48-1992.

Printed in the United States of America

For Brett, Maurice, and Enid Fried

Contents

Acknowledgments

I AM INDEBTED TO MY HUSBAND, BRETT FRIED, WHO IS ALWAYS MY first reader and best critic. I am also grateful to my colleagues in the Research Society for Victorian Periodicals who provided valuable feedback on my work, especially Maria Frawley, Laurel Brake, Linda Peterson, and Linda Hughes. I would like to thank Jim Curley, Pamela Corpron Parker, Lynette Felber, Mary Spongberg, Barbara Todd, and Geoffrey and Linda Skippings for their assistance as I researched individual chapters of the manuscript. Fernando Sanchez and Shandi Wagner provided valuable editorial support as I prepared the final manuscript for publication. Talia Nadir, JoAnn Toussaint, and Faith Bonitz of the University of St. Thomas (UST) O'Shaughnessy-Frey Library provided crucial support for this project as did Pamela Nice and Susan Chaplin of the UST Center for Faculty Development. I am also grateful to Marisa Kelly, Dean of the College of Arts and Sciences, for her generous financial assistance. Finally, I would like to thank my colleagues in the English Department at UST for their collegiality and encouragement as I brought this project to completion.

Introduction

WHY DID VICTORIANS BECOME OBSESSED WITH LITERARY CELEBRITIES in the second half of the nineteenth century? How was the development of the discourse on literary celebrity linked to changing conceptions of gender, national identity, and canonicity? *Literary Celebrity, Gender, and Victorian Authorship* addresses these questions by examining the instrumental role of popular print culture in shaping our understanding of the relationship between literary celebrity and national identity from 1850 to 1914. With the proliferation of new media—travel guidebooks, mass-market newspapers, illustrated periodicals, and gossip columns—came a corresponding obsession with the lives, homes, and bodies of literary celebrities. Located within expanding networks of representation, authors came to be viewed as exemplary men and women who embodied the anxieties and ideals of modern life. At the same time, they were viewed as the engines of popular print culture whose works met the burgeoning demand for literary commodities.

The interest in literary celebrities was fueled by the desire to create a coherent national history, a narrative that would justify and facilitate social progress. By retelling history and marking the landscape with memorials to great writers past, the cult of celebrity fostered an illusion of stability during a time of rapid social change. Although celebrity culture was premised on reconstruction of the past, it was also focused on the ephemeral world of the day-to-day literary marketplace. The demand for new literary products and personalities was met with a proliferation of magazines and newspapers focused on gossip and sensation. The gender, sexuality, and marital arrangements of popular authors were of particular interest throughout the second half of the nineteenth century, a fascination that reflected broader questioning of the conventionalities associated with middle-class domestic life. Popular interest in the lives of literary celebrities provided new opportunities for employment in emerging culture industries, especially for women. Because women were expected to take an active interest in the homes and lives of others, they were able to find employment as historic preservationists and lifestyle newspaper columnists. Women also manipulated the new celebrity media as a way of promoting their own careers, advocating for social causes, and retelling history from a woman's perspective.

Victorian celebrity culture was a vast field of intersecting texts and professional activities focused on exciting interest in the bodies, lives, and homes of popular authors. Yet the discourse on literary celebrity was as much premised on what could be seen and known about popular authors as it was focused on the mysterious and unknowable aspects of their lives and works. Although famous writers came to represent both the continuity of the past and the dilemmas of the present, they remained essentially enigmatic. The lack of complete knowledge about authors' lives and homes justified the search for further biographical details and thus fueled the new media—tourist guidebooks, exposés, photo essays, and gossip columns—that offered incomplete answers to an increasingly curious public.

For women writers, obscurity was required to maintain social respectability, yet women found it necessary to balance privacy with visibility to enhance public interest in their lives and work. Too little exposure could mean invisibility in a fiercely competitive literary marketplace, yet too much exposure could mean being cast aside as the latest vulgar literary fad. Even with these contradictions inherent in the discourse on celebrity, women were remarkably successful in their self-marketing techniques. Yet the high-profile visibility associated with popular authorship at the fin de siècle made it difficult for women to establish a place for their work within the emerging literary canon. As women were featured in interviews and profiles, they were increasingly associated with the ephemerality of the popular press and were often excluded from emerging narratives of British literary history, which defined great literature as having timeless appeal. Press attention seemed to have a more positive effect on men's literary careers because they were expected to construct public identities. The secrets and scandals associated with male authors' lives most often served as an incitement to discourse rather than as a precursor to marginalization within the emerging canon. Nevertheless, in some cases, media exposure had the effect of sensationalizing and pathologizing the bodies of male authors. With the development of protofeminist criticism and historiography, the life stories of male writers were often used to expose unhealthy domestic relationships and to imagine ideal forms of British masculinity.

Literary Celebrity is divided into three sections: celebrity and literary tourism, celebrity and historiography, and celebrity and fin de siècle print culture. The chapters included under these major headings incorporate a wide range of genres and texts, including autobiographies, contemporary histories, travel guidebooks, celebrity periodicals, literary magazines, medical journals, and the publications of literary and spiritualist societies. The chapters in the first section explore the practice of literary tourism in Britain from midcentury to the 1910s, emphasizing the importance of gender and nationalism in the interpretation of literary homes and landscapes. Through their encounters with the homes and haunts of famous writers, literary tourists hoped to experience the Britain of the past, which was nostalgically preserved as the home of the British author, and the Britain of the present, which was carefully marked with sites of cultural interest. Literary tourists found truth on an individual basis through intimate encounters with personally meaningful authors and places. At the same time, they situated their individual experiences within a network of broader national and cultural meanings.

The growth of the literary tourism industry was inseparable from the practice of bio-geographical criticism that emerged in the periodical press during the same period. The periodical press was a key medium within a dense network of discourses that defined "the author" in increasingly personal and invasive ways. It thus linked literary texts to specific biographical and geographical details that could be experienced virtually, through reading periodicals and other texts, or in actuality, by handling personal relics or viewing literary shrines. Periodical reviews constructed a sense of British national identity by locating the literary shrines of London and those of Great Britain more generally at the center of a growing transatlantic literary culture. Yet they simultaneously revealed the inevitable fracturing of the British claim to cultural centrality and exposed the unknowability of the author as a literary construct and multimedia enterprise.

The first chapter, titled "The Virtual City: Literary Tourism and the Construction of 'Dickens's London,'" explores the development of literary tourism focused on visiting the shrines associated with the works of Charles Dickens. During the late nineteenth and early twentieth centuries, journalists returned again and again to Dickens's novels as a way of reconstituting the cultural meanings of the urban landscape. As critics attempted to define works of permanent value through the process of canon formation, they simultaneously attempted to identify "timeless" literary shrines in the city. In the eyes of many critics and journalists, Dickens's novels had assigned permanent cultural meanings to London's landmarks, even if the spaces themselves seemed always in danger of disappearing entirely due to suburban sprawl and urban renewal. As long as the "real" London remained in Dickens's oeuvre, so, too, would the nation's image of itself remain untarnished and unchangeable. The fact that the landmarks in Dickens's London were difficult to locate with complete assurance produced both frustration and pleasure as tourists searched for meaning in a city that was increasingly meaningless, for certainty in a city that was increasingly uncertain. The act of literary tourism relied on the assumption that the literary text was "real" and the city was "unreal"; that is, it assumed that the city could only be made authentic through careful reading, a process of collapsing the world of the literary text onto the world of the urban environment. By referring to the literary text as a marker of the real, the literary tourist constructed an imagined city that promised to embody a cohesive national heritage and culture. Key to the nation's understanding of itself was the concept of domestic masculinity— the idea that male authors such as Dickens embodied middle-class domestic values. After Dickens's death in 1870, guidebooks and periodicals thus became increasingly focused on imagining the writer as an ideal domestic patriarch.

The identification of nationally significant literary shrines and landscapes was premised on gender ideology. Male writers such as William Shakespeare, Walter Scott, William Wordsworth, and Charles Dickens were readily assimilated into narratives of British literary history. As the literary tourism industry developed in London during the late nineteenth and early twentieth centuries, three significant literary shrines devoted to male authors were erected by literary societies: Carlyle's House (1895), Dickens's House (1925), and Keats's House (1925). Nineteenth-century women writers were more difficult to locate on the literary map of London. Accounts of their lives in an urban context often depict them as spectral presences, neither fully present nor absent within the city landscapes they once inhabited. Chapter 2, titled "The Haunting of Victorian London: Christina Rossetti, Elizabeth Barrett Browning, and

George Eliot," examines the spectral metaphors associated with the discourse on literary tourism. The authors of literary guidebooks referred to the "ghosts" of authors and explored their "haunts" as a way of constructing a unique British cultural heritage. However, at the same time, use of spectral metaphors emphasized the difficulty of knowing or interpreting the past. The idea of the literary "ghost" had important implications for women writers because domestic ideology mandated their invisibility in the public realm. In literary guides to London, the spectrality of women authors is particularly apparent. Even though most women writers of the period lived and worked in London, there were no homes clearly identified as literary shrines. Nevertheless, journalists scoured the city, searching for the homes and haunts of Victorian women writers. Most often, their former homes were described as being vacant, overgrown, or otherwise unknowable. Guidebooks seemed to have difficulty imagining the life of a working woman writer or a practice of literary tourism that would make the city inhabitable by literary women. Focusing on Christina Rossetti, Elizabeth Barrett Browning, and George Eliot, this chapter explores how the homes and haunts of women writers were simultaneously constructed and effaced by journalists as they composed maps of literary London. Such an effort was closely linked to the marginal status of women writers within the emerging literary canon at the fin de siècle.

Of course, some women writers took matters into their own hands by constructing their own public images and capitalizing on the new celebrity media. Chapter 3, titled "The Woman of Letters at Home: Harriet Martineau and the Lake District," explores how Martineau facilitated the emergence of her home, the Knoll, as a tourist destination by publishing works focused on the landscape and culture of the Lake District. This included her *Autobiography*, published posthumously in 1877; "A Year at Ambleside," published in *Sartain's Union Magazine* in 1850; "Lights of the English Lake District," published in *Atlantic Monthly* in 1861; and *Complete Guide to the English Lakes*, published in five editions from 1855 to 1876. In these texts, Martineau situated her home and the narrative of her own rise to fame within the literary history of the Lake District region. Through her guidebooks, she reinforced the literary significance of her home as a tourist destination while simultaneously emphasizing her own domestic virtues. Martineau's engagement with the discourse on literary tourism demonstrated her ability to construct and publicize her own celebrity. By depicting herself as both a domestic paragon and successful author, she provided a model of how women could achieve literary fame without losing middle-class respectability. Martineau's efforts at self-promotion were premised on using print media to establish her own literary significance. Throughout her career, these efforts became increasingly literalized as she attempted to heighten interest in the material relics of her illustrious career.

Popular historiography, like the literary tourism industry, was focused on the promise of authenticity and the reconstruction of the past. The second section of *Literary Celebrity* focuses on the ways that historiography was informed by the development of celebrity culture during the mid- to late Victorian period. I begin by returning to Harriet Martineau, whose work as a historian can best be understood within the context of her self-marketing strategies and protofeminist ideology. Chapter 4, "Harriet Martineau: Gender, National Identity, and the Contemporary Historian," explores the publication history of Martineau's *History of England during the Thirty Years' Peace* (1849–50), highlighting the strategies Martineau used to establish herself as a celebrity historian in a male-dominated field. Covering roughly the same time period as the *History*, Martineau's *Autobiography*, written in 1855, can be viewed as its companion text. In the *History*, Martineau provided a somewhat depersonalized account of contemporary British history, while at the same time emphasizing the importance of establishing the historicity of women's experiences. In the *Autobiography*, she further establishes the importance of women's history by inserting her own life story into the broader narrative of national progress. By linking the two texts, she makes a case for the historical significance of her own achievements as an author and social reformer. Martineau's *History* and *Autobiography* are complementary texts in the sense that they demonstrate how she worked across genre, writing contemporary history in a way that challenged conventionally masculine and feminine forms of historiography.

The celebrity home played an important role in the development of a protofeminist historiography. Chapter 5, titled "Rooms of the Past: Victorian Women Writers, History, and the Reconstruction of Domestic Space," explores how women capitalized on popular interest in celebrity lives as a means of establishing careers in the emerging culture industries, particularly the field of historic preservation. Women's involvement in the restoration and reinterpretation of literary homes as tourist destinations grew out of their participation in architectural reform movements. As they imagined ways that the home could be redesigned to promote social progress, women used celebrity homes as examples to illustrate the problems associated with gender inequity in the domestic realm. Through the process of historical interpretation, women were able to retell the narrative of literary history in ways that highlighted women's dilemmas and achievements. By interpreting the shrines and relics of famous writers, women were able to merge their architectural and literary avocations, thus seizing new opportunities for professional advancement. In this chapter, I focus on the opening of Carlyle's House in 1895 and the formation of the Brontë Society in 1893 as case studies for investigating the new spheres of professional activity afforded by the development of literary tourism and the establishment of literary societies. However, I also demonstrate how the interpretation of women's literary works within the context of their life stories and domestic spaces had the effect of diminishing their achievements as writers. The late Victorian discourse on literary celebrity highlights the important role of historic preservation in the development of feminist historiography. At the same time, it demonstrates the limitations of biographical criticism, which links women's achievements to the material remnants of their domestic lives.

The third section of *Literary Celebrity* focuses on the emergence of celebrity media as a major cultural preoccupation in print culture at the fin de siècle. Chapter 6, "Women Writers and Celebrity News at the Fin de Siècle," focuses on representations of women in celebrity periodicals, particularly how women authors were figured in interviews and profiles. Often featured as "news," the woman author garnered public attention in exciting new ways. On one hand, interviews and profiles of women writers demonstrated the compatibility of domestic life and literary careers. However, such news coverage also mystified and sensationalized women's private identities by alluding to scandals and secrets associated with their domestic relationships. Focusing on Charlotte Robinson, Mary Braddon, and Marie Corelli, I demonstrate how the publicity associated with celebrity journalism heightened interest in women writers' lives and works, thus enhancing their marketability in an increasingly competitive literary marketplace. Yet due to the time-sensitive nature of celebrity news, women writers were often depicted as objects of ephemeral consumer interest, commodities in the literary marketplace whose images, as much as their books, would satisfy the desire for sensation and novelty. As women's bodies became ubiquitous marketing devices in illustrated periodicals, women writers came to be seen as diversions or fads rather than as significant figures in British literary history.

The celebrity body was not only the object of keen interest in mass-market newspapers and periodicals but in specialist journals as well. Chapter 7, "Representations of the Authorial Body in the *British Medical Journal*," examines the use of Victorian authors as case studies in the field of medical journalism. The sensationalist treatment of authorial ailments and symptoms played an instrumental role in the professionalization of medicine. On one hand, the *British Medical Journal* (*BMJ*) employed the conventions of mainstream literary journalism, highlighted literary controversies, and cited auto/biographical narratives to attract general interest readers and to authorize itself as a domain of high culture. The health of the genius, contributors argued, was inseparable from the health of the nation. However, at the same time, the authorial body was used as a site for distinguishing between the subjective interpretations of literary authors and the more objective interpretations of medical analysts.

The *BMJ* was involved in a number of controversies over the medical histories of Victorian authors. In this chapter, I begin by focusing on the debate over Harriet Martineau's alleged cure by mesmerism in 1844 and then turn to the dispute over the causes of infertility and discord in the marriage of Thomas and Jane Carlyle. Finally, I examine the controversy over the alleged criminality of Ernest Hart, who served as editor of the *BMJ* from 1867 to 1898. When addressing these controversies, the *BMJ* referenced the authorial body as a way of establishing a self-consciously literary identity; however, it also used authorial case studies as a means of demarcating medical analysis from more literary forms of viewing and reading. The specialized medical gazes inscribed in the *BMJ* were defined as "masculine" in the sense that they were viewed as providing an alternative to sentimentalized assessments of medical history provided by women authors and their biographers. Yet the emergence of the woman doctor at the end of the century challenged and destabilized the confident masculinity of the medical gaze in the *BMJ*. An investigation of the link between medical journalism and biographical literary criticism highlights the ways that the literary celebrity and the doctor, as interlinking tropes, were used to delimit and extend the boundaries of medical discourse at the fin de siècle.

At the fin de siècle, the discourse on literary celebrity was used not only to authorize the medical profession but also to depict landscapes in increasingly detailed and politicized ways. Chapter 8, "The Celebrity Cause: Octavia Hill, Virtual Landscapes, and the Press," demonstrates how Octavia Hill used the press in a strategic way to foster popular support for the open space movement. Hill's campaigns for purchasing and managing urban parks in the second half of the nineteenth century eventually led to the formation of the National Trust in 1895. These intersecting movements were crucial in the development of the British culture industries because they promoted the idea that landscape should be interpreted as shared national heritage. Hill was able to promote the preservation of open spaces by using the press to popularize her own name as a celebrity advocate. The increasing emphasis on signature and celebrity authorship in literary journals such as the *Fortnightly Review, Macmillan's Magazine,* and the *Nineteenth Century* enabled Hill to form a link between her public identity and the open space movement. The fact that these journals often published contributions by women authors and increasingly incorporated visual images made them ideal vehicles for Hill's public relations campaign. Although Hill worked with a small army of activists, it was her name more than any other that came to be associated with the movement's public identity. As a pioneer of the "celebrity cause," Hill demonstrated how to work strategically within the conventions of popular print culture, mobilizing popular sentiment and private fund-raising in support of her open space projects.

Octavia Hill, like many of the women writers featured in this study, was able to use the media strategically for her own advantage. Yet her self-marketing strategies did not result in lasting fame. Her writing, like the work of so many other Victorian women of letters, was soon forgotten. Yet, as I demonstrate in the conclusion to this study, the process of canon formation during the late nineteenth and early twentieth centuries was decidedly unpredictable and uncertain. Like other commemorations of national culture, the literary canon was subject to negotiation and change.

Literary Celebrity sheds new light on the works and careers of a number of key Victorian literary figures, including Elizabeth Barrett Browning, Charlotte Brontë, Thomas Carlyle, Charles Dickens,

George Eliot, Harriet Martineau, and Christina Rossetti. In addition, it explores the careers of writers who are less familiar to literary critics but are nonetheless crucial figures in the discourse on literary celebrity, including Ernest Hart, Octavia Hill, and Charlotte Robinson. To date, there has been very little attention given to the role of celebrity culture and literary tourism in these writers' careers. Thus, my book brings to light a variety of fresh materials and critical insights that illuminate the ways Victorian writers shaped and were shaped by celebrity media. *Literary Celebrity* highlights the work of Harriet Martineau, who was particularly adroit at manipulating the media to further her own career. Scholarly interest in Martineau has been on the rise since the publication of her complete letters in 2007 and the republication of *Life in the Sickroom* and selections from *Illustrations of Political Economy*.[1] My extensive treatment of Martineau's engagement with the discourse on literary celebrity addresses the need for increased understanding of her work and career.

Scholarly interest in the field of literary celebrity has never been greater than it is at the present time. Recent and forthcoming essay collections, such as Nicola Watson's *Literary Tourism and Nineteenth-Century Culture* and Ann Hawkins and Maura Ives's *Women Writers and the Artifacts of Celebrity in the Long Nineteenth Century*, highlight the importance of situating the careers of nineteenth-century authors within emergent culture industries and celebrity media.[2] I build on these studies by focusing on particular themes and authors in the discourse on literary celebrity during a more narrowly defined historical time frame: 1850–1914. *Literary Celebrity* also extends scholarly understanding of the ideological role of literary tourism and celebrity culture as theorized in Nicola Watson's *The Literary Tourist: Readers and Places in Romantic and Victorian Britain* (2008), David Lowenthal's *The Past Is a Foreign Country* (1985), Dean MacCannell's *The Tourist: A New Theory of the Leisure Class* (1976), James Buzard's *The Beaten Track: European Tourism, Literature, and the Ways to Culture*, 1800–1918 (1993), and John Glendening's *The High Road: Romantic Tourism, Scotland, and Literature* (1997).[3] These works provide a broad framework for my own investigation of particular case studies in the discourse on celebrity at the fin de siècle.

Literary Celebrity also relies on recent scholarship in the field of Victorian gender studies. I examine women writers' self-marketing strategies within emerging celebrity media and demonstrate how the decanonization of their work was linked to the emergence of the culture industries at the fin de siècle. *Literary Celebrity* builds on my first book, *First-Person Anonymous: Women Writers and Victorian Print Media* (2004), which contextualized the development of women writers' careers within the publishing conventions of periodical journalism, particularly anonymous publication.[4] In *Literary Celebrity*, I extend this earlier work by exploring the ways women writers shaped and were shaped by the emerging culture industries and celebrity culture in the second half of the nineteenth century. My interdisciplinary approach to the history of women's authorship relies on several crucial works in the field of Victorian gender studies, including Mary Poovey's *Uneven Developments: The Ideological Work of Gender in Mid-Victorian England* (1988), Joanne Shattock's *Women and Literature in Britain, 1800–1900* (2001), Linda Peterson's *Becoming a Woman of Letters: Myths of Authorship and Facts of the Victorian Market* (2009), and Marysa Demoor's *Marketing the Author: Author Personae, Narrative Selves, and Self-Fashioning, 1880–1930* (2004).[5] Likewise, my arguments about the role of gender in the development of feminist historiography would not have been possible without foundational works such as Mary Spongberg's *Writing Women's History since the Renaissance* (2002) and Rohan Maitzen's *Gender, Genre, and Victorian Historical Writing* (1998).[6]

Literary Celebrity demonstrates how changes in gender roles were linked to the expansion of urban development, the rise of feminist historiography, the formation of an organized women's movement, the development of mass media, and the growth of domestic cultural travel. At the same time, I focus on how increasing professional specialization led to the development of sexology, architecture, English studies, and medicine as discrete yet intersecting fields of inquiry. At the center of these movements was the literary celebrity, who served as secular hero but also as a case study for investigating problems and dilemmas within Victorian culture. The discourse on literary celebrity relied on the assumption that investigation of the homes, haunts, and bodies of literary authors would bring coherence and meaning to modern experience. However, because the goal of recovering a unified British national culture was inherently unattainable, the search was always incomplete and unfulfilled. The search for a coherent national literary history thus came to be seen as an end in itself, a means of posing, though never fully answering, key questions about gender, sexuality, and the lives of literary celebrities.

Literary Celebrity, Gender, and Victorian Authorship, 1850–1914

I
Celebrity and Literary Tourism

1

The Virtual City:
Literary Tourism and the
Construction of "Dickens's London"

In the second half of the nineteenth century, London was viewed as the very center of nineteenth-century literary culture. It was here that most of the great Victorian writers had lived and worked. Yet due to rapid urbanization during the second half of the nineteenth century, the literary landmarks of London were increasingly difficult to identify or interpret with any degree of certainty. Where was it possible to experience the cultural heritage of Great Britain if not in London? Yet the city was "constantly shifting," as Francis Miltoun put it in 1903, expanding into the suburbs and abandoning traditional centers of meaning.[1] Lamenting the loss of a cultural center, writers of the late Victorian era attempted to preserve the city's landmarks through various forms of representation. Periodicals, guidebooks, and photographic inventories all served as media concerned with locating and describing London's cultural landmarks. In determining what was worth preserving, journalists turned to the emerging canon of British literature and more specifically to the novels set in the city during the time of Britain's cultural and economic ascendancy. Thus, the "reading" of London—the search for the city's timeless cultural landmarks—was simultaneously a reading of literary texts.

The realist novel produced during the Victorian era seemed to promise the kind of accuracy of vision that would provide a complete picture of the London of earlier days and thus a map for reading the modern city. Novel in hand, the literary tourist wandered through the city searching for evidence of national progress and, at the same time, lamenting the loss of a simpler, more narratable urban landscape. Consequently, the experience of viewing London was premised on the notion that the city could only be known by returning to the literary texts that "produced" it. This quest was inseparable from the process of canon formation at the fin de siècle. At the same time that critics were attempting to identify "timeless" literary texts, they were also attempting to locate the city's "eternal" literary shrines.

Inevitably, the works of Charles Dickens were the focus of these interconnected discourses. In the eyes of many travelers and journalists, Dickens's novels had assigned permanent cultural meanings to the city's landmarks, even if these locations seemed always in danger of disappearing entirely. As long as the "real" London remained in Dickens's oeuvre, so, too, would the nation's image of itself remain untarnished and unchanged. The search for the sites associated with Dickens's novels was by definition a quest for meaning in a city that was increasingly meaningless, a desire for certainty in a city that was increasingly uncertain. Yet it was the search itself—sorting through the dross of urban life, examining layers of reconstructed architecture, and investigating the city's labyrinths—that was infused with meaning. The act of literary tourism relied on the assumption that the literary text was "real" and the city was "unreal." That is, it assumed that the city could only be made authentic through careful reading, a process of collapsing the world of the literary text onto the world of the urban environment. By referencing the literary text as a marker of the real, the literary tourist reimagined London within the context of a cohesive national heritage and culture.

The purpose of this chapter is to explore the development of literary tourism in London focused on the life and works of Charles Dickens.[2] Late Victorian journalists interpreted the city through the lens of Dickens's texts, reimagining the urban culture of an earlier era and at the same time reconstructing the masculinity of Dickens himself as a product of this constructed environment. As we will see, literary tourists responded in droves, combing the city for signs of the lost "Dickens's London." All the while, the literary tourist was haunted by the knowledge that the process of "reading" London through the lens of literary texts was an attempt to revivify or sentimentalize a world that no longer existed or had never existed except in the pages of literary texts. Such touristic readings of London were of course inseparable from the expansion of commodity culture at the end of the nineteenth century, the development of what Jean Baudrillard calls the "hyperreal" or the "meticulous reduplication of the real," which relies on the "fetishism of the lost object: no longer the object of representation, but the ecstasy of denial and of its own ritual extermination."[3] As journalists lamented the absence of referents for sites depicted in Dickens's novels, they simultaneously facilitated the search for the undiscovered originals of Dickens's literary creations. Piecing together "facts" from the novel and from the existing urban landscape, tourists created Dickens's London as an imagined world of coherence and meaning.

An investigation of the practice of literary tourism in fin de siècle Victorian culture is an exploration of the ways that notions of realism were negotiated and debated in literary criticism of the period. Could a novel by Dickens accurately depict London? Was London narratable given the ephemeral nature of all urban environments? At the same time that journalists addressed these questions, they participated in what Jonathan Crary has called a "reorganization of the observer," which provided a "new valuation of visual experience" premised on "unprecedented mobility and exchangeability, abstracted from any founding site or referent."[4] Thus, at the same time that the realist novel emerged as a dominant literary genre, it was challenged by new ways of seeing premised on seeking but never finding the absent referents of locations described in literary texts. Consequently, London emerges at the end of the nineteenth century as what Nicholas Freeman calls a symbolist "labyrinth, which is not only unknowable in itself but a suggestion of all that cannot be known."[5] The investigation of the urban landscape is a key component of the modern spirit, where the viewer, like the reader, attempts to bridge the gap between city and text but at the same time realizes the impossibility of definitive understanding.

DISAPPEARING DICKENSLAND

To define Dickens's London is to understand the complex and contradictory place of the city in the late Victorian consciousness. The city's streets and neighborhoods were often effaced through the process of urban renewal. Consequently, many of the buildings that had supposedly served as originals for the fictional places in Dickens's novels were in danger of being lost entirely. On one hand, this loss was met with celebration. After all, urban renewal meant that sanitation, housing, and employment opportunities were rapidly improving. For example, in 1892, Frederic Harrison praises "bold and useful public works" such as the Embankment and Holborn Viaduct projects and pleads for further development that will enhance "municipal progress."[6] Yet other journalists worried that the "rebuilding" of Victorian London would destroy the city's most treasured literary landmarks. In a 1901 article, Walter Dexter emphasizes the ways that misguided notions of urban redevelopment had razed literary landmarks associated with Dickens's novels. "To make London a city of wider streets and a healthier dwelling-place for its toiling millions," he writes, "old buildings and narrow streets are being ruthlessly swept away."[7] He includes photographs of a few of the remaining Dickens shrines as a way of making a "more permanent record of the places we visit ere they are 'picked down' and shovelled up by the hands of the 'improver'" (547).[8]

In the eyes of many critics, urban expansion and renewal had made the city unintelligible. The comprehensive vision of city life promised by Dickens's work was thus viewed as an impossibility in the modern age.[9] In 1905, Ford Madox Ford writes in *The Soul of London*, "Dickens, posting as the Uncommercial Traveller towards France over Denmark Hill, may almost have had an impression of a complete and comparatively circumscribed London. But so many things—as obvious as the enormously increased size, as secondary as the change in our habits of locomotion—militate against our nowadays having an impression, a remembered bird's-eye-view of London as a whole."[10] The comprehensive vision Dickens "almost" achieves is unattainable in the modern age because the city has sprawled beyond perceivable boundaries. There can be no Dickensian "bird's-eye-view" in the early twentieth century, not only due to the vast size of the city but also due to the fragmentation of experience produced by the subway, the train, and other "habits of locomotion," which offer only fragmentary glimpses of the urban environment and thus prevent comprehensive vision.

Even if the sites associated with Dickens's novels were disappearing and the city was becoming increasingly incomprehensible, journalists nevertheless strove to capture the evanescent reality of Dickens's London. It was the promise of comprehensive vision, rather than its realization, that inspired the literary tourism industry. The fragmentary nature of the modern city acted as a catalyst to journalists and literary tourists, prompting them to piece together disparate scenes and locations into a coherent whole. Indeed, in the late nineteenth and early twentieth centuries, scores of articles on Dickens's London were published in popular journals, including *Munsey's Magazine, Temple Bar, Chambers's Journal*, and *Pall Mall Magazine*. American periodicals, including the *North American Review* and the *Lamp*, also published articles on Dickens's London during this period.[11] In the years following Dickens's death in 1870, several book-length guides were published, including T. Edgar Pemberton's *Dickens's London* (1876), Charles Dickens, Jr.'s *Dictionary of London* (1879), Robert Allbut's *Rambles in Dickens' Land* (1886), Francis Miltoun's *Dickens' London* (1903), H. Snowden Ward and Catherine Ward's *The Real Dickens Land* (1904), and Frank Green's *London Homes of Dickens* (1928).[12] These guides were often richly illustrated with images of the sites associated with Dickens's novels, for example, his home on Doughty Street and the ruins of Marshalsea Prison.

In guides to Dickens's London, photography became the medium of choice for documenting literary shrines. The impulse to photograph these sites was also a desire to make permanent the literary significance of London's urban geography and preserve the cultural markers of the past—the moral vision of Dickens himself. Yet by employing a technology that was very much of the present—photography—the discourse on literary tourism aimed to promote a modern kind of cultural travel. For example, an anonymous article published in the *Strand* in 1907 provides one hundred photographs of the sites associated with Dickens's novels.[13] Each photograph is captioned with a location and a literary reference point. For example, photo six is captioned "Staple Inn, Holborn, *Edwin Drood*," thus connecting place to text. The tourist is invited to overlay the narrative of Dickens's novel onto the scenes of London. Photographs documented these sites as real locations in the city while also presenting them as literary settings peopled by fictional characters.

The use of nonphotographic illustration in guidebooks and periodical essays was equally significant as a device for collapsing fictional and extrafictional worlds. For example, in Frank Green's *The London Homes of Dickens*, illustrations of Dickens's homes are interspersed with images of the Artful Dodger, Captain Cuttle, Mrs. Bardell, and other characters from Dickens's novels.[14] Such illustrations seem intended to populate the sites of London with characters from Dickens's fiction—almost to suggest that they, too, lived in London and were just as real as Dickens himself. As guidebook author Robert Allbut puts it, "We never think of them as the airy nothings of imaginative

OUR "100-PICTURE" GALLERY.

Every article in this series contains at least a hundred pictures.

VII.—THROUGH DICKENS-LAND.

THE land of Charles Dickens is spread out over a large part of the map of England. At the same time Londoners have some reason to claim Dickens as the novelist of London, inasmuch as it contains probably about half the scenery of his novels. Born at Portsea, he came to London at the age of eleven, living with his poverty-stricken family at Bayham Street, Camden Town. He went to school at Wellington House, Hampstead Road ("Our School," in sketches from "Reprinted Pieces"), from which he was removed to become a solicitor's clerk in Lincoln's Inn and afterwards in Gray's Inn, where he began to obtain that knowledge of the legal purlieus shown in his novels. At South Square, Gray's Inn (formerly Holborn Court), he found lodgings for Traddles ("David Copperfield"), whilst just across Holborn the old houses of Staple Inn easily lent themselves to romantic fancy, particularly as regards Mr. Grewgious and his pretty ward ("Edwin Drood"). In Took's Court, Cursitor Street, renamed by Dickens "Cook's Court," was the house of Mr. Snagsby, the law stationer in "Bleak House," only two minutes' walk from Lincoln's Inn Hall, the old Chancery Court in which the great law-suit of Jarndyce v. Jarndyce in the same novel was fought. At 58, Lincoln's Inn Fields, we shall find the residence of Mr. Tulkinghorn, the solicitor in the case; whilst at Ely Place, a short distance away, may be

1. Dickens's Birthplace, Portsea

5 Front of Staple Inn, Holborn
· BLEAK HOUSE. Etc ;

2. Bayham Street, Camden Town:
Where Dickens Lived

6. Staple Inn, Holborn
EDWIN DROOD ,

3. Dickens's School, Hampstead Road

8. Old Chancery Court,
Lincoln s Inn ; BLEAK HOUSE

9 58, Lincoln's Inn Fields
· BLEAK HOUSE

4. South Square, Gray's Inn
(DAVID COPPERFIELD

7. Took's Court, Cursitor Street
("BLEAK HOUSE ·

10. Ely Place
(DAVID COPPERFIELD)

11. St. Dunstan's Church,
Fleet Street (·THE CHIMES)

Figure 1. "Our '100-Picture' Gallery: Through Dickens' Land," *Strand Magazine* (April 1907): 411.

fiction, but regard them as familiar friends, having 'a local habitation and a name' amongst us."[15] William Hughes, in *A Week's Tramp in Dickens-land* (1893), goes so far as to assert that Dickens's characters "are more real than we are ourselves, and will outlive and outlast us, as they have outlived their creator."[16]

Much of the discourse on the realism of Dickens's characters was based on the idea that they were portraits of particular individuals Dickens had known during his lifetime. In his preface to Allbut's *Rambles in Dickens' Land*, Gerald Brenan tells the story of a literary pilgrimage to Dover where he encountered a woman who claimed to have proof that the characters in *David Copperfield* were real. "It is quite evident that you have never lived in Dover," she tells him. "Miss Betsy Trotwood a myth, indeed! Let me tell you that my own mother knew the dear woman well—yes, and that delightful Mr. Dick too; and she remembered seeing Mr. Dickens drive up in a fly from the railway station to visit them."[17] The existence of the "original" thus proves the "reality" of the literary construction. As a result, the world of the novel and the world of the actual become duplicate realities. Later in the preface, this sense of duplication becomes even more apparent when Brenan describes a trip to "old Hungerford Stairs," where the tourist "may visit the spot where the two boys—the real and the imaginary—Charles Dickens and David Copperfield, spent so many hours while working for a scant pittance" (xvi–xvii). Brenan is careful to distinguish the "real and the imaginary," but by placing them imaginatively in the same space, they become doubles, each representing the other without the real being privileged over the fictional.

An 1888 article by J. Ashby-Sterry goes so far as to place readers inside Dickens's texts, allowing them to imagine what it would be like to experience the city as one of his characters. Ashby-Sterry presents himself as a virtual guide, asking the "confiding reader" to "take my arm, trust in me" as he directs him "through one of the pleasantest provinces of Dickensland."[18] One of the first sights he invites the reader to visit is the London Bridge steps, the "exact spot—with precisely the scenery of half a century ago—of the interview [in *Oliver Twist*] between Nancy, Rose Maylie, and Mr. Brownlow" (106). He then invites the reader to "go there about twelve o'clock on a dark night" and "lurk around the pilaster at the bottom of the flight and play at being Noah Claypole" (106). The invitation to impersonate Noah Claypole at the "exact spot" depicted in the novel is also an invi-

and existence has altogether
altered. During that period
London and London life have become absolutely metamorphosed. On all hands has
there been the demolition of old buildings and
the erection of new. Old thoroughfares have
been closed and new streets opened, while ancient
landmarks and records of the past have been
altogether obliterated.
And yet it is strange
to find that with
all this demoli-
tion and re-
volution,

one of
the principal
scenes in *Oliver
Twist* remains ex-
actly as it was when
the book was written, down
to the most minute
detail. If you take
the left-hand side of
London Bridge, when
you are crossing to the
Surrey side, and
descend the flight
of steps to
the river,
hard by the
Bridge House Hotel,
you will find yourself
in the exact spot—with
precisely the scenery
of half a century ago—
of the interview between
Nancy, Rose Maylie, and
Mr. Brownlow. If you go there about twelve
o'clock on a dark night you will realize the
picture to perfection. Indeed, you may lurk
round the pilaster at the bottom of the flight
and play at being Noah Claypole. You
should first however take the precaution to
assure the policeman who happens to be
hovering about the neighbourhood that you

LONDON BRIDGE STEPS.
From a Drawing by A. D. M'CORMICK.

have no intention of committing suicide, and
you should next take care that you do not
fall into the river by accident, for the lower-
most steps are very slippery.

The last time I heard Charles Dickens
read, he gave that most forcible and thrilling
of all his readings—" Sikes and Nancy."
Standing on the very spot, which he pictured

Figure 2. A. D. McCormick, "London Bridge Steps," in "Charles Dickens and
Southwark," by J. Ashby-Steery, *English Illustrated Magazine* 62 (November 1888):
106.

tation to merge conceptions of fictional narrative and real-life experience. Later in the article, after guiding readers though a Southwark building depicted in *David Copperfield*, Ashby-Sterry remarks, "I cannot allow you to accompany David any farther or you will be getting clear of Southwark altogether" (111). Thus, the reader is not only following a virtual guide, accessible only through the written text, but also is simultaneously following David Copperfield through fictionalized versions of Southwark neighborhoods. The overall effect is one of both familiarization and de-familiarization of urban landmarks; the city is at once fictional and real, virtual and experiential.

London was thus interpreted as a world of firsthand experience and a "world" created by Charles Dickens. "Anywhere, I repeat, one might wander," exclaims William Sharp in a 1903 article, he is sure to be "in Dickens-land, of coming upon some house, court, street, square, or locality associated with the personages of that marvelous tragic-comedy, the 'world' of Charles Dickens."[19] The experience of touristic "wandering" is linked to the actions of Dickens himself, who is often depicted rambling through the city, searching for materials for his latest novel. For example, a 1912 article published in the *Bookman* remembers Dickens as an urban wanderer, who, ghostlike, was spotted in the "oddest of places and most inclement weather," often "trudging along the Seven Sisters Road at Holloway, or bearing, under a steady press of sail, underneath Highgate Archway, or pursuing the even tenor of his way down the Vauxhall Bridge Road."[20] Dickens, like the literary tourist, canvasses the city, searching for meaning, constructing narratives. For readers of the *Bookman*, this means that "there is no part of London or of what were its suburbs in his time, that is not associated in some way with his [Dickens's] books. Houses, streets, hotels, effigies, pumps, monuments, have become familiar to us through that association and have added glory to existences which otherwise would never have been noticed at all. In this way it may be said that Dickens discovered London for the Londoner, and has made him acquainted with its streets quite as much as he has made him acquainted with persons who walk them" (241).

By fictionalizing the city, Dickens makes it more "familiar" to Londoners, who otherwise perceive it as an unreal or unfamiliar environment. Dickens produces this familiarity by linking seemingly disconnected urban landmarks into a cohesive fiction. Likewise, by acquainting his readers with fictional urban types, he acquaints them with the people who otherwise would go unrecognized and unacknowledged. For readers, the result is a comforting narrative, the idea that the city and its people are coherent and significant. Indeed, the article concludes with the confident statement that "London to-day is still Dickens's London" even though the "flight of time and the house-breakers have swept much away" (246). The term "house-breakers" would seem to refer to developers who demolish buildings during the process of urban renewal, thus "robbing" the city of its literary heritage. However, at the same time, it suggests that the destruction of literary shrines is a threat to urban domesticity, which relies on Dickens's landscapes as ground on which to build British conceptions of home. Those who take the time to seek out Dickens's London, then, will be rewarded with feelings of continuity and domestic security.

Yet such a vision of urban life—viewed, as it were, through the lens of Dickens's novels—was often interpreted as being accessible only to knowledgeable insiders. W. Kent, writing for the *Bookman* in 1920, notes that there are a "few memorials for those who are not Dickensians"; however, "for the initiated, Dickens, dead just fifty years, speaks everywhere in London streets."[21] For these "Dickens topographers," who have studied the surface of the city, revealing its fictional meanings, "such a pilgrimage would furnish more knowledge of the haunts of struggling men than materials for national history" (108, 110). In Kent's view, it is the social history of the great city, rather than any broader national history, that is illuminated by the act of literary tourism. By defining themselves as social historians, Dickensians imagined their touristic activities as being more scholarly and meaningful than those of the uninitiated masses.

The process of uncovering Dickens shrines was of course not just perceived as an activity for enlightened insiders. The appearance of American tourists in Dickens's London prompted a variety of satirical responses. For example, a 1902 article published in *Chambers's Journal* recounts a literary pilgrimage led by a British guide who takes an American, James Fairfield, on a search for the Hatton Garden police court as depicted in *Oliver Twist*. "I've no doubt all the detail set out in the book was photographically correct," the American tourist says.[22] When they finally locate the site that seems to fit Dickens's description, the tourist exclaims, "In that very room, sir, the magistrate sat behind a bar at the upper end—that means the end farthest from us—and on one side of the door—the very door that gives upon the entrance hall—was a sort of wooden pen in which they put Oliver; . . . Man alive! can't you picture the whole scene?" (384). In response, the narrator makes a "philistine remark to the effect that the whole scene was fictitious" (384). Of course, the American tourist is the philistine; his imposition of fictional references on the city landscape is meant to seem ridiculous. The article thus demonstrates late-Victorian self-consciousness about the ways that simulations—in this case, literary texts—tend to stand in place of verifiable reality. And literary tourism is depicted as a kind of cultural colonialism carried out by all-too-avid American readers, who insist on experiencing the "real fiction" of the city as depicted in a Dickens novel.

Of course the cultural colonization associated with literary tourism operated in the reverse direction as well. At the same time that Americans were invading London, Dickens enthusiasts were establishing literary shrines abroad. Gerald Brenan likens the process of literary tourism to the experience of viewing the "flutter of one's country's flag in foreign lands" because it stirs "our better nature."[23] Later in the introduction, he makes the claim that the boundaries of "Dickens' Land" extend into other national contexts. He writes that there is a "Dickens' quarter in Paris" as well as "small colonies of Dickens' Land across the wide Atlantic" (xii). The colonizing metaphor suggests that Dickens is an emblem of Britishness that can be exported abroad. At the same time that American tourists traveled to Britain in search of sites associated with Dickens's novels, literary enthusiasts were expanding the boundaries of Dickens's London far beyond British national borders.

The growth of a tourist industry focused on Dickens's novels, both at home and abroad, was met with some anxiety as unscrupulous tour guides capitalized on the expansion of cultural tourism. An 1892 article in the *Bookworm* warns readers of the "artful dodgers" who recount stories of the great author in exchange for cash.[24] "Visitors to places of note both at home and abroad invariably meet with this class of irresponsible historians," the article points out (78). Thus, it warns, books such as William Hughes's *A Week's Tramp in Dickens-land* should "not be taken as 'gospel'" (78). Charley, Dickens's son, also took on the project of debunking myths perpetuated by professional guides who misidentified literary shrines based on limited evidence. Charley believed that American tourists were especially vulnerable to charlatans. "Indeed," he writes, "it is not too much to say that it is almost entirely among the pilgrims to English literary shrines and

the indefatigable and omnivorons general sightseers from the great
Western Continent that the professors of this singular and deceptive
industry find their prey."[25] He resents the "vast army of untrustworthy
people who have taken the great sights and shrines of the world into
their peculiar keeping" (670). In addition to criticizing the tendency
of tour guides to create their own fictional representations of Dickens's London, Charley points out that his father's creative process
problematized any direct referentiality between text and city. The
process of literary creation, he argues, performs the function of syn-
thesizing details of the external world rather than representing reality in a photographic likeness. In "Notes on Some Dickens Places and
People" (1896), he writes, "In their wish to verify as closely as possible
the places with which the Dickens books deal, people run a considerable danger of losing sight of the rather important fact that the imagination of the writer has . . . raised so considerable a superstructure on
the basis of the original fact as to make it practically unrecognizable.
. . . Photographic accuracy must not be demanded in these cases."[26]
Without a direct physical referent in the urban landscape, textual
description refers only to itself.

Of course, Charley capitalized on his father's fame in order to
promote his own writing career,[27] creating a small industry of writing
tour guides to the literary shrines associated with his father's novels.[28]
Charley published *Dickens's Dictionary of London* in 1879 as well as a
number of articles on the same subject in popular periodicals such
as the *English Illustrated Magazine,* the *North American Review,* and *Pall
Mall Magazine.*[29] Indeed, as Joss Marsh has pointed out, he succeeded
in "codifying his father's superficially 'eccentric' vision of London,
creating conventions by which touristic, urban, and literary posterity
would live."[30] The replication of the name *Charles Dickens,* affixed to
Charley's books and journalistic essays, often with the *Jr.* omitted,
demonstrates the ways that an authorial name—even when it is associated with the descendents of a famous writer, rather than their
"original"—carries a cachet that can be employed in the process of
self-marketing. The intimate ties of kinship implied by the Dickens
name suggest that the author is a literate insider who has privileged
insight into the novels and the places and people that inspired them.
Yet, at the same time, the replicability of the name problematizes its
referentiality, calling into question the notion of a single "Charles
Dickens" whose knowledge and identity can be contained and known.
In a similar way, the process of misidentifying the "originals" of the

people and places in Dickens's novels leads to a multiplication of sites and identities. In "Notes on Some Dickens Places and People," Charley writes, "I do not think that, when I was travelling all over the country giving Dickens Readings, and being hospitably entertained at all sorts of houses, and acquiring a remarkable experience of all sorts of hotels, I heard of more than fifty originals of Sam Weller."[31] He points out that most of his father's characters were "compound[s] made up from observation of many men" (353). Dickens, Jr., thus serves as a "double" of his father while at the same time criticizing the replication of the "originals" of his father's characters. The real Charles Dickens or the real Sam Weller cannot be known except through encounters with their duplicates.

During his lifetime, Charles Dickens was sensible to the fact that his books and identity had become replicated commodities in the literary marketplace. In an 1856 letter, Dickens indicates his dislike of the "multiplication of my countenance in the Shop-Windows."[32] On one hand, this replication of images, as a form of hero worship, would seem to highlight Charles's Dickens individuality; however, this process of mass replication actually had the effect of effacing his identity, converting his image into mass produced objects of exchange: *cartes de visite* and collectible photographs. As Jim Barloon points out, Dickens's fiction demonstrates the ways that the "city tends to dislocate and diffuse individuals," highlighting how they become lost in the urban labyrinth.[33] The process of photographic mass production has a similar effect, replicating the individual into nonexistence. "The photograph," Jonathan Crary notes, "becomes a central element not only in a new commodity economy but in the reshaping of an entire territory on which signs and images, each effectively severed from a referent, circulate and proliferate."[34] Far from being simply an instrument of documentary realism, the photograph takes on a life of its own through replication and dissemination.

Within the discourse on literary tourism, the photograph and its subject, like the text and its originals, become duplicates, each "authentic" in its own way without a clear privileging of the original over the reproduction. For some critics, the only way to capture this notion of doubleness was to use supernatural metaphors. Dickens and his characters were imagined as spectral presences, ghosts and spirits who haunted the streets of London. The ghost, like the photograph or literary text, is related to its original yet leads an independent life. Neither here nor there, alive nor dead, the ghosts of the literary past informed many experiences of Dickens's London. "One may meet as many ghosts of Dickens's characters within a half-mile radius of Chancery Lane as in all the rest of London," a writer for the London *Times* notes in 1914.[35] This reference to the ghostly quality of Dickens's characters points to the ways that the text "haunted" the city for many tourists. Indeed, Henry James called it a kind of "pressure" that had been "laid upon" his generation to "feel Dickens, down to the soles of our shoes."[36] After meeting Dickens, James describes the relationship between author and acolyte as a "relation between benefactor and beneficiary, or debtor and creditor" (388). He continues, "No other debt in our time has been piled so high, for those carrying it, as the long, the purely 'Victorian' pressure of that obligation" (388). Dickens thus becomes a kind of cultural burden that James must carry. Like a ghost, this burden is an invisible presence that informs his craft and inhabits his body to the soles of his shoes.

DICKENS AT HOME

Concomitant with the proliferation of journalistic representations of Dickens's London was the formation of the Dickens Fellowship in 1902, the founding of the *Dickensian* in 1905, and the opening of the Dickens House in 1925.[37] These quasi-scholarly enterprises, monitored by relatives of the late author, had an important role to play in the reinterpretation and preservation of Dickens shrines. Indeed, the narrative surrounding the formation of the Dickens House Museum depicts the fellowship as an instrument of urban restoration. "In the summer of 1922," an early guide to the museum reads, "No. 48, Doughty Street, was in danger of demolition, and a few members of the Council of The Dickens Fellowship determined to buy and preserve it."[38] Although Dickens had lived in the house for less than two years, its availability on the market made it an ideal site to serve as a headquarters for the fellowship and a focal point for literary tours. Indeed, one guide calls it the "Mecca of all Dickensians" and insists that "no lover of Dickens should be guilty of not having visited 48, Doughty Street."[39]

Before the Doughty Street house was opened to the public, the focal point of Dickens's London was the supposed original of the Old Curiosity Shop, a wastepaper shop on Portsmouth Street near Lincoln's Inn Fields. Francis Miltoun remarks in 1906, "There is no ques-

THE (REPUTED) "OLD CURIOSITY SHOP"

Figure 3. "The (Reputed) 'Old Curiousity Shop,'" in *Dickens' London*, by
Francis Miltoun (Boston: Page, 1903), 126.

tion but what it is *the relique* of the first rank usually associated with
Dickens' London, as witness the fact that there appears always to be
some numbers of persons gazing fondly at its crazy old walls."[40] The
owner of the shop, he notes, capitalizes upon this reputed association
by selling "souvenirs, prints, drawings, etc.," to the crowds of visitors,
particularly Americans (127). Indeed, he reports, an American "col-
lector" has offered to buy the shop and transport it to America as a
way of saving the "humble shrine" from demolition (127). The identification of the Portsmouth Street storefront as the original of the
Old Curiosity Shop in the novel was viewed as specious by most journalists, including Charley Dickens, who called the shrine "bogus,"[41]
and his son, Charles Dickens III, who referred to the building's "false
sanctity."[42] As evidence of its misidentification, Charles quotes from
the text of his grandfather's novel, which pointedly notes that the
"old house had been long ago pulled down" (834). Amusingly, the
literary text becomes a means of calling into question the authenticity
of a physical building in a particular London location. Yet for Fran-

cis Miltoun, the building's authenticity had little to do with textual evidence; rather, the tourist "must decide for him or herself."[43] Thus, in the debate over the Old Curiosity Shop, the literary text is both relevant and irrelevant. For some readers, the shrine was "real" only inasmuch as it was authenticated by the literary text, but for others, the "truth" of the shrine was constructed in more subjective terms as the imaginative reconstruction of Dickens's world in an urban context. Rather than experiencing what Miltoun calls the "disappointment that the visitor often feels when comparing his impression of London, as it really is, with the London of his imagination," the tourist instead imposes his own notion of Dickens's London on existing urban landmarks as a way of making the landscape meaningful and resonant.[44] However, the attempt to create resonance for the Old Curiosity Shop as a literary shrine would soon come to an end. The shop was demolished in the early twentieth century, thus ending any controversy over its supposed authenticity.

The search for an urban shrine or home that would serve as a focal point for tours of Dickens's London went hand in hand with the desire to reimagine Dickens's masculinity within the context of middle-class notions of domesticity. After Dickens's death in 1870 and the subsequent sale of his household goods, the practice of literary tourism became increasingly focused on collecting his personal effects and imagining his domestic life. The search for the "real" Dickens was thus premised on the desire not only to "find" him in London but also to interpret his legacy within the context of his domestic life. This desire was part of a broader reconfiguration of gender roles, which defined masculinity in relation to domestic habits and responsibilities. As John Tosh points out, the "place of the home in bourgeois culture could be summed up by the proposition that only at home could a man be truly and authentically himself."[45]

Initially, the search for the "authentic" Dickens drew tourists outside the boundaries of the urban environment to Gad's Hill Place. Through various representations in biography and journalistic reportage, Gad's Hill became a symbol of the "real" Dickens: the family man, the father, the domestic paragon.[46] In an 1871 article, Hans Christian Andersen described a visit to the shrine, giving a detailed account of his experiences, writing, "It was a fine new house with red walls, four balconied windows, and a portico resting on small pillars. . . . A thick hedge of cherry-laurel stood close up against the house, which looked over a carefully-tended lawn to the high-road, and beyond the road to a back-ground of two mighty cedars of Lebanon."[47] Once inside, he remarks, "The room in which we and some of the children sat down to breakfast, was a model of comfort and holiday brightness. The windows were overhung, outside, with a profusion of blooming roses" (29). Mrs. Dickens presides over the idyllic domestic scene with a "certain soft, womanly repose," and the great writer "took the house-father's place, at the head of the table; and, according to English custom, he always began the meal with a short quiet grace" (29–30). In this way, Dickens's life at Gad's Hill comes to represent a domestic ideal intended to resonate with middle-class readers.

Other representations of Dickens at Gad's Hill reinforce the performative nature of his domestic avocations. An article in the *London Journal* published in 1870, for example, includes the following paragraph:

> The dwelling, as will be perceived from the illustration, is not pretentious; but it was large enough for Dickens, and long will the neighbors recollect the pleasant sight presented by him, his daughters, and youthful guests, playing croquet on the lawn on bright summer afternoons. Alas! never again will his hearty laugh ring over that lawn—never again will his bright eyes glance with saucy humor at the, perhaps, too curious lookers-on of his exercise with mallet and balls! But none of them, nor the thousands in London, who know him well will ever forget the marked characteristics of his personal appearance. The face and figure of Charles Dickens were unmistakably conspicuous.[48]

Here Dickens is imagined as a jolly father who enjoys lighthearted domestic pursuits and is just as unpretentious as his home. Yet, at the same time, he is a "conspicuous" performer who is remembered by "too-curious" neighbors. These onlookers, like literary tourists, construct a mythology surrounding Dickens's home life, which is then communicated broadly via the periodical press. Such anecdotes would certainly fuel the literary tourism industry, which relied not only on nostalgic representations of Dickens's London but also on idealized accounts of Dickens's domestic performances.

Gad's Hill, as Dickens's last home, promised to provide insight into the private life of the great writer and his family. Indeed, after Dickens's death, the house was temporarily opened to the public.[49] Yet for some enthusiasts, it proved to be an inadequate shrine to the late author. American tourist Moncure Conway, for example, recounts his pilgrimage to Gad's Hill in September of 1870, just three months after Dickens's death. Upon arrival in the evening, he is greeted by a closed "fortress" with a sign posted on the door stating, "no admission after four."[50] Once he announces that he is an American, though, the doors are opened, and he is shown around the house with "affability and attention" (614). As he ponders over the remaining household objects, he is haunted by the "vacant chair" and empty bookshelves (614). The Gad's Hill house, once a focal point for understanding Dickens as a domestic patriarch, has become a field of empty signs. Once the writer and most of his belongings have been removed from the space, it becomes less satisfying as a spectacle of domestic life.

As Dickens enthusiasts strove to remember the late writer at home, they ultimately turned again to London, where relics were contextualized within meaningful domestic settings. American journalist Caroline Ticknor, writing for the *Lamp*, describes a visit to the home of one of Dickens's sons, Henry Fielding Dickens, at Egerton Place in southwest London. Here the relics of the great writer's life form the center of a happy family circle: "On the left as one enters, is Mr. Dickens's study, used also as a reception room, where in the bay window stands the desk at which the author wrote nearly all of his novels. If one happens in, late in the afternoon, he is likely to find a gay group of young people assembled here drinking tea by the big fire-place."[51] After dinner, the family retires to the "Dickens room," where the "walls are completely covered with autographs, illustrations, bits of manuscript, and what is of chief interest, a large collection of portraits of Charles Dickens, representing him at all stages of his career" (35). These relics create a room that is "pervaded by the strong personality of the departed" and a persona who is still "alive" in the memory of his relatives (36). This intimate, personal monument stands in place of any public shrine (other than the tomb at Westminster Abbey). As Ticknor points out, it was Dickens's dying wish that no public "monument, memorial, or testimonial" be erected in his memory (36). Instead, his "published works" and his enshrinement in the "homes of those who loved him best" will serve as his monument (36). Yet this form of memorialization also serves to efface Dickens's memory in significant ways. Once again, through the replication of mass-produced images, multiple portraits, multiple novels, and multiple descendents, all of whom claim to speak for (almost as) him, the "real" Dickens becomes inaccessible.

The solution to the problem of locating Dickens in London was of course the purchase of the Doughty Street house in 1925, which contained the writer's furniture and household effects and served as a "museum" that was open to the public. The museum provided interpretations meant to capture fantasies associated with Dickens's domestic life, thus creating what the museum web site (in 2010) calls an "authentic and inspiring surrounding." [52] As tourists walked through the house, they were invited to fantasize and dream, not only about Dickens's domestic habits but about the fictional locations he created as well. The current exhibits, for example, include the "attic window through which Dickens gazed as a boy, when living in Bayham Street, Camden Town," and the "pantry window from a house in Chertsey," which served as a model for the window in the "burglary episode of *Oliver Twist*." The combination of the biographical and the fictional enhanced the experience of Dickens's London by giving Dickens enthusiasts a place where they could feel at home. The Doughty Street museum became an imagined domestic space created at the intersection of Dickens's novels, his biography, and the artifacts of the past.

Dickens World

As a starting place for urban investigation, the Dickens Museum formed the center around which Dickens's London could be mapped, even if it could never be fully understood. As Joss Marsh has pointed out, "For Dickens the novelist, tour-guide was to be a life-long (even posthumous) role. To understand the city, to understand Dickens, is to slice through multiple layers of its riotous growth; to negotiate the novels is to learn their methods of metropolitan mapping." [53] To traverse Dickensian London, literally or imaginatively, was to seek a set of signifiers for the real London of the past. If the discourse on literary tourism exposed the fictionality and inaccessibility of these real locations, it also defined them as truths worth searching for. Reading the late Victorian city was like reading a Dickens novel, threading one's way through labyrinthine streets, untangling multiple plots, and searching for elusive meanings.

The process of seeking Dickens's London would of course continue in the twentieth and twenty-first centuries. With the development of new technologies came new opportunities for viewing the city as a Dickensian text. The 2007 opening of Dickens World, an indoor theme park in Chatham, Kent, can be interpreted as an extension of the earlier discourse on literary tourism of the late nineteenth and early twentieth centuries. This attraction, built in a hangarlike facility, features scale models and amusements inspired by scenes from Dickens's novels, including the "Haunted House of 1859," "Great Expectations Boat Ride," a "4D cinema show at Peggotty's Boathouse," and an 1832 "Victorian School complete with nasty schoolmaster."[54] The attraction promises that visitors will "come face to face with some of Dickens' literary characters in their magnificent rendition of a Victorian town courtyard." Some journalists have welcomed the attraction, including Dana Huntley, who praises developers' attempts to make the historical detail "as accurate as possible to Dickens' times and novels."[55] The experience of visiting the attraction, she notes, "might well spur a child's interest in reading the stories that inspired such a cool place."[56] Not surprisingly, however, the development of the theme park has been met with disapproval from other Dickens scholars, who object to its trivialization of Dickens's work. Judith Flanders, for example, expresses "great forebodings" about the project, particularly its "domestication" of the "wildness and fierceness" of Dickens's engagement with key social issues of his day.[57] She asks, "With Magwitch's boat-ride, do we learn about the Bloody Code and penal reform?"

The development of a simulacrum focused on Dickens's works can be seen as a logical extension of the discourse on literary tourism in the popular press of the late nineteenth and early twentieth centuries. When visiting Dickens World, tourists of today view a fake city designed to imitate a London that had, after all, always been a kind of fiction. "Faux worlds," journalist Dea Birkett notes, "are always cleaner, happier and more ordered places that the gritty, flawed world we actually inhabit."[58] Such "worlds" have always been the product of literary tourism, which reconstructs landscape imaginatively in idealized terms. The tourist industry focused on the works of Charles Dickens, including Dickens World, promises a reference back to "reality" in the same way that Dickens's realism promised an understanding of the urban environment. Yet the effect was a layering of fictional narratives on the material facts of urban life. In fact, Dickens World is situated in an area that had long been associated with Dickens tourism in the Rochester-Chatham vicinity.[59] Gad's Hill Place, which will be opened as a Dickens visitor center in 2012, is just five miles away, and the theme park itself is built near the site of the Royal Dockyards where Dickens's father worked as a clerk. Dickens World thus acts as a literalization of a long-standing imaginative practice among Dickens enthusiasts, which involved superimposing narrative upon narrative as a way of understanding and interpreting an increasingly fragmented urban landscape.

2

The Haunting of Victorian London:
Christina Rossetti, Elizabeth Barrett Browning,
and George Eliot

As NOTED IN CHAPTER 1, REFERENCES TO LITERARY "GHOSTS" WERE ubiquitous within the discourse on literary tourism during the second half of the nineteenth century. Literary guidebooks encouraged tourists to visit the "homes and haunts" of famous writers as a way of communing with their "spirits." One of the earliest of these texts was William Howitt's *Homes and Haunts of the Most Eminent British Poets* (1847). Later examples include Walter Thornbury's *Haunted London* (1865), Theodore Wolfe's *A Literary Pilgrimage among the Haunts of Famous British Authors* (1895), Marion Harland's *Where Ghosts Walk: The Haunts of Familiar Characters in History and Literature* (1895), H. B. Baildon's *The Homes and Haunts of Famous Authors* (1906), and E. Beresford Chancellor's *The Literary Ghosts of London: Homes and Footprints of Famous Men and Women* (1933).[1] Spectral metaphors were also employed in the periodical press, which popularized a "homes and haunts" approach to literary criticism by emphasizing the connection between authorial biography, British geography, and the experience of reading literary texts. Periodicals and guidebooks suggested that literary tourism was a ghost hunt and that readers could commune with the spirits of authors by visiting the locations associated with their lives and works.

The first part of this chapter will explore how authors of guidebooks invoked literary ghosts and explored their haunts as a way of asserting the existence of a unique British cultural heritage while at the same time pointing to the difficulty of knowing or interpreting the past. As noted in chapter 1, London was a vital center within nineteenth-century British literary culture and thus was a logical focal point for the literary tourism industry. Due to urban expansion and renovation, however, the literary landmarks of the city had become increasingly difficult to identify and interpret. Consequently, London was viewed as a city inhabited by literary specters, signifiers of a lost British cultural history that must be rediscovered and preserved. The ghostly quality of literary London served as an incitement to discourse as literary tourists sought the elusive identities and truths associated with the city's illustrious literary past.

The use of spectral metaphors in literary guidebooks had important implications for women writers, whose ghostly invisibility was a product of the intersecting discourses on literary tourism and domestic ideology. The second part of this chapter will explore how the London homes and haunts of three women writers—Christina Rossetti, Elizabeth Barrett Browning, and George Eliot—were simultaneously constructed and effaced through the discourse on literary tourism. For women writers, ghostly invisibility was reinforced by domestic ideology, which mandated women's absence in the public sphere and their reticence as national heroes. This sense of invisibility was reinforced by the act of reading, which, like the act of literary tourism, facilitated the disembodiment of women writers by emphasizing their "remains": the book, the relic, and the home.

The disincorporation of women writers was premised on the idea that their participation in the public realm was problematic, particularly within urban environments.[2] While the lives and works of male writers, particularly Charles Dickens, were closely associated with the topography of London, women were more difficult to "locate" on a literary map of the city. In a culture informed by domestic ideology, women's participation in London's literary marketplace, let alone their physical presence on the streets of London, was viewed as potentially compromising. Of course, as Lynda Nead has pointed out, respectable women *did* occupy urban spaces, thus "forcing constant renegotiation of modern identity in the urban context."[3] Indeed, literary fame in late Victorian culture increasingly depended on visibility in the urban environment. Linda Shires reminds us that successful authorship during the nineteenth century depended on "being seen—seen at certain places, with certain people, and in particular outfits or poses."[4] Nevertheless, public display was still problematic for women writers as they struggled to balance the need for public visibility with the desire for social respectability. As a consequence,

Shires points out, writers relied on withholding themselves from public view as a strategy for stimulating public interest in their lives and careers.[5]

Although self-imposed invisibility may have stimulated tourist activity focused on women's homes and haunts in London, it also served to efface the details of their working lives. Guidebooks and periodicals suggested that women writers should not be seen in city spaces or understood as products of an urban environment. Women's homes and haunts in London are most often described as being vacant, overgrown, or otherwise unknowable. The writers of literary guides to London seemed to have difficulty imagining the life of a working woman writer or a practice of literary tourism that would make the city "inhabitable" by literary women. As Virginia Woolf remarked in 1932, London was a city of "great men's houses."[6] Even today, although there are many blue plaques marking literary women's homes in London, there is no literary shrine devoted to a woman writer equivalent to Keats's House, Carlyle's House, or Dickens's House. Yet some of the most important women writers of the Victorian period—including Christina Rossetti, Elizabeth Barrett Browning, and George Eliot—lived and worked in the city. Although London was considered the center of the literary world and was the center of many Victorian women's literary lives, there could be no representative home for the woman writer in the urban environment. Yet women haunted London just the same, emerging as half-materialized presences and disembodied spirits. The interplay of presence and absence in women's literary careers and urban experiences served as a catalyst for literary tourism, which focused on the mysteriousness and spectrality of women's participation in the public realm.

LITERARY SPECTERS

When visiting the "homes and haunts" of famous writers, literary tourists were responding to a specific form of bio-geographical criticism in Victorian popular print culture. For many critics, the "environment" was a logical starting point when composing biographies of Victorian authors. Leslie Stephen, for example, writing about George Eliot, notes that it is usual "at the present day to begin from the physical 'environment' of the organism whose history we are to study."[7] Employing a metaphor from natural science, Stephen points to the ways in which biography and geography are mutually reinforcing. W. Robertson Nicoll, editor of the *Bookman*, further describes his approach: "Interest in an author's work is greatly stimulated by knowledge of the author's life. In fact, no author can be understood without some acquaintance with his personality, his outward environment, and his circumstances."[8] Reading a literary text was not only a means of entering another world and getting to know the "person" behind the literary text but also a way of preparing for direct experience of the spaces and scenes associated with the author's life and work. As Peter Mandler has pointed out, reading served as a means of "priming the imagination with the vocabulary of the past which could then be unleashed by the unique physical encounter."[9]

The spectral metaphors associated with the practice of literary tourism suggest that writers are always both present and absent in the environments associated with their lives and work. Likewise, the biographical author is "behind" the written text but at the same time is essentially inaccessible to the reader. As Julian Wolfreys has argued, "all forms of narrative are, in one way or another, haunted."[10] This is because "to tell a story is always to invoke ghosts, to open space through which something other returns, although never as a presence or to the present. Ghosts return via narratives, and come back, again and again, across centuries, every time a tale is unfolded."[11] Like a ghost, the writer is extant yet never fully materialized. In the home of the deceased literary idol, the writer is likewise at once "present" due to biographical and literary constructions of the local environment but is at the same time absent to the physical eye.

This interplay of presence and absence creates a sense of the uncanny because the author is at once inside and outside the tourist's immediate experience.[12] The result is a disruption of conventional notions of individual identity. As Nicholas Royle has argued, the uncanny evokes a "sense of what is autobiographical, self-centered, based in one's own experience" while at the same time conveying a sense of "ghostliness" or "strangeness given to dissolving all assurances about the identity of a self."[13] For literary tourists, the experience of reading text and landscape not only problematized notions of the inviolate self but also produced a kind of enchantment where the supernatural haunted the apprehension of the real. For example, after visiting Stratford-upon-Avon, Washington Irving writes,

I could not but reflect on the singular gift of the poet; to be able thus to spread the magic of his mind over the very face of nature; to give to things and places a charm and character not their own, and to turn this "working-day world" into a perfect fairy land. He is, indeed, the true enchanter, whose spell operates, not upon the senses, but upon the imagination of the heart. Under the wizard influence of Shakespeare, I had been walking all day in a complete delusion. . . . I had been surrounded with fancied beings; with mere airy nothings, conjured up by poetic power, yet which to me had all the charm of reality.[14]

Through the lens of Shakespeare's texts, the region's geography casts a "spell" on Irving. The scenes around him become uncanny in the sense that they are real yet magically transformed by Shakespeare's literary texts. He thus experiences what Freud would later call *unheimlich*: when the "boundary between fantasy and reality is blurred, when we are faced with the reality of something that we have until now considered imaginary, when a symbol takes on the full function and significance of what it symbolizes."[15] The touristic experience becomes enchanted with the "charm of reality," the momentary union of landscape, self, and text.

The uncanny effects of reading literature were produced not only by touring the homes of dead writers but also by visiting the spaces associated with living authors. Although alive, celebrity writers were absent to tourists, except as they appeared as presences "behind" written texts, buildings, or landscapes. The half-materialized presence of the living author was interpreted via virtual or physical travel through those spaces frequented, or "haunted," by the writer. Guidebooks that encouraged literary ghost hunting were always careful, when speaking of living writers, to maintain a boundary between "knowing" a writer through reading and tourism and viewing the writer through literary stalking. E. Beresford Chancellor, for example, remarks, "Perhaps one should not pry too curiously into the habits of contemporaries; but even Browning, in a famous poem ["House"], agreed that it might be permissible to peep through the poet's window, though not to pass over the threshold; and so one ventures to indicate the locality, but not that actual home of a few of those whose privacy should be considered."[16] Chancellor is careful to demarcate the boundaries of acceptable touristic practice, yet his account relies on the notion of authorial spectrality. To be a celebrity writer is to be only half-materialized, both intimately knowable and never fully apprehended.

Of course, the spectral metaphors associated with literary tourism have religious analogues. The search for the "spirit" of a writer can be interpreted as a quasireligious quest. Indeed, in guidebooks, literary tourism is often referred to as "pilgrimage," and the sites of literary interest are called "shrines." Likewise, the objects associated with literary lives are sometimes referred to as "relics."[17] The literary tourist, like the religious aspirant, was encouraged to have faith in the unseen, to seek mysterious and unverifiable truths based on spiritual encounters in hallowed places and on careful readings of sacred texts. Literary pilgrimage, as a quasispiritual activity, involved traveling to specific locations where one could commune with "spirits" that most represented British moral or cultural goodness. Tourists sought spiritual fulfillment through encounters with relics and sacred landscapes, marked and made meaningful by literary texts. They thus sought "truth" on an individual moral basis through intimate encounters with personally meaningful authors and places; at the same time, they were encouraged to situate themselves within a national heritage, which contextualized the individual within a broader network of cultural meanings.

The quasispiritual character of literary tourism was linked to the expansion of the spiritualist movement in Great Britain in the second half of the nineteenth century.[18] As Lisa Brocklebank has pointed out, spiritualist practices such as telepathy were often conflated with the process of reading because both enabled individuals to "extend their identity through sympathetic identification."[19] Reading was imagined as a psychic activity in the sense that it was a "means of rendering fluid and permeable the borders of individual consciousness."[20] It is not surprising, then, that the sympathetic union between reader and author enabled by the reading process would be interpreted as psychic experience. With the death of great Victorian writers came a corresponding interest in invoking their spirits through séances, automatic writing, and other spiritualist practices. The spirits of Tennyson and Wilde, for example, were invoked by mediums in the years following their deaths, and both famously "dictated" new writings telepathically via spiritualist intermediaries.[21] Such spiritualist activities were closely linked to the practice of literary tourism. An article in W. T. Stead's spiritualist periodical *Borderland* not only included discussion of Tennyson's spiritualist activities and postmortem appearances but also incorporated illustrations of his homes.[22] In this way, Stead suggests that

Tennyson's spirit was closely associated with the spaces he had inhabited during life.

In the same issue of *Borderland,* Elizabeth Barrett Browning is featured as a "Borderlander" who maintained her spiritualist beliefs despite her husband's disapproval.[23] She, like Tennyson, is depicted as
having a spirit existence after death, appearing to Bayard Taylor as a
ghost in her Casa Guidi home.[24] Such accounts no doubt stimulated
tourist activity by highlighting the link between Barrett Browning's
"spirit" and the authorial home, "which her pen immortalized" (366).
Borderland thus highlights Tennyson and Barrett Browning as spiritualist heroes, asserting that "all great poets are Borderlanders," because
they have "psychic gifts" and "embody in verse the sublimest aspirations of the race."[25] Indeed, great writers, both alive and dead, were
often viewed as being more spiritual than corporeal. Their spectrality infused the literary pilgrimage with spiritual meanings, prompting tourists, like spiritualist mediums, to channel beloved authors
through intimate encounters with landscapes, relics, and texts.

HAUNTED LONDON AND THE
GHOSTS OF WOMEN WRITERS

London was viewed as an especially important stop on a literary tour
of Great Britain due to its libraries, literary societies, and publishing
houses. As R. R. Bowker remarked in 1888, London was the "chief
literary centre of the world."[26] At the same time, however, the city was
expanding beyond recognizable boundaries, thus becoming "many
centres in one."[27] As noted in chapter 1, during the late nineteenth
century, London was perceived as being on the verge of losing its
literary significations along with its spiritual/cultural center. Due to
expansion and renovation, the city was represented as a shifting space
that was difficult for literary tourists to "read" or interpret. As a result,
London was often depicted as a city of ghosts. Walter Thornbury, in
his 1865 guide, *Haunted London,* interprets the city as space layered
with historical significations. "This book deals not so much with the
London of the ghost-stories," he writes, "as with the London conse-
crated by manifold traditions—a city every street and alley of which
teems with interesting associations, every paving-stone of which marks,
as it were, the abiding-place of some ancient legend or biographical
story; in short, this London of the present haunted by the memories

III.—OUR GALLERY OF BORDERLANDERS.

I.—TENNYSON.

◆

> " The veil
> Is rending, and the Voices of the Day
> Are heard across the Voices of the Dark."

ALL great poets are Borderlanders. The possession of certain psychic gifts is almost invariable in prophets, founders of great religions, and the men and women who have been privileged to embody in verse the sublimest aspirations of the race. They are all more or less seers, who dwell on the Borderland, seeing things that are invisible to ordinary men, and, therefore, are properly described as Borderlanders.

While writing out the " Penny Poets," I was much impressed by the constant reference to the other world in English poetry. To our greatest poets that other world is as real as this material one, which alone is recognised by the majority of men. From Shakespeare and Milton downwards the poets nearly all bear testimony, more or less emphatic, of the existence of other beings than the embodied spirits whom we call men and women. Shakespeare abounds with references to spiritual beings capable of exercising more or less influence upon the lives of mortals. Milton asserted in the strongest way that millions of spiritual creatures walk the earth unseen by mortal eye.

But of all our poets, few have been so constantly

SOMERSBY RECTORY, WHERE THE POET WAS BORN.

psychic as Lord Tennyson. In the case of other poets the vision was more or less unconscious ; with them it is part of themselves ; they did not know how it came or whither it went. Tennyson was more conscious of his unconsciousness—if I may use a paradox—and was well aware that most of his best work was due to the intrusion of the other world into this life, or rather to his ability to rid himself of his material surroundings, and enter into that other world which to him was much more real than that which is but as the shadow that passes away.

The appearance of the Memoir of the late Poet Laureate by his son, Hallam, the present Lord Tennyson,* naturally supplies some partial insight into the

psychic life of the poet. Judging from the Memoir, it is probable that most readers will draw up the conclusion that the psychic gift which the father possessed to such an extraordinary degree has not been inherited by the son. The tendency of the biographer is to minimise instead of emphasise the fact that his father was emphatically a dweller in Borderland ; that his genius was largely the result of his psychic life ; that he was able to charm, instruct, and inspire men of his generation, because in his higher moments he dwelt habitually on a mystic plane to which they seldom or never gain access. A biographer who was more in sympathy with occult things would easily, by a very few touches, have conveyed a much more impressive picture of Tennyson as a mystic—of Tennyson as a dweller in the realm of spirit. But even in this Memoir the fact is

* " Tennyson." A Memoir by Hallam, Lord Tennyson. In two vols. Macmillan & Co. 36s.

of the past."[28] London's rich cultural associations were located in the material remnants of history, which must be "dredged up from the Sea of Oblivion" because "Time, the Destroyer and the Improver" was "erasing tombstones, blotting out names on street-doors, battering down narrow streets" (vi). Thornbury's personification of time as a violent destroyer suggests that the city is a dangerous place where precious cultural knowledge is constantly under threat of annihilation. Similarly, in *The Literary Ghosts of London*, E. Beresford Chancellor writes that it is not "altogether superfluous to recall what London has been in the past, as the home of famous literary men whose ghosts (if ghosts do walk) must find it not a little difficult to avoid the vastly increased material crowd that throng the streets, and especially the traffic which makes those streets often enough places of terror and not infrequently scenes of tragedy."[29] Wandering among the London crowds, literary ghosts of the past find themselves in a dangerous urban landscape, where individual lives, along with cultural memories, are effaced and consumed.

Westminster Abbey would seem to promise a permanent home for London's wandering literary spirits. Yet it was depicted as memorial to decay and cultural loss. In *Poets' Corner* (1892), Fred Weatherly writes,

> Where are the mighty poets gone?
>   Where are their burning spirits fled?
> Is it beyond the stars and sun,
>   And do they sleep among the dead?
> Or who will wake their songs again,
>   Or strike their silent harps once more,
> And sing, in these sad days, a strain
>   Of chivalry and love of yore? (1–8)[30]

In the "sad days" of the present, even Westminster Abbey seems to have been vacated by the "burning spirits" of the past. By the end of the poem, however, the denizens of Poets' Corner are revealed to be "alive" after all. Weatherly concludes,

> And then I tread the Abbey dust,
>   And scan the legends speaking fair,
> The storied urn, the sculptured bust,
>   And think to find them sleeping there.
> But no! They ask not such a bed,

> Death hath for them no lot, or part,
> The Poets live! They are not dead,
>   They live within their people's heart! (17–24)

In this stanza, writers are figured as absences, yet they are "not dead." Christlike, they have risen from the tomb and "live." The memorials at Westminster Abbey are false signifiers in the sense that they mark deaths that are not "real" to the literary tourist. Moving from a melancholy "I" at the beginning of the stanza to a celebratory reference to the "people" in the last line, the poem suggests that the process of literary tourism can heal a sense of isolation and cultural loss, reintegrating individuals into a coherent national culture.

The publication of guidebooks to various literary sites in London enabled the "ghost hunt," which would allow tourists to link the "live" spirits of the literary past to the "dust" of the material present. Exploring the haunts of Charles Dickens and other male writers was the primary object of the London literary pilgrimage, and the city was full of physical reminders of their presence in the city, including several tombs in Westminster Abbey. Shrines to women writers were more difficult to locate in the abbey or in London more generally. During the Victorian era, there was only one woman author memorialized in Poets' Corner, Mary Eleanor Bowes (1749–1800), and there were few blue plaques marking women's homes and haunts elsewhere in the city.[31] Because women writers were so difficult to place on a tourist map of London, they were interpreted as being even more ghostly and invisible than their male counterparts. This invisibility was of course reinforced by domestic ideology, which problematized the relationship between literary fame and feminine respectability.

CHRISTINA ROSSETTI

Only as disembodied spirits could women be imagined as city dwellers, let alone as professional writers working in a competitive literary marketplace. Christina Rossetti, for example, spent the majority of her life as a working author in London, writing and publishing books of poetry and prose. Yet even during her lifetime, readers imagined Rossetti as a ghostly presence in the city landscape. Critics emphasized the "spirituality" of Rossetti's poetry not only to highlight its importance as devotional literature but also to suggest ways that it evoked the ghost of the living writer, who was always part spirit.[32] By virtue of having read Rossetti's poetry, readers claimed to know the writer on a personal level, yet they could never see or fully understand her due to her reclusiveness, her status as ghostly, half-materialized other. R. R. Bowker, for example, writing for *Harper's New Monthly Magazine,* contends that "Christina Rossetti's deeply spiritual poems are known even more widely than those of her more famous brother, Dante Gabriel Rossetti. She still lives in London, an invalid and recluse, with that same sad, sweet face of the *religieuse* which her brother had so often delighted to paint, producing 'hymns and spiritual songs' as the spirit moves her."[33]

When journalists describe meetings with Rossetti, their encounters take on an otherworldly quality. In an article titled "Some Reminiscences of Christina Rossetti," published in the *Bookman,* Katharine Tynan Hinkson describes a meeting with Rossetti in this way: "Cheerfulness in that house seemed a little discordant. Entering it you felt the presence of very old age, a silence that draped and muffled the house. . . . It was heavy and seemed to darken, as well as to muffle sound."[34] The house, like a mausoleum, is dark and quiet, sealed off from the bustling city. Indeed, Hinkson reports Rossetti as saying that she has "few visitors from the outside world" (28). She is "colourless, as a person who kept the house much and led a sedentary life," although she maintains the "strong spiritual beauty of the face her brother painted as the young Mary, predestined to superhuman sorrows" (29). Likewise, Hinkson describes Rossetti's heavy eyelids as "strangely heroic and strangely spiritual" (29). By the end of the article, Hinkson confesses that Rossetti is now "in heaven" (29). Yet given Rossetti's entombment in her home and her colorless life, the reader wonders whether she hadn't been dead years before. The marking of her death seems redundant given her ghostly presence during life.

Rossetti, like other urban poets of the period,[35] addressed the spectrality of the author in her work by employing supernatural motifs. For example, in a poem titled "At Home," Rossetti writes from the perspective of a woman who haunts her former house after death:

> When I was dead, my spirit turned
> To seek the much frequented house:
> I passed the door, and saw my friends
> Feasting beneath green orange boughs;

> From hand to hand they pushed the wine,
>   They sucked the pulp of plum and peach;
> They sang, they jested, and they laughed,
>   For each was loved of each. (1–8)[36]

Here the poetic persona is a ghost who passes through the rooms of those who are taking part in the sensory pleasures of wine, food, and love. "I, only I, had passed away," the speaker laments as she listens to the others talk of "tomorrow" (22–23). Ungrounded in the sensory realm, she can only "stay and yet to part"—neither here nor there, caught in a liminal space where she resides yet cannot be seen. On one level, the poem expresses the fear of being forgotten after death, but on another level, it expresses concern about the spectrality of authorship itself, which seems to require a woman author to be both present and absent, both in the text and outside of it, inseparable from domestic space yet separate from it.[37]

After Rossetti's death, her homes were marked on the literary map of London by a few articles and guides. However, although the homes were carefully described, they were depicted as being unsatisfactory markers of the writer's life. For example, in *Little Journeys to the Homes of Famous Women* (1897), Elbert Hubbard describes his tour of Rossetti's homes as an exploration of tantalizingly vague literary references. Hubbard first takes a room in the home that was Rossetti's birthplace: 38 Charlotte Street, Bloomsbury. This stay offered "nothing further than the meagre satisfaction of sleeping for two nights in the room in which Dante Gabriel Rossetti was born, and making the acquaintance of the worthy ticket taker [the current owner] who knew all four of the Rossettis, as they often passed through his gate."[38] The house at 166 Albany Street is similarly vacant, but he notes that "on one of the windows of a little bedroom we found the word 'Christina' cut with a diamond. . . . I have recently heard that the signature has been identified as authentic by a man who was familiar with the Rossettis' handwriting" (163–64). This is a significant moment because the scratched name, like a literary text, can be "authenticated" and evokes the persona, the "hand" that created it. Scrawled by a dead writer, the name seems almost a message from another world that is left as "code" for the literary tourist to interpret. Is it a defiant expression of self? Or is it, like prison cell graffiti, a cry for release? The inability of readers and tourists to answer such questions based on a single literary relic refuels the process of reading and tourism.

The writer is both tantalizingly "there" in Rossetti's texts and homes yet always elusive. A window, like a literary text, promises to allow readers to "see in," yet in Rossetti's case, it denies complete vision. The inability to obtain full knowledge engages the reader in a pleasurable process of detection, seeking that which can only be half-revealed truth. If the "real" Christina Rossetti could be found, her contemporaries suggested, it could only be outside the city. In an 1893 review, Edmund Gosse writes, "I have no reason for saying so beyond internal evidence, but I should be inclined to suggest that the county of Sussex alone is capable of having supplied all the imagery which Miss Rossetti's poems contain."[39] Although Rossetti spent a great deal of time at her grandfather's country home, there was no shrine literary tourists could visit that would explicitly link the imagery of Rossetti's poetry to the geography of rural England. This was partly due to that fact that Rossetti's poetry was not regional or otherwise specific in its geographical references. Alhough Gosse finds "internal evidence" sufficient to suggest a geographical connection between poetry and place, most other readers did not. No industry of literary tourism sprang up around her rural homes and haunts. Yet in London, Rossetti is still present for the literary insider who traces Rossetti's spectral presence through her texts and haunts.

ELIZABETH BARRETT BROWNING

Like Christina Rossetti, Elizabeth Barrett Browning spent many years in London, yet guides to literary London often overlooked the shrines associated with her life and career. Although Barrett Browning wrote prolifically while living in London, she was most often associated with the literary landscapes of Italy, particularly Casa Guidi in Florence, which was interpreted as the location of her "real" identity. According to the usual narrative, Elizabeth Barrett Browning achieved self-actualization by escaping the confines of London and entering into a romantic and literary partnership with Robert Browning. She could only achieve this self-fulfillment by leaving Great Britain and making her home in a more hospitable climate. When guidebooks mentioned Barrett Browning's London homes,[40] they interpreted them as isolated locations having little to do with the surrounding urban environment.[41] Barrett Browning's interaction with the literary marketplace is usually figured as a visit from a male supporter or a messenger who "waited at the door and begged to exchange the bank-notes for MS."[42] The marketplace never penetrates Barrett Browning's domestic privacy, thus enabling her to pursue a literary career in a hermetically sealed environment. Descriptions of Barrett Browning's early life in London stress the physical darkness of her bed chamber, interpreting it as a metaphorical tomb out of which the spiritually "dead" woman would later be reborn. H. B. Baildon's description of this metamorphosis is typical: "*Her* long invalid life was passed in the upper darkened chamber of a cheerless house situated in 'that long unlovely street' of Wimpole. Mutual love, which gave to her renewed life, gave to them both ambient emancipation."[43] As was the case with Rossetti, Barrett Browning's childhood homes in rural Britain were not interpreted as viable shrines for memorializing the great author. Although many guidebooks pictured a young Barrett Browning longing for "her happy childhood among the beautiful hills and orchards of the West country," they could not fasten on a particular rural location that would forge a connection between her life and the life of the nation as a whole.[44]

Nowhere is the inability to locate Barrett Browning on the literary map of Great Britain more apparent than in contemporary disputes over the location of her birthplace. The fact that biographers were unable to fasten on a particular site reveals their inability to "map" Barrett Browning and to narrate her life as a product of a particular British environment. Elbert Hubbard begins his introduction *Little Journeys to the Homes of Famous Women* with the following caveat: "But I will not tell where and when Elizabeth Barrett was born, for I do not know. And I am quite sure that her husband did not know. The encyclopaedias waver between London and Herefordshire, just according as the writers felt in their hearts that genius should be produced in town or country."[45] In this way, Hubbard points to the constructedness of the literary birthplace as well as its indeterminacy. The debate over Barrett Browning's birthplace began in 1886, when Anne Thackeray Ritchie, writing an entry on Barrett Browning for the *Dictionary of National Biography*, listed her birthplace as Coxhoe Hall, Durham.[46] John H. Ingram, in his biography on Barrett Browning published in 1888, argues that she was born in London.[47] He provides evidence based on biographical research and a birth announcement published in the *Tyne Mercury*. These "facts" were disputed by Robert Browning himself, who claimed that his wife was born "on March 6, 1807, at Carlton Hall, Durham, the residence of her father's brother."[48]

Ingram refutes this claim by pointing out that "Carlton Hall was not in Durham, but in Yorkshire, and, I am authoritatively informed, did not become the residence of Mr. S. Moulton Barrett until some time after 1810."[49] Today, scholars of course know that Anne Ritchie was correct in identifying Coxhoe Hall, Durham, as Barrett Browning's birthplace. The Victorian debate over her birthplace reveals the public's desire to situate the writer in geographical space, a local environment that produced the imagery of her poetry and the personality behind the myth. Yet it also reveals the frustration of this desire—the inability of critics to otherwise locate Barrett Browning on the literary/geographical map of England. She is from Great Britain but not of it.

After Barrett Browning's death, her London homes were interpreted as literary shrines on the verge of losing any specific cultural meanings. Elbert Hubbard describes his visit to 74 Gloucester Place, one of the Barretts' Marylebone homes, in this way: "It is a plain, solid brick house, built just like the ten thousand other brick houses in London where well-to-do tradesmen live. The people who now occupy the house never heard of the Barretts and surely do not belong to a Browning Club."[50] After lingering in front of the house for an hour, Hubbard departs, noting that his presence is monitored by servants and the police. In Hubbard's account, the literary shrine fades into insignificance by virtue of its unremarkable architecture and the neglect of the current generation of inhabitants, who have never heard of the great poet. The literary tourist becomes a loiterer, whose presence in the neighborhood is interpreted as a danger to both privacy and security. The loss of the literary shrine thus becomes a loss of status and purpose for Hubbard as a Barrett Browning enthusiast. Meanwhile, Casa Guidi in Florence remained a significant tourist destination. H. B. Baildon writes in 1906 that the home "has become a name sacred to English people for its poetic and human associations, and not an English-speaking visitor who comes to Florence omits a pilgrimage to the Via Maggio to see it."[51] Barrett Browning's career thus can only be interpreted outside British national boundaries.

Indeed, after Barrett Browning died in 1861, she was buried in Florence, not Poet's Corner. The gravesite immediately became a popular shrine for literary tourists, who, to the annoyance of Robert Browning, took pieces of the monument as relics.[52] When Robert Browning died in 1889, his remains were interred in Westminster Abbey, and for a time there was talk of transferring Elizabeth's remains to the abbey as well. However, these plans soon failed, and the two graves remained in separate countries. However, Barrett Browning is commemorated with an inscription at the foot of her husband's grave in Westminster Abbey, which reads "His wife Elizabeth Barrett Browning is buried in Florence. 1806–61." As Samantha Matthews has shown, the discourse over the burial of the two poets reveals Barrett Browning's "symbolic and rhetorical assimilation into his [her husband's] nationally significant grave."[53] Even after death, Elizabeth Barrett Browning could not be located within the British national landscape or cultural heritage. To "know" or to "locate" her, literary tourists must visit Italy; that is, they must immerse themselves in another country's system of cultural and national significations.

George Eliot

George Eliot, like Christina Rossetti and Elizabeth Barrett Browning, spent a significant portion of her working life in London, yet she, too, was difficult to locate on a literary map of the city. During the 1870s, when Eliot lived in London, her homes were unofficial stops on literary tours of London. Literary pilgrims from England and America flocked to the Priory at St. John's Wood to visit the sage writer. Alfred Austin, for example, described a visit to the Priory in this way: "But there I found pervading her house an attitude of adoration, not to say an atmosphere almost of awe, thoroughly alien to my idea that persons of genius, save in their works, should resemble other people as much as possible, and not allow any special fuss to be made about them."[54] Indeed, Eliot's homes are described in a number of memoirs and guidebooks.[55] Yet these descriptions are often carefully focused away from Eliot's urban context. Even while a resident of a bustling city, George Eliot is most often depicted at home or in parks and green spaces: Regent's Park, St. John's Wood, and Hampstead Heath. In guidebooks, these natural environments are seen as a necessary antidote to literary labor and urban life. One writer, discussing Eliot's and George Henry Lewes's tendency to walk in Hampstead Heath, notes that "when their literary tasks brought on weariness and indisposition occasionally, George Eliot and Lewes would stroll across the fields to the beloved Hampstead haunts, and, after a few hours, return with fresh zest to their respective labours."[56]

Even after her death and burial in Highgate Cemetery, George Eliot was located within the physical confines of the city yet was represented as being spiritually "outside" the urban environment. In *A Literary Pilgrimage among the Haunts of Famous British Authors*, Theodore Wolfe begins his tour of George Eliot sites with a description of her grave: "From the terraces above her bed we look over the busy metropolis, astir with its myriad pulses of life and passion, while its rumble and din sound in our ears in a murmurous monotone."[57] To begin with George Eliot's grave is significant because it establishes her as dead yet alive in the sense that her spirit lives on in the margins of the city. Wolfe provides no other representations of Eliot's urban experiences; instead, he provides a lengthy tour of the sites associated with Eliot's novels in the English midlands. Because Eliot was born in the country, she was easy to locate within a rural environment, which could be read as the reference to or source of her major novels. Leslie Stephen, like many other critics of the era, found her novels provided the "most vivid picture now extant of the manners and customs of the contemporary dwellers in the midland counties of England."[58] Nuneaton, as the writer's birthplace, provided a convenient center for exploring "George Eliot Country," which included not only her childhood homes and haunts but also the originals for the characters, houses, and landscapes in her novels. Indeed, a museum display honoring George Eliot was erected at the Nuneaton Museum and Art Gallery in the 1970s. Significantly, a display in the museum recreates Eliot's London drawing room, including her desk and grand piano. To memorialize Eliot as a London sage, the literary pilgrim must go to the country, that is, to a space that is physically separated from the urban environment. Other memorials, including an obelisk (1952) and a bronze statue (1986), soon became points of interest on a tour of George Eliot Country. Today, Nuneaton remains the jumping off point for literary tourism in the region, especially excursions associated with the George Eliot Fellowship, founded in 1930.

"George Eliot Country" was established as a subset of a broader system of cultural landmarks in the midlands region. Charles Olcott, writing in 1910, notes that at the "southern extremity" of the region, "is the birthplace of Shakespeare, visited annually by thousands of tourists from all over the world."[59] At the center is Kenilworth, "immortalized by the pen of Sir Walter Scott," and to the north is Coventry, "with its three spires and its legend of Lady Godiva, which Tennyson has put into imperishable verse" (5) Yet further north is

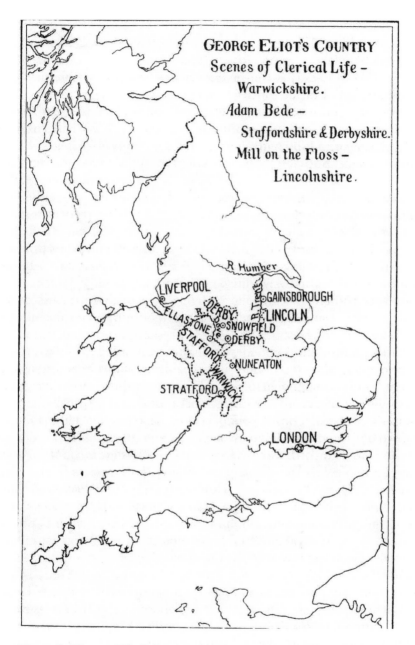

Figure 5. "George Eliot's Country," in *George Eliot: Scenes and People in Her Novels*, by Charles Olcott (New York: Crowell, 1910): 6–7.

Nuneaton, "near which George Eliot was born and passed the first twenty-one years of her life" (6). In this way, Olcott establishes George Eliot's birthplace within a network of cultural landmarks, a circuit of literary references that can be experienced on a single literary tour of the region. Indeed, Sidney Lanier establishes Eliot's greatness by emphasizing the geographical proximity of her birthplace to Shakespeare's Stratford-upon-Avon: "We have the greatest English man and the greatest English woman born, though two centuries and a half apart in time, but a few miles apart in space."[60] The bio-geographical emphasis here suggests that greatness is produced not only by the midlands landscape but also by a similar propensity for genius. Indeed, Olcott points out, the two writers viewed "life through the same environment."[61]

The construction of George Eliot Country was accomplished through a variety of written texts that forged a triangular relationship between the author's biography, her literary works, and the environments that "produced" them. The introduction to the 1908 edition of the *Mill on the Floss* is typical: "The scenery of the novel is supposed to be in Lincolnshire, and the town of St. Ogg's to present Gainsborough, but the details are those of George Eliot's native district, and her old neighbors recognised her by the closeness of her descriptions."[62] Interestingly, the introduction emphasizes that Eliot's neighbors recognize "her" through her literary text, by which they seem to mean the memory of her as a child, the ghostly persona of the past who now haunts Eliot's "native district" and can be invoked through acts of literary tourism. It was thus only through traveling to rural British environments that tourists could experience the "real" homes of women authors, where visions of domestic femininity could be successfully reconciled with conceptions of the woman author. To truly "know" George Eliot, one must go to the country, to explore the "homes and haunts" of the past, those formative natural environments that retain her "spirit" or "essence" through constructions in literary texts.

The practice of tourism, as Dean MacCannell has pointed out, is a symptom of modernity in that it attempts to "overcome the discontinuity of modernity, of incorporating its fragments into unified experience."[63] The same can be said of the discourse on literary tourism, which attempts to construct not only a coherent narrative of the past but also a coherent reading of literary lives and texts. This process was inseparable from the process of canon formation during the second half of the nineteenth century. The difficulty of locating Rossetti and Barrett Browning on the map of literary Britain was concomitant with their decanonization in the early years of the twentieth century. Although they remained tantalizing "ghosts" to the most epicurean literary tourists, their lives and works were difficult to integrate into a coherent narrative of British literary history. George Eliot, of course, achieved canonical status in the years just following her death. However, the tourism industry could not imagine Eliot as an urban denizen and thus invented George Eliot Country, a rural location that connected meaningfully to the locations described in her books. Such a rural location was no doubt assimilated more easily into the nation's vision of itself. Likewise, a young Marian Evans of Nuneaton was in many ways easier to understand than the sage writer of the Priory who had lived with a married man and had operated so effectively (if somewhat stealthily) within the London literary marketplace.

Of course, literary tourism, like the late Victorian literary canon, was subject to continual reinvestigation and change. Even Poet's Corner, which seemed to promise a sense of cultural permanence, was subject to alteration. In a 1900 article published in the *Monthly Review*, William Archer refers to Poets' Corner as "an academy of the dead" that is quickly outstripping available space in the abbey.[64] "For the past fifty years at least," he notes, "space in the Poet's Corner, and in the Abbey generally, has been at an enormous premium" (119). The lack of available space is complicated by the fact that "there is also a far larger number of would-be geniuses clamouring for consideration, and therefore far more chance of real greatness passing unheeded in the welter of mediocrity" (121). Archer makes a case for adding memorials to Christina Rossetti and Elizabeth Barrett Browning, writers who are deserving of "national hero-worship" (125).[65] Further, he finds it shocking that George Eliot's grave is "hidden in the crowded purlieus of Kensal Green" instead of Westminster Abbey (125). Meanwhile, Elizabeth Gaskell and Margaret Oliphant are among those "doubtful cases" of authors who fail to meet the standard of permanent value (125). Yet Archer remains unsure of his own choices. If the writers on his "doubtful" list had been enshrined, "would any great harm have been done?" (125). He continues, "The age of pompous epitaphs is past, and there can be no very withering irony in the mere carving of a name, to which future generations are free to accord whatever tribute they think fit—a tear, a smile, a shrug, or an unrecognizing glance" (126). Archer thus constructs a Victorian "academy of the dead," making an argument for which authors would best represent the apogee of literary genius of the nineteenth century. At the same time, he questions the whole idea of canon formation, suggesting that such selections are arbitrary, the creations of a particular historical moment.

The process of canon formation, like the process of literary memorialization, was in a state of flux during the late nineteenth century and certainly continues to be so more than one hundred years later. Like the process of canon formation, the practice of literary tourism is always in a state of fracturing and differentiation, where minor narratives and microreadings of landscape interrupt and complicate those constructed within dominant print culture. As Dean MacCannell points out, the coherence promised by modern tourism is "doomed to eventual failure," because "even as it tries to construct totalities, it celebrates differentiation."[66] The same is true of the process of literary tourism, which offers pleasure to tourists not only by enabling them to visit those sites that have already been established as culturally significant on a national level but also by allowing them to discover the spectral presences of writers who have been forgotten and whose "homes and haunts" are only visible to the discerning eye. The woman writer, due to her ghostlike invisibility brought on through the related processes of literary canonization and literary tourism, becomes the special object of desire for cultural tourism. The study of women's literary history, whether through revising the canon or rediscovering cultural landmarks, is a process that emphasizes the ability to know the past and points to its inacessibility. At the same time that tourists or readers construct literary heroes or literary shrines, they are reminded of the ephemerality of these objects of devotion—their ghostlike spectrality that eludes the reader, producing both investigative frustration and readerly pleasure.

3

The Woman of Letters at Home:
Harriet Martineau and the Lake District

HARRIET MARTINEAU, PERHAPS MORE THAN ANY OTHER VICTORIAN woman writer, understood the importance of capitalizing on celebrity culture as a way of ensuring her own enduring fame as a woman of letters. By situating her home in the Lake District and demonstrating the compatibility of literary and domestic pursuits, she provided a model for how women could make a name for themselves while still maintaining middle-class respectability. By the 1870s, the Knoll had become a regular stop on literary tours of the Lake District. This was of course partly due to the fact that Martineau's literary reputation had established her as a central figure in most major political and social controversies of the day, including industrial relations, women's rights, and abolition. By the time she came to settle in the Lake District, Martineau had already published more than a dozen successful works, including *Illustrations of Political Economy*, *Society in America*, and *Deerbrook*.[1] She had also published numerous articles in periodicals such as the *Westminster Review*, *Tait's Edinburgh Magazine*, and the *Monthly Repository*.[2]

Just as important to the emergence of the Knoll as a literary shrine were Martineau's own efforts at self-promotion. This chapter will explore how Harriet Martineau participated in constructing her own public image as a literary icon by first building and then publicizing her Lake District home. Martineau facilitated the emergence of the Knoll as a tourist destination by publishing works focused on the landscape and culture of the Lakeland region. These efforts included her *Autobiography*, published posthumously in 1877; "A Year at Ambleside," published in *Sartain's Union Magazine* in 1850; "Lights of the English Lake District," published in *Atlantic Monthly* in 1861; and

Complete Guide to the English Lakes, published in five editions from 1855 to 1876. In these texts, Martineau traces her own rise to fame and domestic fulfillment and tells the stories of other Lakeland settlers: William Wordsworth, Dorothy Wordsworth, and Fredrika Meyer. Working both inside and outside notions of domestic femininity and Wordsworthian fame, Martineau provided a model of how women could capitalize on the emerging industry of literary tourism as a way of enhancing their status as literary celebrities. At the same time, she drew attention to the ways that women could assume positions of agency and independence through their engagement with the natural world.

Martineau used her Lake District publications as a means of fusing her identity with the local geography, which was already rich with literary associations. Beginning in the middle of the eighteenth century, the Lake District became a popular destination for artists and writers. As Ernest de Selincourt points out, "In the last quarter of the eighteenth century no part of England was more often the subject of description and illustration."[3] During this period, the Lake District was considered a prime location for viewing picturesque scenery.[4] Many writers of the period, including Ann Radcliffe and Thomas Gray, popularized the area through their writings and experiences as travelers in the region.[5] However, these literary associations were soon eclipsed by the emergence of the Lake Poets, who altered perceptions of the region through literary representations of the landscape as well as through accounts of their own lives as Lakeland residents.

For literary tourists, the homes and haunts of William Wordsworth held a special fascination throughout the nineteenth century. Wordsworth's meteoric rise to success, beginning with the publication of *Lyrical Ballads* in 1798 and culminating with his poet laureateship in 1843, provided an important model of literary success that was grounded in a particular geographical locale. As a marker of this achievement, in 1813 Wordsworth moved to Rydal Mount, a home that soon became a destination for literary tourists and celebrities. For Wordsworth, establishing a substantial residence in the Lake District was a marker of having arrived as a poet and thinker. Harriet Martineau was no doubt well aware of this history when she relocated to the Lake District in 1846. Like Wordsworth, she constructed her home as a marker of her growing literary fame. However, for Martineau, the construction of a home also meant refashioning her identity to harmonize her professional career with Victorian stereotypes of domestic womanhood.

In her engagement with the discourse on literary tourism, Martineau was participating in a rapidly expanding field of literary activity that encompassed a variety of popular print media, including guidebooks, maps, pamphlets, memoirs, and the periodical press. As noted in previous chapters, the practice of literary tourism had become a full-fledged industry by the end of the Victorian era. These touristic activities were focused not only on London as a literary center but also on sites located outside the urban context. As the British middle classes gained increasing mobility due to the expansion of railway travel, they began touring the homes and haunts of their favorite authors as a form of secular pilgrimage. On one hand, as James Buzard points out, Victorian tourists sought "authenticity" through uncovering the "true" or "real" version of British culture that was "off the beaten track" and accessible only to a few.[6] On the other hand, they sought a group experience that would enable them to see the packaged version of the sites and points of interest that promised a sense of unifying vision. This "view of acculturation," Buzard notes, is by definition a "double and potentially self-contradictory process, requiring gestures of both self-distinction (to separate oneself from the crowd) and solidarity (to appeal to an imagined small group of independent spirits)."[7] Such attempts were of course related to the broader project of constructing national identity. At the same time that the British Empire was becoming increasingly fragmented and decentered, the British industry of literary tourism began to package Britain as a coherent geographical space made real and significant through a variety of literary references. Thus, Britain could be fully understood only by those who had carefully studied literature and literary biography, which enabled them to see beyond the trivial, the chaotic, and the superficial. Martineau's writings on the Lake District, then, perform the function of establishing her own literary celebrity while at the same time participating in the construction of "Great Britain" as a geographical space that is knowable only through study of literature and literary auto/biography.

The pervasive image of the writer at home in nineteenth-century print culture was also significant as a product of debates over the domestic ideal. Was it possible for women to pursue careers without compromising the sanctity of the "feminine" sphere? How might conceptions of "home" be reconfigured to be more inclusive of women's new literary practices? Such questions fueled the discourse on literary tourism as it related to the homes and haunts of women writers. By visiting women's homes, tourists could visualize and vicariously experience the contradictions and pleasures of the literary life.

Harriet Martineau, perhaps more than any other writer of her time, capitalized on this desire to know and view the woman author by fusing her identity with the landscape of the Lake District and by constructing and publicizing her own home as a literary point of interest. Her Lake District writings illustrate the ways that women could make use of the discourse on literary tourism, constructing the landscape through literary texts as a means of self-promotion. At the same time, these writings demonstrate the limitations of literary discourse in constructing national or local landscapes; that is, they reveal the inevitable failure of all attempts to mark the landscape or mediate the experience of place through literary acts of self-memorialization.

BUILDING A HOME

Martineau began constructing the Knoll in 1845, when she was forty-three years old. The construction of a house marked the end of her six-year confinement to the sickbed and her miraculous cure by mesmerism. Martineau claimed in her *Autobiography* that her decision to settle in the Lake District was motivated by her "thirst for foliage" as well as her desire for a "domestic life . . . among poor improvable neighbors."[8] Yet on some level, Martineau's decision may have been motivated in part by her desire to put herself on the literary map of England, both literally and figuratively. By 1845, Martineau was well known as the author of *Illustrations of Political Economy, Society in America,* and *Deerbrook.* During her years as an invalid, Martineau found it difficult to maintain the kind of publishing agenda that would ensure her literary reputation. She published several works during this period, including *The Hour and the Man, Life in the Sickroom,* and *Letters on Mesmerism.* Although these works succeeded in keeping her in the public eye during her illness, they did not enhance her literary reputation in a significant way. In fact, looking back on the period of her illness, Martineau decided to "ignore altogether the five years at Tynemouth . . . and proceed as if that awful chasm had never opened

in my path which now seemed closed up, or invisible as it lay behind."[9]
A move to the Lake District was a way of resuming her earlier life of
health, domestic enjoyment, and literary productivity. The process
of building a house was inseparable from the goal of rebuilding her
life. She writes to Emerson in 1845,

> It is with as much wonder as pleasure that I write to you. Here I
> am, looking out on blue Windermere, on the mountains all sun and
> shadow,—feeling myself full of health through my whole frame,—
> strong, peaceful, *well* in mind and body . . . For the first time in my
> life I am free to live as I please;—and I please to live here. My life
> is now (in this season) one of wild roving, after my years of help-
> less sickness, I ride like a Borderer,—walk like a pedlar,—climb like
> a mountaineer,—sometimes on excursions with kind and merry
> neighbors,—sometimes all alone for a day on the mountains. I can-
> not leave this region. London must give way. Before you get this, I
> shall probably have paid for a field opposite Fox How, for which I am
> in treaty, and have begun to build my cottage.[10]

In this passage, Martineau's mobility and engagement with the landscape are reflected in the syntax of her sentences: running phrases
and active verbs set off by commas and dashes. This gives the prose
a sense of movement that, toward the end of the passage, settles in
short end-stopped sentences and, finally, in the building of her cottage. The cottage thus serves as a stationary point of reference in the
passage and in Martineau's immediate life experience—a home base
upon which to center her physical and literary activity.

In her *Autobiography*, Martineau describes the construction of her
home as the creation of a distinctly literary space. One of the reasons
she decides to build rather than rent is that her bookcases are too tall
to fit into the local cottages.[11] Indeed, in her plans for the Knoll, the
study dominates the ground-floor design. James Payn would later remark that "there were bookshelves everywhere at The Knoll."[12] After
the success of her translation of Comte's *Positive Philosophy* in 1853,
Martineau rewards herself with a "first-rate regular Chancery-lane
desk, with all manner of conveniences."[13] But most importantly, in her
Autobiography, Martineau demonstrates the compatibility of literary
and domestic pursuits within the space that she has constructed. She
describes a typical day in 1854 this way: "Two or three hours, after
the arrival of the post (at breakfast time now) usually served me for
my work; and when my correspondence was done, there was time

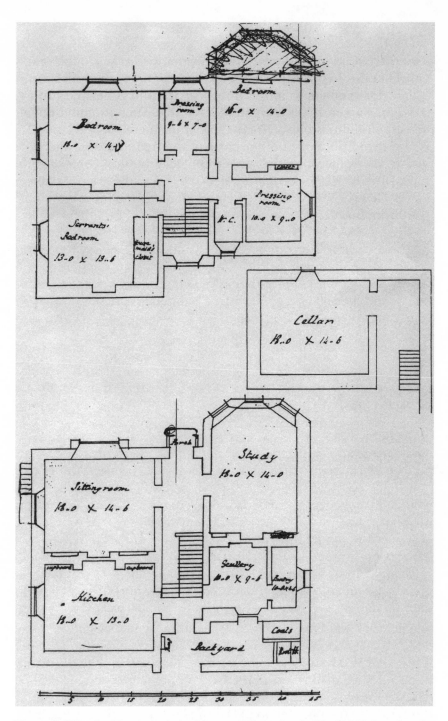

Figure 6. "Harriet Martineau's Architectual Plans for the Knoll," University of Birmingham Library, Harriet Martineau Papers, HM 1302. Reproduced with permission.

for exercise, and the discharge of neighborly business before dinner. Then,—I have always had some piece of fancy-work on hand,— usually for the benefit of the Abolition Fund in America."[14] In this passage, Martineau's literary work is distinguished from her domestic responsibilities but is inseparable from them. This relationship is also demonstrated in other parts of the *Autobiography*, where she locates the scene of writing within the geographical context of the Lake District. When recounting her first trip to the area, Martineau writes, "It was on the 2nd of September that we drove through Ambleside, from Bowness to Grasmere, passing the field in which I am now abiding,—on which I am at this moment looking forth" (2:138–39). The inclusion of illustrations of the Knoll in the *Autobiography* adds to this sense of Martineau's writing location as an essential part of her book's appeal. As the author and protagonist of her *Autobiography*, she defines herself as a Lake District habitué, whose home, as much as her life and work, is designed to fascinate readers—and ultimately to inspire literary tourism.

Chronicling the Lake District: Periodical Essays

Indeed, by the time the *Autobiography* was published in 1877, just after Martineau's death, the Knoll had already become a well-known tourist destination, partly due to Martineau's own efforts. During the 1840s and 1850s, Martineau published articles on the Lake District in literary periodicals.[15] Two of the most important of these articles were written for an American audience: "A Year at Ambleside," a series of essays published in *Sartain's Union Magazine* in 1850, and "Lights of the English Lake District," an essay published in *Atlantic Monthly* in 1861. These articles, aimed at a middle-class audience of men and women, were intended to entertain armchair travelers and literary tourists with personal accounts of the landscape and culture of the Lake District. They also reveal how Martineau conceived of her relationship to the landscape and literary history of the region, especially the ways she actively promoted literary tourism and attempted to remap the district according to the details of her own life experiences.

"A Year at Ambleside" describes changes to the Lake District landscape month by month and highlights the region's scenic and literary points of interest. Martineau is careful to point out the Swan Inn, where Walter Scott had "his daily draught and chat with the landlord," and Dove Cottage, "where Wordsworth lived with his sister before he married."[16] She even depicts herself as a literary tourist who sometimes stops at the local parsonage to "hear something of Mrs. Hemans (who was guide and friend to the curate in his youth)" (96). Throughout her description of the literary sites of the Lake District, Martineau adopts the narrative persona of a tour guide. For example, in her description of the Rydal Valley, she gives the impression that readers are participating in a guided walking tour:

> We now see the recess of Fairfield, its whole cul-de-sac, finely, unless mists are filling the basin, and curling about the ridges; and Rydal Forest stretches boldly up to the snow line. Lady Le Fleming's large, staring, yellow mansion is a blemish in the glorious view; but a little way back, we saw near it what puts all great mansions out of our heads—Wordsworth's cottage [Rydal Mount], a little way up the lower slope of Nab Scar.—the blunt end of the Fairfield horseshoe. Of that cottage we must see more hereafter; it does not lie in our road now. (49)

Here and elsewhere in the narrative, Martineau describes her surroundings with precision, including the locations of various homes and the identities of their inhabitants. This reveals the level to which Martineau's narrative was shaped by the discourse on literary tourism, which relied on specific, spatially located descriptions of literary relics and points of interest.

Punctuating Martineau's walking tour of the region are segments of personal memoir and nature writing that seem aimed at fusing her literary identity with the Lake District landscape. The organizing principles for the first half of the series are not only the seasonal changes in Ambleside but also the stages in the construction of Martineau's home. She describes selecting the land and watching the house take shape. In the articles focused on her garden, she describes how she plants trees, establishes a garden, and walks ten miles to collect ferns and mosses (61, 70). Martineau thus invites readers to participate in the process of constructing her home and to view creative inspiration as an organic process that begins in winter, grows in the spring, and flowers in the summer months as a completed project.[17] Like Martineau, Mother Nature herself is "eternally busy," reshaping the landscape through landslides, floods, and windstorms. And like Martineau, she focuses her energy on gardening and home improvements:

> She is for ever covering with her exquisite mosses and ferns, every spot which has been left unsightly, till nothing appears to offend the human eye within a whole circuit of hills. She even silently rebukes and repairs the false taste of uneducated man. If he makes his dwelling of too glaring a white, she tempers it with weather stains. If he indolently leaves to the stone walls and blue slates unrelieved by any neighboring vegetation, she supplies the needful screen by bringing out tufts of delicate fern in the crevices, and springing coppice on the nearest slopes. (75–76)

Here Martineau brings together the two themes of the first half of the book: the passing of the seasons and the building of domestic space. And she, like Mother Nature, works on improving her surroundings and repairing the mistakes of the "uneducated."

Indeed, the second half of the series is dominated by a second construction project: Martineau's plan for building cottages for the local workers, who live in ignorance of modern advancements in education and sanitation. "I made up my mind," she writes in her October installment, "that the true way to improve the health and morals of our neighborhood was, by putting the people in the way of providing wholesome dwellings for themselves" (134). She institutes a series of lectures for working people and establishes a local building society. Once the autumn season commences, bringing illness and hardship to the workers, Martineau hatches a plan for the construction of a "hamlet of thirty or forty wholesome dwellings" to be completed over a term of thirteen years (137).[18] She also reports that a Board of Health has been established in the region and that "large subscriptions have been made for building a new church—partly for the sake of a new place of burial" away from the village to prevent the outbreak of disease caused by an overcrowded and unsanitary churchyard (137–38).

Martineau thus depicts the Lake District as a location constantly in flux, due not only to seasonal changes and the work of Mother Nature but also to her own tireless activity, which is directed toward improving and shaping her surroundings. Her efforts to construct houses and gardens are mirrored by her construction of a literary text, which recreates these spaces yet again for an American audience. Martineau finds the Lake District an ideal site for these activities because she is surrounded by women who live lives of useful activity. Anticipating Elizabeth Gaskell's *Cranford*, Martineau points out that the region is inhabited primarily by "Amazons" (52). She notes that "gentlemen soon grow tired" of country life and "go off somewhere to find something to do—some business, or foreign travel, or hunting" (52). Because there are so few men at home, "three times out of four, our little parties are composed wholly of ladies; and they happen to be such ladies as leave nothing to be wished" (53). Even Wordsworth, the most famous man in the region, "likes to see his friends at home, but does not visit" (52). Thus, the Lake District social and geographical space is interpreted by Martineau as a female-dominated environment, ruled by Mother Nature herself, where women are able to achieve freedom from the social constraints faced by those in more conventional environments. In her description of one of the Lake District Amazons, a German boatbuilder named Fredrika Meyer, Martineau remarks, "What grace there is in her freedom of action! Who would have thought of boat-building being a graceful operation? Yet now, when she cannot hold her hand off the work, how beautifully she uses the hammer, and rapidly makes a row of copper-headed nails shine along the side!" (96–97). Fredrika often reappears in the series as a symbol of the sort of independent feminine spirit that dominates the region. In addition to building boats, she is an avid fisherwoman, artist, and walker (97). Like Martineau, she has traveled widely and is a gifted storyteller (98).

In a sense, Fredrika becomes an externalization of what Martineau feels she cannot tell about herself: that she is an artist. Martineau makes few references to her own artistic life in "A Year at Ambleside," perhaps because she wants to focus on her domestic virtues. Because Martineau had the reputation of being an unwomanly writer due to the political subject matter of her work, she no doubt felt the need to present her feminine side to the world.[19] When she does mention her literary pursuits, it is usually in the context of discussing her engagement with the landscape as a builder and walker. In her December segment, she describes taking an early morning walk and then returning home to feel the "glow from exercise, and one's mind all awake for the work of the day!" (149). The nature of this work is left ambiguous, although on some level readers familiar with Martineau's career could imaginatively insert the word *writing* into her sentence. Although she makes only indirect reference to her literary pursuits, she does demonstrate in one anecdote the way that her books contribute to the shaping of her home. During the period in which she is establishing her lawn, she awakens one day to discover that grass sods have been placed over her wall as an anonymous gift. She writes,

> They were of the finest grass, neatly rolled and piled. Our first idea was, that a neighboring gardener had mistaken my enquiry for an order, and had involved me in an expensive purchase; but the gardener knew nothing about it, and could not imagine where such sods were to be had. . . . Fine as they were, they did not cover much ground; and in two or three nights more another load was deposited in the same place. . . . After an interval of a week, a large quantity—probably a wagon load—was found, and finally, a fifth portion, which sufficed to cover every bare spot, and left some grass over. Under this last pile lay a letter—studiously vulgar in its external appearance, and with bad spelling within. . . . It pretended to be from two poor poachers, who affected gratitude to me for having written against the game laws [in *Forest and Game Law Tales*], and begged to show it by thus secretly presenting me with what I most wanted for my garden. (83–84)

The building of the house is facilitated by her writing, which produces the kind of good will that benefits the writer by helping her to construct a domestic space, rather than providing public accolades or monetary reward. Writing thus becomes a kind of good work that, through a barter system, produces good trade that indirectly facilitates the writer's craft.

Although references to Martineau's writing life are often indirect or vague, her presence as a narrator reminds the reader that she is the creator of the narrative. Martineau sometimes uses diarylike techniques: present tense verbs and dated entries. She also emphasizes the inclusivity of her narrative by using the pronoun *we* to describe her jaunts outdoors. In her description of a hike to the top of Kirkstone Pass, for example, she writes,

> Well: to this house we are first to mount—taking our time for the steep and almost continuous ascent of three miles and a half. How steep it is! How soon we look down into the church tower, and see the valley mapped out below us, and find the lake spreading and lengthening, and little Blelham Tarn now glittering beyond it, over the nearer hills—and the Langdale Pikes rearing their crests above the

> Grasmere range—and line upon line of ridges, grayer and fainter,
> extending westward towards the sea! (74)

Throughout "A Year at Ambleside," Martineau retains this sense of
vividness in her description and presents her own perception as a
filter through which the reader can participate in constructing the
landscape. In this way, she invites American readers to come to the
region and see the Lake District through her eyes.

Perhaps even more importantly, Martineau reinforces the connection between place and her individual identity by fashioning her own
home as a site of literary interest. She establishes the noteworthiness
of her home as a tourist destination not only by emphasizing its connection to her own domestic activities but also by marking its association with the life and career of William Wordsworth. For example,
in her description of the construction of her garden, Martineau tells
this tale:

> On this spot it was that the most important planting of all took place.
> I had asked Mr. Wordsworth whether he would plant a tree for me,
> and he had said he would. . . . Mrs. D. sent to her gardener for a
> young oak; but Mr. Wordsworth objected that an oak was too com-
> mon a tree for a commemorative occasion—it should be something
> more distinctive. So we selected a vigorous little stone pine, and off
> we went. Mr. Wordsworth struck in his spade on a spot under the ter-
> race wall, just overhanging the little quarry from which the stone for
> that wall was taken. . . . In most workman-like fashion he set the little
> tree, and gave it its first watering. Then he washed his hands in the
> watering-pot, took my hand in both his, and gave his blessing to me
> and my dwelling. (62–63)[20]

This account establishes the stone pine tree as an object of tourist
interest.[21] The phrase "on this spot," when followed by other par-
ticularizing detail, would seem to invite readers to locate and then
view the tree (along with Dove Cottage and other sights) on their
visits to the Lake District. In focusing on this commemorative tree,
Martineau was calling on a tradition that was well established in the
literary tourism industry. For example, an article titled "Literary Relics," published in *Chambers's Edinburgh Journal* in 1846, discusses the
tourist activity surrounding the mulberry tree honoring John Milton in the garden of Christ's College, Cambridge. The article notes
that the "smallest fragments from this tree are religiously cherished

by the poet's numberless admirers."[22] Likewise, by focusing on the Wordsworth tree located on her property, Martineau creates a historical relic that memorializes Wordsworth's visit while at the same time emphasizing her own literary celebrity. After all, the tree is planted in her honor.

In "A Year at Ambleside," Martineau depicts Wordsworth as a literary associate whose fame was necessary for establishing the touristic value of the Lake District and her own home. In addition to mentioning the locations that inspired Wordsworth's poems, she depicts herself as an intimate of the Wordsworth family who is invited over for tea and attended Hartley Coleridge's funeral. Indeed, in her letters and essays, Martineau often speaks of Wordsworth as an important mentor and role model.[23] However, Martineau also often identifies him as a literary competitor, whose work and lifestyle could be usefully contrasted to her own achievements.[24] In her *Autobiography*, Martineau claims to have "worshipped Wordsworth" in her youth, but she goes on to claim that his work produced "more disappointment than pleasure" in her later years.[25] She complains that his work lacks "sound, accurate, weighty thought" as well as "genuine poetic inspiration" (2:238). She continues, "Those who understand mankind are aware that he did not understand them; and those who dwell near his abode especially wonder at his representation of his neighbors" (2:239). She then recounts how Wordsworth entertained five hundred literary tourists per year by guiding them in groups around his terraces, "relating to persons whose very names he had not attended to, particulars about his writing and other affairs which each stranger flattered himself was a confidential communication to himself" (2:241). Martineau suggests that Wordsworth's approach to writing, like his approach to entertaining tourists, is superficial and self-aggrandizing.

If William Wordsworth's career served as a kind of master narrative she must both replicate and challenge, then Dorothy Wordsworth's story served as a cautionary tale. In her essay "Lights of the English Lake District," Martineau tells literary anecdotes associated with the region, focusing her attention primarily on the Wordsworths. In her descriptions of William Wordsworth's career and domestic life, Dorothy haunts the text, appearing as a specter of a woman whose gift was consumed by a masculine literary genius. When describing the Wordsworths' decision to settle at Dove Cottage, it is Dorothy's writing, not William's, that takes center stage. "Many years afterwards,"

Martineau reports, "Dorothy *wrote* of the aspect of Grasmere on her arrival that winter evening,—the pale orange lights on the lake, and the reflection of the mountains and the island in the still waters. She had wandered about the world in an unsettled way; and now she had cast anchor for life,—not in that house, but within view of that valley."[26] Martineau seems to identify with Dorothy Wordsworth's search for a home and her desire to process this experience through writing. Indeed, this passage recalls Martineau's own epiphany as described in her *Autobiography*: her own spontaneous decision to set down roots in the Lake District. Although Dorothy Wordsworth's journals would not be published until 1897, Martineau's references to Dorothy's writing in "Lights of the English Lake District" imply that she was aware of Dorothy's literary activity. Martineau is careful to note that Wordsworth possessed the "true poet's, combined with the true woman's nature" (545).

Although Martineau seems to identify with Dorothy, she also draws attention to her loss of purpose and mental balance. Martineau writes, "Too late it appeared that she had sacrificed herself to aid and indulge her brother" (545). According to Martineau, Mary Wordsworth explains Dorothy's loss of sanity as the consequence of overexercise from accompanying her brother on extended walking excursions in the district. "To repair the ravages thus caused she took opium," Martineau reports Mary Wordsworth as saying, "and the effect on her exhausted frame was to overthrow her mind" (545). Martineau allows this explanation for Dorothy Wordsworth's decline to stand until later in the essay, where she finally discounts it, although only indirectly. Martineau tells of how the Wordsworths accused her, too, of the "mischief of overwalking" and "took up the wholly mistaken notion that I walked too much" (556). By extension, their explanation for Dorothy Wordsworth's decline is also mistaken. Indeed, Martineau suggests that Dorothy "had sacrificed herself to aid and indulge her brother" in other ways, perhaps by suppressing her own talent (545).

Refusing to be cast in the same mold as Dorothy Wordsworth, Martineau seems to view the older woman's life as a warning—a ghostly reminder of the possible fate of a spinster aunt with frustrated literary ambitions. In the end, Martineau reports that Dorothy Wordsworth becomes a haunting presence at Rydal Mount: "The poor sister remained for five years longer [after William died]. Travellers, American and others, must remember having found the garden-gate locked at Rydal Mount, and perceiving the reason why, in seeing a little garden-chair, with an emaciated old lady in it, drawn by a nurse round and round the graveled space before the house. That was Miss Wordsworth, taking her daily exercise" (557). In this narrative of Dorothy Wordsworth's final years, she becomes a name-less object. The traveler notices the chair before noticing the "emaci-ated old lady," whose identity is unknown until revealed at the end of the passage. She becomes a kind of antirelic for literary tourists, who come to Rydal Mount to gaze upon the familiar and significant objects that help to recall the memory of William Wordsworth. In this case, the gate is locked and the space is defamiliarized by the presence of an unknowable, objectified individual.

On some level, Martineau's depictions of Dorothy Wordsworth in "Lights of the English Lake District" express her fears about her own career and domestic life in the Lake District being effaced by the mythology surrounding the life and works of William Wordsworth. Would her life and her home become empty signifiers, fragments of the literary past interpretable only by a select few? Would tourists head straight for Dove Cottage and Rydal Mount without stopping at the Knoll? Clearly, Martineau fears the loss of identity that befalls women who sacrifice their talent for the men in their lives. Unlike Dorothy, she depicts herself as a solitary woman who continues to walk and to write, a presence embodied in the narrative voice of the essay itself, which confidently speaks to an American audience. Mar-tineau emphasizes the congruence between her engagement with the landscape and her literary output, thereby once and for all put-ting to rest the idea that such an engagement will produce mental instability.

MARTINEAU'S GUIDES

In 1854, a local publisher named J. Garnett persuaded Martineau to publish the first in a series of guides to the Lake District. The suc-cess of Martineau's *Guide to Windermere* (1854) led her to write *Guide to Keswick* (1857) and, even more significantly, the *Complete Guide to the English Lakes*, which was published in five editions between 1855 and 1876.[27] As the most comprehensive of Martineau's guidebooks, the *Complete Guide* proved to be something of a challenge. Soon af-ter agreeing to undertake the project, she writes to her friend Mrs.

Ogden, "I have been very sorry not to be able to get over to call. But this Guide Book has made me work 'double tides' for a month past; & I have been obliged to refuse all invitations but two."[28] According to James Payn, Martineau researched the guide by taking friends on coach tours and walks in the district.[29] He writes, "It was very literally a labour of love, nor did the pleasure to be derived from it come, I think, short of her expectations. We made up a little party together, and 'did' the district . . . in ten days or so."[30]

In undertaking the *Complete Guide*, Martineau was of course following in the footsteps of Wordsworth, who began publishing his own guides to the region in 1810.[31] Wordsworth's *Guide* went through nine editions before being repackaged in 1842 as *Hudson and Nicholson's Guide to the Lake District*.[32] Although Hudson and Nicholson dropped Wordsworth's name from the guidebook's cover in 1842, they included an introductory essay by Wordsworth and advertised the poet's name on the title page. Hudson and Nicholson's *Guide* continued to be published until 1864. Thus, Martineau's guide and "Wordsworth's" guide were in direct competition from 1854 to 1864.[33] The two guidebooks were similar in structure and price. Both included foldout maps, engravings, itineraries, and lists of native plants. They were more scientific than earlier guides in the sense that they included tables recording the heights of waterfalls, the depth of lakes, as well as lists of native plants and geological features of the region. Such an approach was appropriate for the mass influx of tourists that began after the construction of a railway to Windermere in 1847.[34] These tourists required practical information that would help them make the most of their holidays: suggested hotels, restaurants, walks, and points of interest. As Clement Shorter put it, "Mr. Baedeker discovered that the German and the Englishman alike were principally concerned with their dinner, and that their wives were principally concerned with the price of it. And so guide-books reduced themselves to concise collections of hard facts."[35] Indeed, Martineau's *Guide* contains a wealth of such practical information, including the names and addresses of all residents of the region, but it provides a great deal more as well.[36] She includes personal anecdotes describing her walks (127), locations for experiencing blissful solitude (57), social changes in the region (138), and the effects of railroads as a positive economic force (141).

Her descriptions of sights, walks, and outdoor activities in the region provide a great deal of practical information, but they sometimes become more decidedly literary, thus requiring a closer, more sensitive reading. Martineau's nature descriptions, many of which are taken directly from her periodical essays, seem written as much to inform as to delight. Here, for example, is Martineau's description of Easdale Tarn:

> The water and the track together will shew him the way to the tarn, which is the source of the stream. Up and on he goes, over rock and through wet moss, with long stretches of dry turf and purple heather; and at last, when he is heated and breathless, the dark cool recess opens in which lies Easdale Tarn. Perhaps there is an angler standing besides the great boulder on the brink. Perhaps there is a shepherd lying among the ferns. But more probably the stranger finds himself perfectly alone. There is perhaps nothing in natural scenery which conveys such an impression of stillness as tarns which lie under precipices: and here the rocks sweep down to the brink almost round the entire margin. For hours together the deep shadows move only like the gnomon of the sundial; and, when movement occurs, it is not such as disturbs the sense of repose;—the dimple made by a restless fish or fly, or the gentle flow of water in or out; or the wild drake and his brood, paddling so quietly as not to break up the mirror, or the reflection of some touch of sunlight, or passing shadow. (51)

Such passages were no doubt intended to be read by tourists after reaching the point of destination. Martineau provides enough information to guide the reader to Easdale Tarn and also provides vivid images and a ponderous tone that are designed to help tourists appreciate their surroundings. Indeed, elsewhere in the *Guide*, she sometimes locates the reader and the reading process in the outdoors. For example, in a passage describing the ascent of Skawfell Pike, Martineau retells Wordsworth's story about being caught on the peak in a rainstorm and then concludes with this exclamation: "May the tourist who reads this on the Pike see every cloud vanish from every summit!" (160). The guidebook is thus defined as a necessary addition to the literary walker's kit bag, the book that will guide and shape the traveler's experience of the natural setting. Thus, the traveler experiences geography through the lens provided by a famous writer, whose interpretation of the landscape is more authentic, and therefore more real, than the literary tourist's unmediated experiences and impressions of place. The literary tour becomes what Peter

Newby has called "as much a voyage of the mind as one of the body."[37] That is, the landscape is experienced physically as the tourist moves through space but also virtually though the mediating influence of the literary text.

Martineau, like Wordsworth, made the literary focus of her guidebook even more transparent by including her own name on the title page and integrating a variety of literary references to the region. Thus, Martineau's homes, writings, and social relations form part of the guidebook's appeal. This makes the guidebook seem as if it were designed specifically for literary tourists rather than for a more generalized traveler. Martineau mentions many Lake District luminaries in her *Complete Guide*, including Felicia Hemans, Robert Southey, Samuel Taylor Coleridge, and Hartley Coleridge. However, she gives special notice of Wordsworth's Dove Cottage and Rydal Mount as well as the location of various other stops on a Wordsworth tour of the region, including the location of the grammar school where he studied at Hawkshead (29) and the "old square church tower, beneath whose shadow Wordsworth is buried" (49). In addition to making reference to these literary shrines, Martineau employs a variety of strategies that locate her own home on literary tours of the Lake District. In most editions of the *Complete Guide*, Martineau mentions the Knoll in her description of walks around Ambleside. For example, in describing the approach to Ambleside from Rydal, she writes, "The house on the rising ground behind the chapel is the Knoll, the residence of Miss H. Martineau" (55). Besides displaying her own name prominently on the book's cover and title page, Martineau includes a picture of the Knoll as a frontispiece in some editions. The 1876 edition also includes an advertisement for notepaper and postcards featuring illustrations of Martineau's home.

What are we to make of all these references to the Knoll in Martineau's guidebook? On one hand, Martineau, like Wordsworth, wanted to emphasize that she was a resident of the Lake District, not a tourist, and thus had greater authority in describing the sights, geography, and culture of the region. However, she may also have intended to capitalize on her celebrity as a marketing strategy for selling her guide. Given the fact that Martineau's *Guide* was modeled after Wordsworth's—and was at the same time literally in competition with it—it is likely that Martineau was also establishing her own authority as the creator of a *literary* guide to the district. By locating

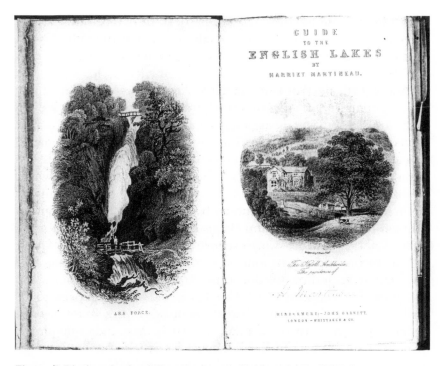

Figure 7. Lindsey Aspland, Frontispiece to *Guide to the English Lakes*, by Harriet Martineau (Windermere: J. Garnett, 1876).

herself and her home within the hallowed geography of the Lake District, Martineau establishes her place within the literary landscape as a major author whose fame rivals Wordsworth's and whose home is equally rife with literary associations. This tendency toward self-promotion is reinforced by the fact that Martineau, like Wordsworth, claimed to detest tourists. In fact, as she points out in her *Autobiography*, soon after moving to the Lake District, she made a practice of letting her house during the summer months to avoid the "unscrupulous strangers who intrude themselves with compliments, requests for autographs, or without any pretence whatever."[38] "Every summer," she writes, "they come and stare in at the windows while we are at dinner, hide behind shrubs or the corner of the house, plant themselves in the yards behind or the field before; are staring up at one's window when one gets up in the morning, gather handfuls of flowers in the garden, stop or follow us in the road, and report us to the newspapers" (2:266).[39]

But was not this just the kind of attention Martineau was hoping to promote (or at least expected to endure) as a result of her tourist guides and essays? This is, of course, the same question we might ask about Wordsworth's guides to the Lake District. In his discussion of Wordsworth's guidebooks, James Buzard draws attention to this contradiction and explores ways that Wordsworth promoted a different kind of tourism focused less on itineraries and defined points of interest than on deep forms of viewing and experiencing place.[40] Likewise, Peter Newby points out that Wordsworth's "use of place was important for the tourist industry because it demonstrated where the experiences that gave rise to his philosophy and new standards of taste could also be experienced by others."[41] However, I am not convinced that improving tourist taste was the primary motivation of Wordsworth's *Guide*.[42] More crucially, Wordsworth, like Martineau, seemed to view the publication of a guidebook as a self-authorizing act meant to forge a connection between a sense of place and a sense of his own career as a writer. By creating textual representations of the landscape through literary acts of self-representation, both writers hoped to locate themselves and their writing careers on the map of England. Thus, their guidebooks, like their autobiographical texts, can be seen as a kind of self-memorialization. As Stuart Semmel points out in his article on Waterloo, the study of tourism is an investigation of how individuals "conceived their relationship to history" while at the same time coming "face to face with the *problem* of memorialization, the *difficulty* of capturing the past."[43] In a sense, the challenge both writers faced was how to create links between their work and the Lake District landscape that would make one unreadable without the other.

Such connections were of course tenuous. Both Wordworth's and Martineau's guides went out of print in the late nineteenth century, reemerging as short-run reprints in the twentieth.[44] Thus, the specific associations between text and landscape established by the guides become reduced to a few points of interest: Dove Cottage, Rydal Mount, Wordsworth's grave, and the Knoll. For some late nineteenth-century critics, these sites were in danger of losing their significations due to their commodification as tourist destinations.[45] For example, in an 1898 article, Clement Shorter notes that, although the "memory of Wordsworth . . . overrules this scenery," Dove Cottage itself has become a vulgarized symbol of the poet's career.[46] After the cottage was acquired by the Wordsworth Society, it is overtaken by a "multitude of visitors, who pay their sixpence readily enough to see the simple cottage" (7). As a result it is "too tidy, too well organised to have much suggestion of poetry, and when one of its little rooms is crowded up with all kinds of spick and span books about Wordsworth, most of them worthless, the last touch will be given to the vulgarising of the place" (7). Martineau, according to Shorter, has become only a "vague memory," whose books have lost their appeal but whose house "will always be pointed out" (8).

Certainly by century's end, Martineau's home—the richly nuanced and significant literary destination she had carefully constructed in her Lake District writings—was reduced to a single commodified image, an obligatory and empty stop on the tour of Ambleside. However, in the years just following Martineau's death, the complex significations of her life and work were revivified by her friends and admirers, who wrote narratives about their experiences at the Knoll.[47] Maria Weston Chapman, for example, in her "Memorials" published as part of Martineau's 1877 *Autobiography*, focuses on domestic objects as signifiers for Martineau's life and character. She gives a tour of Martineau's home, making note of the garden, décor, and relics associated with Wordsworth and other famous literary visitors. She highlights the "costly sun-dial" in the garden, the "stone-pine planted by Wordsworth," and Martineau's magnificent library, "probably the best woman's library extant."[48] She also minutely describes the gifts of Martineau's friends and family that adorn the Knoll, including a "marble-mounted sideboard, sent by her friend H. Crabb Robinson" and an "ebony *papeterie*, the gift of Florence Nightingale" (381).

Moving from room to room, Chapman positions these objects in three-dimensional space for the armchair traveler, providing a virtual tour and inventory of relics. Chapman writes, "What touching stories ought to be told of so many another useful and ornamental object, all brought together from different nations and kindred tongues and people" (381). The Knoll thus becomes a collection of objects that recall Martineau's broad social, political, and cultural affiliations, especially her transatlantic political connections. At the same time, the Knoll becomes a microcosm for the Empire itself, which makes a similar claim about binding together nations and "kindred tongues." For Chapman, these layers of meaning and association make the Knoll a sacred space. Here, for example, is her description of Martineau's library:

> Imagine,—between globes and little stands for precious objects, with
> here and there casts of Clytie and the Huntress Diana,—the bay-win-
> dow, filled with geraniums, and the library-table with her *chaise-longue*
> behind it, and you have a general idea of this room, which seemed
> less a library than an oratory, consecrated as it was by a devotedness
> to the world's welfare so instinctive as to have become unconscious;
> but visitors were always conscious of it, and stepped softly and spoke
> low, as if the place were holy. (384)

In this way, Chapman establishes the posthumous list of must-see
items relating to Martineau's domestic life. Indeed, memorial essays
such as Chapman's fueled interest in the Knoll in the years just following Martineau's death. In the 1870s and 1880s, her home became
an essential stop on a literary tour of the region. As one Ambleside
resident quipped, "If I had a penny for every time they stop the coach-
man to ask where Miss Martineau lives, I should be a rich woman."[49]

However, this revival of interest in Martineau soon faded, and the
Knoll all but disappeared from the literary map of England. At the
end of the nineteenth century, some guidebooks make brief mention
of the Knoll,[50] but just as many guidebooks of the same period drop
Martineau's home from their lists of important sights.[51] By the early
twentieth century, references to Martineau became even sparser,[52]
and by the beginning of the twenty-first century, they became all but
nonexistent.[53] Even today, the location of Martineau's home can only
be determined by consulting the Martineau Society or the staff of the
Armitt Library, Ambleside.

Martineau's attempts to construct her home as a literary shrine
would thus appear to have been only temporarily successful. Because
her books were rarely taught or read during the twentieth century,
her home lost its literary significations to all but a select few. To
these scholars, Martineau's home became a tourist destination experienced on a personal level and with the memory of the earlier
mass of tourists in mind. Thus, with the rediscovery of a forgotten
person and experience, modern scholars infuse the home with feelings of nostalgia. As David Lowenthal points out, "Like memories,
relics once abandoned or forgotten may become more treasured
than those in continued use; the discontinuity in their history focuses attention on them."[54] As scholars look upon the Knoll, they
remember and resignify those places that have been forgotten, reas-
serting Martineau's vision of the land and its relics. They do so with
an awareness that they are creating textual geography—land shaped

and marked by literary texts. The recovery of women writers is thus also a reinterpretation of geographical space—a remapping of literary landscapes, the places tourists visit, the relics they reconstitute as significant. Martineau, perhaps more than any other Victorian writer, understood (and was able to capitalize on) this concept of textual geography. She thus serves as an excellent case study for exploring the ways that landscape is written and read by successive generations of literary scholars.

II
Celebrity and Historiography

4

Harriet Martineau:
Gender, National Identity, and
the Contemporary Historian

THE PRACTICE OF LITERARY TOURISM WAS PREMISED ON THE IDEA that readers, writers, and tourists had important roles to play in retelling nineteenth-century literary history and situating these micronarratives within a broader contemporary cultural history of Great Britain. As noted in chapter 3, Harriet Martineau was a crucial figure in the discourse on literary tourism due to her self-conscious attempts at self-memorialization. By marketing herself as a Lake District celebrity, Martineau managed to recount contemporary cultural history on her own terms, locating her work both literally and figuratively on the literary map of Great Britain. During the 1850s, Martineau was involved in two additional writing projects concerned with narrating contemporary history: *The History of England during the Thirty Years' Peace*, published 1849–50, and her *Autobiography*, written in 1855. These complementary texts illustrate Martineau's efforts to authorize herself as a contemporary historian and literary celebrity. They also demonstrate her desire to integrate women's stories and experiences into the broader narrative of British history.

Harriet Martineau's *The History of England during the Thirty Years' Peace* was one of the most widely read historical studies of its day.[1] A review of the 1864 edition published in the *National Quarterly Review* proclaimed that "with the sole exception of [Thomas Babington] Macaulay's History, no similar work written within the last twenty years has been more extensively read in England."[2] The popularity of Martineau's *History* was in part due to its focus on contemporary British history, 1816 to 1846, which had an immediate sense of relevance to readers who struggled to make meaning out of the social turmoil

95

of the 1830s and 1840s. As Rosemary Jann has pointed out, Victorian historical writing was intended to provide "comfort in history's assurance that the direction of change was ultimately toward the good."[3] Indeed, Martineau's *History* provides an account that is attuned to its particular historical moment, when debates over parliamentary reform and the "Condition of England Question" were reaching a fevered pitch. Like other Whig histories of the period,[4] Martineau's *History* was intended to document British progress in bringing about social reform, from the achievements of the abolition movement and revisions of the poor laws to anti-Corn Law agitation and the expansion of parliamentary representation.[5] Martineau provides biographical portraits of the "great men" who had brought about triumphant national reform. In so doing, she tells a story of the development of a new idea of Englishness: the emergence of reform-minded sensibilities that had transformed the nation.[6]

Although Martineau's *History* is clearly situated within the conventions of nineteenth-century Whig historiography, her contribution to the field was decidedly innovative. That a woman writer would undertake a four-volume history of Great Britain, negotiating the challenge of retelling events still fresh in many readers' memories, is remarkable indeed. Although many women were engaged in writing history during this period, it was rare for a woman to take on a comprehensive national history, let alone a didactic narrative with specific recommendations for the ongoing progress of contemporary society.[7] In this chapter, I will review the publication history of Martineau's *History*, highlighting the strategies she used to establish herself as a celebrity historian in a male-dominated field. I will also argue for the importance of Martineau's *History* as a pioneering example of British national history that is inflected by a protofeminist sensibility. By including women's history in a masculinist narrative of social progress, Martineau reinforced the historicity of women's lives and suggested that national advancement was in part dependent on the reform of legal and social institutions that oppressed women. The status of women, like the status of the laboring classes or the status of the free-market economy, was a sign of the times, a measure of social evolution.

Covering roughly the same time period as the *History*, Martineau's *Autobiography*, written in 1855, can be viewed as its companion text.[8] If in the *History* Martineau provided a somewhat depersonalized account of contemporary British history, in the *Autobiography*, she reinserted her own life history into the broader narrative of national progress, making a case for the historical significance of her own political and literary achievements. Reading Martineau's *History* in tandem with the *Autobiography* and other auto/biographical texts reveals the ways that she worked across genre, writing contemporary history in a series of intersecting texts that encompassed conventionally masculine and feminine forms of historiography.[9] In this way, Martineau balanced her claim to historical objectivity with an assertion of her own historical significance as a literary celebrity and social reformer.

WRITING CONTEMPORARY HISTORY

As many recent critics have noted, history writing was a major genre within the field of literary publication throughout the Victorian era.[10] There were a number of women writing history in the first part of the nineteenth century; however, their fitness as historians was hotly debated, and the work of male historians was privileged by the critical establishment.[11] Thus, when publisher Charles Knight (1791–1873) appointed Martineau to write the *History*, he was making an unconventional, if not wholly unprecedented, choice.[12] Of course, by the late 1840s, Martineau was a well-known writer, whose works *Illustrations of Political Economy* (1832–34), *Society in America* (1837), and *Retrospect of Western Travel* (1838), though controversial, had established her credentials as a keen social critic of the liberal-radical stamp.[13] Indeed, in his memoir *Passages of a Working Life* (1865), Knight called Martineau "adequately qualified, not only by the power of writing agreeably, but by unwearied industry and a long course of observation upon the social affairs of the country."[14]

Knight took on the project of writing the *History* in 1846 and wrote the first sixteen chapters. However, he soon became overwhelmed with the project and turned it over to Charles MacFarlane (1799–1858) and George Craik (1798–1866), who together wrote the remainder of Book 1. Once Martineau took over the project in 1848, she wrote the remaining monthly numbers, 1849–50. In 1851, she published an introductory volume covering the years 1800 to 1815, and in 1864, she updated the *History* to include recent events, 1846 to 1854. In her preface to the 1864 edition of the *History*, Martineau notes that she initially took on the project in 1848 after "Mr. Craik also gave up."[15] With this simple statement, she depicts her fellow historian as being less fit for the task of writing a national history.

In her introduction to the *History*, Martineau makes no reference to her deficiencies or differences as a woman writer taking on the ambitious task of writing a history of the nation.[16] Rather, she expresses confidence in her ability to tackle the project. Although she, like her male predecessors, at first found the project "overwhelming," she persevered, writing in her 1864 preface, "I undertook to try what I could do."[17] She then reports that she accomplished what her predecessors could not: efficiently completing the multivolume manuscript between the autumn of 1848 and the end of 1849.[18] Martineau's later account of writing the *History*, as retold in her *Autobiography*, is a similarly triumphant narrative. Initially, she notes, writing the *History* was somewhat of a struggle: "The quantity and variety of details fairly overpowered my spirits."[19] However, "in a few weeks," she reports, "I was in full career, and had got my work well in hand" (2:319). She soon developed a system by which she organized and classified the historical sources she would need to write each monthly number, thus bringing order out of "chaos" (2:319). Martineau's sources, which were at least partly provided by Knight and footnoted in the text, were comprised largely of letters, memoirs, diaries, periodical essays, previously published histories, and the *Annual Register*.[20]

In addition to providing Martineau with source materials, Knight supported her with encouragement and editorial feedback.[21] Indeed, by July of 1849, Martineau wrote to W. J. Fox, "I like doing my History,—uncommonly: & Mr. Knight & I are capital friends about it."[22] However, Martineau's relationship with Knight was not always harmonious. This was partly due to the highly politicized nature of writing contemporary history. As Martineau's biographer Maria Weston Chapman later wrote, "There are a thousand risks in taking time as it flies."[23] The contemporary historian, she notes, "must expect the blame, most likely the ill offices, of all who stand condemned as their deeds are placed in line (3:334). Indeed, Chapman points out, Knight was an anxious collaborator whose "frequent changes of mind as to time of publication were very detrimental to the success of the History" (3:336). Chapman reports that Martineau told her about one occasion when Knight expurgated a passage from the *History* without permission after receiving a threatening letter "from a Whig official" (3:336). Martineau was incensed, saying, "I then told him he should never more publish for me" (3:336). In Chapman's recounting of this anecdote, Martineau is revealed to be her publisher's superior in terms of bravery and moral strength. He provides her with vitally important resources and encouragement, yet he lacks the kind of editorial courage necessary to be fully supportive.

When taking over the project from Knight, Martineau also had to contend with one of the previous contributors to the *History*, Charles MacFarlane, who had expected to be chosen as chief writer after Craik abandoned the project. In his 1855 *Reminiscences*, MacFarlane refers to Martineau as an "ill-favoured, dogmatizing, masculine spinster" and complains that Knight "engaged her to do what I in justice ought to have done, that is, to write the history of the thirty years' peace."[24] Indeed, in her negotiations with Knight, Martineau insisted on being "*solely* responsible" for the remainder of the *History*, perhaps specifically hoping to exclude MacFarlane.[25] From MacFarlane's perspective, the addition of Martineau's chapters to the first book of the *History* resulted in a heterogeneous text. "Those who admired Miss Martineau's doing," he notes, "could not tolerate ours."[26] As a result, he claims, the sales of the *History* were poor. An examination of the subsequent publishing history of the *History* suggests that MacFarlane's assessment of the economic viability of the project was probably incorrect. In an 1850 letter to Fanny Wedgwood, Martineau writes that the "History is so popular that it is to be extended at both ends, and republished as a History of the Half Century."[27]

The *History* received positive notices in a variety of British and American periodicals.[28] One of the most interesting of these reviews, written by George Henry Lewes, appeared in the *British Quarterly Review* in 1850. Lewes notes that it bears "traces of haste, of imperfect knowledge, and of imperfect historical art," thus evoking the usual arguments against women's historical writing.[29] However, overall he endorses the book, praising its usefulness as a "history of our own times" (355) and as a chronicle of the "rapidity of European progress" (356). Further, Lewes praises the democratic impulse behind Martineau's narrative: "In looking over the records of these thirty years we are struck with the deficiency in great men, but are compensated by the greatness of the People, who now come more prominently forward on the scene" (360). Indeed, as a pioneer of modern social history, Martineau, like many of historians of the period,[30] took a particular interest in the "unhistorical" details associated with women's and working-class life. In an 1849 letter to Richard Monckton Milnes, Martineau reinforces that the *History* was intended "not for the fastidious aristocracy, but for the great middle & operative class of readers."[31] At the same time that she was writing the *History*, Martineau began a lengthy lecture series intended to benefit her working-class neighbours in Ambleside, including "twenty lectures on the History of England."[32] She notes that it was her aim to "give rational amusement to men whom all circumstances seemed to conspire to drive to the public-house, and to interest them in matters which might lead them to books, or at least give them something to think about" (2:306). Thus, Martineau's interest in writing a people's history of England was grounded in her long-standing zeal for popular education.[33]

Overall, Martineau's *History* can be read as political history that chronologically retraces the affairs of state and popular response. Women play a small role in the narrative as constructed by Martineau. As a contemporary critic for the *National Quarterly Review* noted, the work as a whole displays the "masculine vigor of her intellect," being both "thoughtful and philosophical" as well as "keen and discriminating" in its representation of the historical record.[34] But such a cursory reading does not do justice to the important protofeminist subtext that informs the *History's* broader masculinist narrative of British history. When tracing the progress of various reform movements, Martineau pays particular attention to inadequacies of and revisions to marriage law. She devotes a large part of the first book of the *History* to the Queen Caroline affair, the scandal associated with King George IV's petition for a divorce based on the alleged sexual improprieties of the queen during her years abroad. As Linda Colley has vividly illustrated, the Queen Caroline affair was a pivotal event in a broader narrative of social change where the "feminisation of the British monarchy" served as a rallying point for debating the role of women in public life.[35] As thousands of women came to the defense of the queen, Colley points out, they developed a "focus for their patriotism that was peculiarly their own."[36] Martineau's lengthy account of the affair in the *History* makes a similar case for its centrality as an example of how "the people" might take an issue of public morality into their own hands, delivering an outcome that challenged the king's prerogative. "There was no cause for despondency," Martineau notes, "in seeing how sound was the heart of the English people in regard to the weightier matters of the law—justice and mercy—strong as is the tendency generally to visit such offences as those now in question more severely on women than on men."[37] Further, she notes, when the ministers agreed to pursue divorce proceedings against the queen, "they little understood the woman they had to deal with, or the disposition of the English people to succor and protect the unhappy and oppressed, irrespective of the moral merits or demerits of the sufferer" (2:273). When the king and his ministers decreed that the queen's name would no longer be included in the liturgy, the queen, along with an enflamed public, rebelled: "They did not know the spirit of the English people, or they would have seen that the crown could not be more degraded than by the persecution of a woman, by excluding her from the public prayers of the nation" (2:277). The defeat of the king's case against the queen in 1820, Martineau reports, resulted in unprecedented public celebration (2:285). Thus, for Martineau, the story of the Queen Caroline affair reinforced the power of popular opinion to reform a morally wayward government but also showed how the discourse on gender could be mobilized to bring about a change in national morality. Popular support of the queen was premised on domestic ideology, which depicted women as dependents in need of protection; however, at the same time, debates over the Queen Caroline affair enabled women, including Martineau, to take a public stand, drawing attention to the legal disabilities of women in British society. As Colley points out, separate spheres ideology "could be drawn on in practice to defend the position of women" and "legitimise women's intervention in affairs hitherto regarded as the preserve of men."[38]

In her *Autobiography*, Martineau recounts her personal response to the Queen Caroline affair, retelling public history in private terms. She reports that when her pastor and "two or three other bachelor friends" came to her house for dinner in 1819, she bravely defended the royal family against gossip, pointing out that they "could not reply to slander like other people."[39] However, Martineau was soon thrown into a "fix," she remarks, when her dinner companions criticized her "immorality in making more allowance for royal sinners than for others" (1:81). The dilemma, she notes, ultimately did indeed "fix my attention upon the principles of politics and the characteristics of parties" (1:81). Thus, one kind of "fix" leads to another. At the early age of seventeen, Martineau exchanges a feeling of moral indeterminacy for a commitment to historical objectivity. "Still," she remarks, "how astonished should I have been if any one had then foretold to me that, of all the people in England, I should be the one to write the 'History of the Peace!'" (1:81). Yet her account reinforces her aptitude for historical study, her ability to develop a sense of objective distance from her subject matter, focusing on broad principles rather than on private cases. More importantly, the anecdote emphasizes her own early resistance to patriarchal interpretations of national events, reinforcing her intellectual—and perhaps sexual—independence from the clerical "bachelors" across the table.

The topic of marriage and sexual politics once again emerges in the fourth volume of the *History* when Martineau addresses the passage of the Infant Custody Bill. "The session of 1839 was a memorable one," she begins, "to at least half the nation," because it brought about the passage of the "first act of what must become a course of legislation on behalf of the rights of women; who are in so many ways oppressed by the laws of England."[40] The major objection to the bill, Martineau notes, came from Lord Brougham, who was anxious about addressing a "mass of laws so cruel and indefensible as that all must come down if any part were brought into question" (4:184). Although Brougham spoke against the bill, his speech aided the women's cause through "his exposure of the position of married women in England" (4:186). "They were not represented at all," Martineau reinforces, because the men "supposed, in the works of political philosophy, to represent them, are precisely those against whom legislation is needed for their protection" (4:186). As in the Queen Caroline affair, women, the "virtuous matronage of England," are represented as the wronged victims of an irresponsible male establishment and consequently a biased system of laws (4:186). Martineau then makes reference to an inflammatory article published in the *British Quarterly Review*, which "proceeded on the supposition that all women are bent on mischief, and that the only way to manage them is to place them under the absolute despotism of their husbands" (4:187). In the process, "several of the most eminent ladies in Great Britain were insulted by name, and every woman in the world by implication" (4:187). It is here that Martineau's identity as a woman historian comes most to the surface, her outrage erupting into what is otherwise a largely patriarchal political history of the nation. An insult to a few women is an insult to them all, and the status of women in Britain is linked to the status of women "in the world." In this way, Martineau suggests a global politics of gender, much as she does in *Society in America*, where she famously states, "If a test of civilization be sought, none can be so sure as the condition of that half of society over which the other half has power."[41] For Martineau, both America and Britain inevitably fail this test of civility, and women consequently fall subject to "barbarous law."[42]

Although Martineau's protofeminist chapters represent only a small part of her *History*, they nonetheless perform the function of drawing attention to the need for reform of the social and legal institutions that oppress women. It is easy to see how her overall vision of "progress" might be adapted to the needs of the nascent women's movement, which gained strength after the first Reform Bill and became an organized effort in the 1850s.[43] Indeed, in her chapter on men's clubs, Martineau sets out an argument for women's employment opportunity, an issue that would soon become a major rallying point in the women's movement. Here, Martineau proposes the development of new clubs that will include women, providing them with opportunities for intellectual development outside the home. She writes, "In a state of society like our own at present—a transition state as regards the position of women,—the lot of the educated woman with narrow means is a particularly hard one. . . . It is no longer true that every woman is supported by husband, father, or brother; a multitude of women have to support themselves; and only too many of them, their fathers and brothers too: but few departments of industry are yet opened to them, and those few are most inadequately paid."[44] For this reason, she concludes, "clubbing together" will allow women to "try an experiment of their own," sharing resources of books, music, and food in a more economical way (3:181). This idea of social experiment as a way of addressing women's changing economic roles of course prefigures Martineau's argument for women's employment in her influential article "Female Industry" and anticipates the efforts of the Langham Place group.[45] As I and others have argued, Martineau was an instrumental figure in the history of the Victorian women's movement. Clearly, the *History* was an important contribution to her protofeminist oeuvre.[46] For Martineau, women's history was not separate from men's history; it was an integral part of a broader vision of ongoing national progress.

In addition to focusing on social and legislative measures of national progress, Martineau uses the achievements of individuals to assess the evolution of British society. She concludes selected books of the *History* with a "necrology," a compendium of short obituaries of writers, artists, politicians, and other notables from each historical era.[47] Such obituaries served as markers of a discredited national past, outmoded subjectivities that must be replaced by more enlightened models of individual identity. Byron, for example, is described as the "mouth-piece of the needs and troubles of men in a transition state of society" who "could not produce, except by snatches, what was permanently true."[48]

For Martineau, most women writers of the early nineteenth century were just as irrelevant to the modern age. She refers to Fanny Burney, for example, as the "most popular of female novelists, however we may wonder at the fact" (4:242). Martineau situates Burney within her time period, explaining that the popularity of her work is best understood as a product of the "last century when conventionalism had touched its last limit of excess" (4:242). She writes, "It is now scarcely possible to read her 'Evelina' and 'Cecilia,' with all their elaborate, delicate distresses, which could never have happened to ingenuous people, and which a breath of good sense and sincerity would at any time blow away in a moment; but the enthusiasm about these novels in their day proves that they were true to their time, and that they ought so far to have value with us" (4:243). The books of the last generation, rather than serving as moral touchstones for the present, become interesting only as documents of a fallen historical past, the time before a progressive spirit would prevail.

Even though in the *History* Martineau often derides women of the past, emphasizing the obsolescence of their achievements, she nonetheless gives significant attention to their contribution to literary history. Martineau's inclusion of so many biographies of women writers in her necrology chapters may have been what caused George Henry Lewes to remark that her obituaries were "singularly misplaced, and executed without any sense of proportion," revealing "too much or too little of each person."[49] After all, Burney's obituary was about the same length as Walter Scott's. Indeed, at times Martineau seems to assert the prime importance of women writers in literary history. For example, even though she presents Maria Edgeworth as a voice of the past, she makes an argument for her founding influence on later writers: "She it was who early and effectually interested her century in the character and lot of the Irish; and she did much besides to raise the character of fiction, and to gratify the popular mind, before Scott and Bulwer and Dickens occupied that field of literature."[50] Martineau's metaphor here is telling. Male writers are viewed as "occupiers" of the field first cultivated by a woman writer. In writing the *History*, Martineau of course reverses this equation by "occupying" a largely masculine historical tradition. In fact, she had usurped the project of writing the *History* from a male writer, even if encouraged to do so by Charles Knight. The chapters written by Knight, Craik, and MacFarlane were literally enclosed by Martineau's writing once the introductory volume was added in 1851. Indeed, in an 1850 letter to Fanny Wedgwood, Martineau mentioned that she intended to "rewrite the *dull* chapters of Craik and McFarlane."[51] For Martineau, literary history was thus a series of occupations and counteroccupations of contested literary territory.

According to Martineau, women not only had a place in literary history but a role in the moral history of the nation as well. Martineau first articulated her argument for the historicity of women's culture in *Society in America*, where she asserted that the "nursery, the boudoir, the kitchen, are all excellent schools in which to learn the morals and manners of a people."[52] In her *History*, Martineau builds on this idea not only in her coverage of the domestic lives of British sovereigns, particularly Queen Victoria, but also in her occasional mention of women heroes of a humbler cast. For example, she provides somewhat extensive coverage of the story of Grace Darling, the twenty-two-year-old woman who took part in a daring rescue of the crew of a steamboat that had crashed off the shore of Northumberland in 1838. "Her name flew abroad over the world," Martineau notes.[53] Darling's celebrity resulted in the "impossibility of repose" and consequent death (4:215).

Reading between the lines, it is possible to detect Martineau's own anxiety about the negative effects of celebrity, as described in her article "Literary Lionism," published in the *Westminster Review* in 1839. Her own public adulation, like Darling's, had potentially fatal consequences. Thinking back on her invitations to soirees, she notes, "The drawing room is still the grave of literary promise."[54] Yet Martineau's fame, like Darling's, assured her a place in the national memory. The monument erected to Darling would "preach a lesson of self-sacrifice, and rouse a spirit of heroic good-will, long after the sectarian strifes of the time shall have been forgotten."[55] Here, Darling's contribution to history provides a sense of transcendent moral value that is at once a product of its time period and beyond it. Unlike the history of sectarian struggles, the history of moral virtue will be remembered by the people. By extension, Martineau's own monument, her oeuvre, will outlast the ephemeral historical events she describes. She concludes "Literary Lionism" with a reference to the "few, very few" who have "faith to appeal to the godlike human mind yet unborn—the mind which the series of coming centuries is to reveal."[56] The fact that Martineau signed her article with her well-known initials, "H. M.," and reprinted the article in her *Autobiography* suggests its importance as a document establishing her relationship to history. She presents a vision of her own transcendent historic role, which like Darling's, will withstand the degradations of fame at the same time that it is produced by them.

Indeed, in the *History*, Martineau's presence looms large over her production. Her name is boldly printed on the title page of the first edition, and she prefaces her work by reinforcing her own role as the book's author and source. Contemporary reviewers were well aware of the importance of Martineau's firsthand experiences as source material for writing a contemporary history. In 1866, a critic for the *Christian Examiner* writes, "All of this history she has seen. No little part of it she had been."[57] Likewise, the *New Englander* notes, "We do not regard it as one of those disadvantages that in many of the controversies which agitated the little island during the period in question, the historian herself was an earnest and effective participant."[58] Such commentary is remarkable not only for the way that it acknowledges the influential role of a woman in public affairs but also for the way that it interprets her experience outside the domestic realm as an asset to her work as a national historian.

The emphasis on Martineau's historic role in critical writing of the period is interesting given that Martineau made no direct references to herself in the text of her *History*.[59] Martineau's omission of her own life experience is surprising considering that in *Society in America* and her Lake District writings she frequently drew attention to her own subjectivity and celebrity as a lens through which to read her work.[60] The absence of personal anecdotes or references may have been partly due to Knight's editorial influence. In a letter to W. J. Fox, Martineau notes that Knight afforded her the "*fullest liberty*" in terms of subject matter, yet she would "ponder much before I published any thing of a personal nature of which he decidedly disapproved."[61] Indeed, the idea of interpolating personal details into the writing of history would seem to have violated Martineau's theory of historiography. In an 1866 letter to Fanny Wedgwood, Martineau complains of James Froude's tendencies in the *Reign of Elizabeth* (1864) toward "writing about himself and his sensibilities."[62] "He is the only historian I know of who ever did that," she continues, "and it is sadly out of place in a History" (275). Earlier, in her *Autobiography*, she had attacked Thomas Babington Macaulay for his "loose and unscrupulous method of narrating" and his frequent "inaccuracies and misrepresentations" of historical fact.[63] For Martineau, the best historical texts were depersonalized and well-documented interpretations of historical fact, even if written with the vividness of fiction and from a particular political viewpoint.[64]

Writing a contemporary history certainly had the potential of collapsing the whole idea of history writing as a genre because it would seem to have much in common with the political essay, the memoir, the political pamphlet, and the parliamentary report. However, Martineau was intent on maintaining generic boundaries, tenuous as they might have been in this pre-professional period of Victorian historiography. This was most likely due to her anxiety about the tendency among early feminists, such as Mary Wollstonecraft, to "injure the cause by their personal tendencies," that is, by drawing attention to their personal experiences and complaints.[65] A woman activist, Martineau contends, must "speak from conviction of the truth, and not from personal unhappiness" (1:401). The narration of history, like other forms of political writing, would thus rely on depersonalized truth telling.[66]

WRITING PERSONAL HISTORY

If, on one hand, Martineau seemed intent on distinguishing memoir from history writing in the *History of the Peace*, she seemed to blur these same generic boundaries in her *Autobiography*. The fact that Martineau wrote her *Autobiography* in 1855, just five years after the *History*, suggests that she may have been attempting to assert, retroactively, the importance of her own personal life story within a broader narrative of British national history. The *Autobiography* begins with Martineau's birth in 1802, which roughly corresponds to the beginning of her "introduction" to the *History*, published in 1851, which begins in the year 1800. Likewise, Martineau's *Autobiography* ends in the present moment, 1855, which corresponds to the time frame of the expanded version of the *History*, which ends with the commencement of the Crimean War in 1854. Both texts close with prophetic statements about the state of politics at midcentury. For example, in the *Autobiography*, Martineau writes, "When I look at my own country, and observe the nature of the changes which have taken place even within my own time, I have far more hope than I once had that the inevitable political reconstitution of our state may take place in a peaceable and prosperous manner."[67] In the last chapter of the *History*, she likewise notes that a review of recent history "may be thoroughly delightful, as convincing us of that rapid partial advance toward the grand, slow, general advance which we humbly but firmly trust to be the destination of the human race."[68]

When Martineau does make reference to her own viewpoints in the *History*, she carefully masks her own identity, not only by using *we* in place of *I*, as in the above example, but also by generalizing personal anecdotes. For instance, at the end of the *History*, she makes reference to national improvement in terms of the role of the educator in society, saying, "We find the function of the educator somewhat more respected than it used to be" (4:618). She notes, however, that "there are still suburban villages where the inhabitants are too genteel to admit persons engaged in education to their book-clubs" (4:618). Here Martineau is indirectly referencing her experience of being rejected for membership in an Ambleside book club in 1848. In the *Autobiography*, she recounts the incident, expressing shock and amusement at the idea of "so voluminous a writer, and one so familiar in literary society in London, being black-balled in a country book-club!"[69]

In discussing the economic crash of 1825–26 in her *Autobiography*, Martineau makes a more explicit connection to the *History*. "In the reviews of my 'History of the Thirty Years' Peace,'" she writes, "one chapter is noticed more emphatically than all the rest;—the chapter on the speculations, collapse, and crash of 1825 and 1826. If that chapter is written with some energy, it is no wonder; for our family fortunes were implicated in that desperate struggle, and its issue determined the whole course of life of the younger members of our family,—my own among the rest" (1:128). Here Martineau provides readers with a private history of a public, decidedly "historic," event. In doing so, she establishes an autobiographical lens through which to view her *History*, extending an invitation to read the two texts side by side, illuminating links between her own life story and the history of the nation. Even if she strove for objectivity in writing the *History*, her *Autobiography* suggests a more subjective subtext, one informed by her own emotional "energy" as a woman who shaped and was shaped by economic history. Reading the *History* through the lens of the *Autobiography* thus reveals that, for Martineau, the personal ultimately *was* political. Although she criticized Mary Wollstonecraft for unnecessarily drawing attention to her personal life, Martineau was not above forging a connection between personal and political history in her own oeuvre. By presenting her own life story as both virtuous and exemplary, she makes a case for the historicity of the life of a politically active single woman.

Reading the *History* and the *Autobiography* in tandem further reveals the ways that Martineau viewed autobiography and history as mutually informing source material. This connection becomes particularly apparent in Martineau's description of Queen Victoria's coronation, which is described at length in both texts. In reading Martineau's eyewitness account of the coronation in the *Autobiography*, it becomes clear that the description of the same event in her *History* had been based on firsthand observation. Interestingly, it also becomes clear that Martineau used the *History* as a source when writing her *Autobiography*. Taken together, the accounts consequently reinforce the intersections between Martineau's conception of life writing and historical writing. In the *History*, for example, she makes reference to the sparkling "jewels of whole rows of Peeresses" illuminated by the "first rays of the midsummer sun that slanted down through the high windows of Westminster Abbey."[70] In the *Autobiography*, she uses the same imagery but sharpens her critique of the royal display. She once again mentions the "first gleams of the sun [that] slanted into the Abbey," but refers to the consequent sparkling of jewels as the "self-coroneting of all the peeresses."[71]

More significant is her depiction of the young queen herself, who in the *History* is weighed down by the "ancient Edward's mantle of cloth of gold [which] looked cumbrous and oppressive," symbolizing an outmoded form of royal power based on "divine right."[72] In the *Autobiography*, she writes, "After all was said and sung, the sovereign remained a nominal ruler, who could not govern by her own mind and will; who had influence, but no political power; a throne and a crown, but with the knowledge of every body that the virtue had gone out of them."[73] In both texts, the ceremony is depicted as being absurd due to its outmoded references to royal power and privilege, but in the *Autobiography*, Victoria becomes a complex trope, also evoking the ineffectual political status of women in society more generally. The fact that Victoria can "influence" but lacks direct "political power" suggests that she is like all British women, who have "nominal" but not actual political representation. Taken together, then, the *History* and *Autobiography* reveal how Martineau interpreted cultural tropes in public and private ways, revealing layers of complexity that would be inaccessible in a single text.

The affinities between the *Autobiography* and *History* suggest not only Martineau's virtuosity and complexity as a writer but also her ability to assert her own role as a shaper of national history. In her introduction to the *Autobiography*, she points out that one of her chief motivations in writing the memoir was to "interdict the publication of my private letters" (1:1). In their place, she offers her *Autobiography* as a primary source for understanding her "somewhat remarkable" life (1:1). Indeed, throughout the *Autobiography* she argues for the historicity of her life experience. "I have for a long course of years influenced public affairs," she notes, "to an extent not professed or attempted by many men" (1:402). Thus, by writing the *History*, she had asserted her own vision of national progress, and by writing the *Autobiography*, she documents her own role in bringing about this evolutionary change. Martineau's extensive discussion of the expansion of religious liberty in the *History*, for example, becomes more nuanced and complex when paired with Martineau's accounts of her own campaigns against religious dogmatism as described in her *Autobiography*.

Throughout the *Autobiography*, Martineau cross-references the *History*, inviting readers to study the two texts as complementary histories.[74] For example, in recounting a meeting with Charles Buller regarding Lord Durham's government of Canada, she remarks, "By means of my American travel and subsequent correspondence, I was able,—or Charles Buller thought I was,—to supply some useful information, and afford some few suggestions" (1:341). She follows this remark with "the readers of my 'History of the Peace' must perceive that I had some peculiar opportunities of knowing the true story of that Canada governmental campaign" (1:341). Later in the *Autobiography*, she once again references her firsthand knowledge of Canadian politics: "One of the strongest interests of the year 1838 was Lord Durham's going out as Governor-General of the North American colonies. I have given my account of that matter in my History of the Peace, and I will not enlarge on it now" (2:129). In both instances, she reinforces the connections between her autobiographical and historical accounts of British politics. By cross-referencing the two texts, she encourages readers to turn to the *History* as a way of completing and augmenting their understanding of historical events as recounted in the *Autobiography*.

Martineau's seemingly intentional linking of the *Autobiography* and the *History* suggests that her view of history writing differed significantly from that of her fellow Whig historians. Rosemary Jann has argued that Victorian historians "shared a sense of vocation. Each chose the historian's role to deliver himself of a vision of the past that he hoped would do for society what it had done for him: order and make sense of the present."[75] For Martineau, as a woman historian, this sense of vocation operated in a more complex fashion. For women, the personal did not merely precede the political interpretation of history; it, by necessity, must be reinserted retroactively into a generalized history. Women must simultaneously authorize themselves as "real" historians while arguing for the historicity of their own life experiences. Indeed, in writing the *Autobiography*, Martineau was creating just the kind of text she herself relied on when writing the *History*: a first-person account of momentous events that would inform future histories. At the same time, she was authorizing her earlier history, showing it to be the product of significant firsthand experience as a woman and well-connected political reformer.

Indeed, in the *History*, Martineau subtly situates herself among the great male historians of her age. At the end of the final volume of the 1864 version of the *History*, Martineau departs from her custom of recording the obituaries of great men and women who have died and instead lists those greats "who remained among us at the close of the period," those "few whose social influence was as unquestionable in 1846 as it can ever be to another generation."[76] This list of worthies includes three of her fellow historians: Thomas Macaulay, Henry Hallam, and Thomas Carlyle.[77] This nod to the great historians of her time can on one hand be viewed as a strategy of self-authorization, an attempt to place her work alongside theirs, even if only indirectly. However, a closer reading suggests a more competitive relationship. Martineau praises Macaulay but notes that his "influence as a historian is for a future generation to judge of; for his efforts in that direction have been entered upon since the close of our forty years.[78] Likewise, Hallam's *Constitutional History* "may have been inestimable in a transitional political period" (4:607). And even though Carlyle is the "man who has most essentially modified the mind of his time," his work is "not universally read; and he has long wrought where his works have never appeared, and his name been barely heard" (4:607). Martineau's backhanded compliments are interesting in that they simultaneously valorize and throw into question the greatness of her fellow historians.[79] Later, in the *Autobiography*, she would sharpen her critiques of her fellow historians, referring to Macaulay's *History*, for example, as a "brilliant fancypiece,—wanting not only the truth but the repose of history."[80]

Women historians receive little attention in Martineau's *History*. In her footnotes, she does make reference to two historical texts, Eliza Lee Follen's *The Life of Charles Follen* (1844) and Lady Florentia Sale's *A Journal of the Disasters in Afghanistan* (1843). In addition, she briefly mentions Hester Thrale, the "hostess and friend of Dr. Johnson, and the recorder of much that we know of him."[81] However, neither Anna Jameson (1794–1860) nor Elizabeth Penrose (1780–1837) appears in her compendium of literary giants, let alone Agnes Strickland (1796–1874) or Hannah Lawrance (1795–1875).[82] These omissions imply that Martineau viewed herself as a woman standing virtually alone in a field occupied by male historians, however inadequate they might be.[83]

Yet through her own example, Martineau proved women's fitness for writing history and their ability to write both impersonal and personal accounts of the nation's development. For Martineau, the personal and political were inseparable, even if they must be treated in separate texts or according to different generic rules. As Mitzi Myers has pointed out, Martineau "saw herself as purely the instrument of ideas whose time had come," and it was just this sense of temporality—the intersection of private and public histories in the contemporary moment—that informs both her *History* and *Autobiography*.[84] By encouraging readers to engage in inter-textual reading within her own oeuvre, Martineau suggested ways that historical truth could be produced through multiple textual genres and lenses. Further, she demonstrated how the writing of history and memoir could be used as a tool of self-authorization within a male-dominated publishing industry. Although Martineau did not always allow fellow women writers the same kind of historical role she imagined for herself, she nevertheless still integrated women's biographies and histories into a broader masculinist narrative of national progress, suggesting that the advancement of women was inseparable from the progress of the nation. In this way, Martineau was a Whig historian par excellence as well as a crucial figure in the development of feminist historiography.

5

Rooms of the Past:
Victorian Women Writers,
History, and the Reconstruction
of Domestic Space

For Harriet Martineau, as for many other women engaged in writing contemporary history, the middle-class home was an important site for reimagining women's domestic and social roles. In what ways did existing domestic architecture promote or impede social progress? How might it be reformed? What aspects of the historical past, embedded within the architectural structure of the home, were worth preserving? Throughout the nineteenth century, women played an important role in addressing these questions as journalists, builders, domestic managers, and historic preservationists. On one hand, the home was represented as a remnant of the past, a space that must be rebuilt and reformed to ensure social progress. In another sense, the home was represented as a historical artifact that could be rescued, restored, and interpreted from a woman's point of view.

These two ways of approaching the past—through rebuilding and preserving domestic spaces—informed women's activism in crucial ways throughout the Victorian era.[1] Women's engagement in the architectural reform movements of the 1830s and the historic preservationist movements of the 1890s provided new sites of agency and infused domestic management with new political and social meanings. New research on Victorian women's historical writing has suggested ways that we can begin to appreciate a protofeminist historiography.[2] Because women were often excluded from conventional forms of historical writing and archival research during the nineteenth century, feminist scholars have begun to investigate alternative forms of discourse Victorian women used to construct their relationship to the past.[3] In this chapter, I will explore one of these alternative forms of discourse: women's literary representations of domestic architecture.[4] Although architecture as a profession remained relatively closed to women throughout the century,[5] women engaged in debates over the construction, reform, preservation, and appreciation of domestic space in a variety of quasiprofessional ways. Women were able to capitalize on the interest in celebrity homes and lives in order to establish themselves in the emerging culture industries, particularly the field of historic preservation. It was at the intersection of home and text, at the nexus of architectural and literary study, that Victorian women redefined their relationship to history and imagined new roles and spaces for social activism.

In response to the call for social reform in the 1830s, women were empowered to view domestic architecture as inherently political. They believed that by rebuilding and reforming domestic spaces, they could transform age-old social hierarchies based on class and gender. In the first part of this chapter, I will examine the ways that architectural education for women was promoted in the British popular media during the 1830s and 1840s. Middle-class women from liberal, dissenting backgrounds were the first to respond to the call, publishing their writing in reformist periodicals dedicated to philanthropy, popular education, and social improvement.[6] The work of two of these women journalists, Mary Gillies and Harriet Martineau, will provide an illustration of the ways that the renovated domestic sphere could be used as a signifier of social progress and as a symbol of a new kind of future for women and the working classes.

In the second part of this chapter, I will explore the ways that women's engagement in the discourse on architectural reform was channeled into the historic preservation movement and the activities of literary societies during the 1890s. Earlier in the century, women's involvement in architectural reform movements was implicitly literary in the sense that it was concurrent with their increased participation in the field of periodical journalism. Later in the century, the connection between women's literary and architectural concerns became more explicit as women journalists began to document the history of women's writing lives, emphasizing the professional and domestic barriers they faced in a male-dominated society. In addition, by memorializing and preserving the shrines and relics of famous writers, women were able to retell the narrative of literary history in a way that highlighted women's achievements and experiences.

It was thus within the discourse on historic preservation that women's architectural and literary avocations merged, providing a new array of professional opportunities. Focusing specifically on the opening of Carlyle's House in 1895 and the formation of the Brontë Society in 1893, I argue that literary tourism and literary societies provided new opportunities for women to reconsider their historical roles and discover new spheres of social activity. However, at the same time, I demonstrate how the movement to preserve famous women writers' homes to some extent detracted from the acceptance and appreciation of their literary works by defining their texts as being inseparable from their life stories and domestic spaces. The late Victorian discourse on domestic preservation thus highlights a key theoretical problem in feminist literary historiography: how to reclaim a tangible past and illuminate the barriers faced by women writers in the domestic sphere without forging an essentializing link between their literary works and domestic lives.

REBUILDING THE PAST:
WOMEN AND DOMESTIC REFORM

Through their representations of domestic spaces, women writers attempted to work out their relationship to the historical past in architectural terms. As Gaston Bachelard has pointed out, houses as metaphors are repositories of memory and desire and thus serve as effective maps for exploring the relationship between individuals and history. He writes, "House images move in both directions: they are in us as much as we are in them."[7] Houses are thus "haunted" in the sense that they incorporate images of the past and the present, the visible and the invisible. As Virginia Woolf observed, the past haunts the present "like some immense, collective ghost," which is "here beyond all possibility of exorcism."[8]

For middle- and upper-class women, the Victorian home was a "given," a space inherited from the patriarchal family or assumed through marriage. In this regard, the house "made the woman" just as the family and the historical past shaped her identity and future prospects. Yet the representation of history (and its associated architectural environments) as fixed and unchangeable was countered by a desire to reform and renovate domestic space, to sweep it clean of memories, secrets, and the legacy of patriarchal inheritance. Examined in this light, the house can be seen as "belonging to" the woman in the present as a sphere of activity, a realm of possibility subject to her creative control. It was one place in Victorian society where she could exert a degree of influence and agency (while still falling subject to patriarchal surveillance). As Elizabeth Langland has pointed out, the Victorian wife was far from being just an "angel in the house"; rather, she performed a "significant and extensive economic and political function" in the home as a manager of "class power."[9] This included the "dissemination of certain knowledges" that "helped to ensure middle-class hegemony in mid-Victorian England."[10]

In architectural terms, this meant the management and codification of domestic space through manuals, cookbooks, family periodicals, and other forms of popular media. As Mark Girouard has noted, this enabled the creation of a home that was a "hieratic structure" constructed according to strict rules for the separation of classes and sexes.[11] However, the Victorian home was also seen as a structure in flux, a space in constant need of renovation. Indeed, beginning in the 1830s, women were defined as key players in the effort to reform and modernize domestic architecture. In an 1831 essay published in the *Foreign Quarterly Review*, W. H. Leeds recommends the study of architecture "as a branch of education for young persons of *both sexes.*"[12] However, Leeds makes it clear that he does not mean to suggest that women be trained as draughtsmen. He remarks, "It is not in order that they may be able to draw columns, for that is merely the means not the end of the pursuit, that we would suggest the propriety of ladies applying themselves to what has hitherto never been included within the circle of female acquirements; but that they may thereby cultivate their taste, and ground it upon something less baseless and shifting than mere feminine likings and dislikings" (441). He further argues that architecture, unlike other fields of study, is a "Virgin Art," which is "incapable of receiving or transmitting the least moral taint" (443). Leeds is unable to name a single female architect; however, in a footnote, he mentions a "lady of rank," Lady Stafford, who redesigned Costessey Hall in grand "domestic Gothic" style (443).

While W. H. Leeds imagined architectural study as a polite pursuit for the upper classes, J. C. Loudon, writing during the same period, imagined an even broader role for women in renovating historically significant buildings and improving architectural taste. In *The Ency-*

clopaedia of Cottage, Farm, and Villa Architecture (1836), Loudon identifies as his first object the improvement of the "dwellings of the great mass of society" and as his second object the dissemination of a "taste for architectural comforts and beauties."[13] Loudon claims that the graphic, nonspecialist format of his book is likely to appeal to "young persons . . . especially those of the female sex" (1). Women, he argues, have the potential to facilitate the development of improved architectural taste among all classes of society and thus "materially contribute towards universal adoption of correct and elegant habits of thinking and acting generally" (2). Although Loudon stops short of recommending that women become architects or contractors, he does suggest that women can develop a critical awareness of the connection between the architectural and moral improvement of society. He asks, "If the study of landscape drawing, by ladies, has led to the improvement of landscape gardening, why should not the study of architectural drawing, on their part, lead to the improvement of domestic Architecture?" (2).

Loudon's use of the modifier *domestic* reminds us that the study of architecture was reinterpreted during this period as an extension of women's traditional roles in the domestic sphere as philanthropic ministers to the poor and as practitioners of the domestic and fine arts.[14] Women were viewed as instruments of social progress who were key players in correcting architectural "improvements" of the historical past, which had focused on the "accommodation, arrangement, and exterior beauty of the mansions of the wealthy."[15] Published in the wake of the passage of the first Reform Act (1832), which excluded both women and the working classes from the franchise, Loudon's *Encyclopaedia* links the empowerment of women to the improvement of domestic living arrangements for all classes of society. In doing so, he suggests ways that women can influence society and promote social justice even without the vote.

Indeed, women did become involved in architectural reform movements during the 1830s. Women's desire to improve the homes of the working classes was expressed in myriad ways within popular print culture as a response to debates over urban sanitation in the early 1830s and 1840s. Of special importance was the reformist periodical press, which provided unprecedented opportunities for women to participate in public discourse focused on the condition-of-England debate.[16] For some women journalists, especially those from liberal, dissenting backgrounds, the question of how homes should be rebuilt to promote public health was connected to the question of how women could be empowered as rational mothers and thinkers. They made a connection between the historical construction of the home and outdated conceptions of femininity, which made women narrow-minded and ineffective as domestic managers. This view is especially apparent in a series of articles by Mary Gillies published in *Howitt's Journal* in 1840.[17] Gillies (1805?–1870) was a reformer and children's book author closely associated with William and Mary Howitt and their circle. In her series of essays for *Howitt's*, Gillies proposes a plan for "associated homes" for the working classes and lower middle classes.[18] In meticulous detail, she sets out her plan for a "society of individuals residing under one roof, but in totally separate suites of apartments" (38). Communal spaces include a kitchen, dining room, library, nursery, and in-house school room.[19] For Gillies, the social benefits of such an arrangement are clear. She writes, "The more the subject is considered, the more it becomes apparent that that whole of our social arrangements may be wonderfully improved, and that this co-operative plan is the medium by which it will be elevated" (41).

Gillies is especially interested in exploring ways that women were degraded by unhealthy housing arrangements. She points out that they must skimp and save just to make ends meet and have "no time for reading or mental improvement"; thus, they become "narrow-minded and unfit companions for their husbands" (270). With the "diminution of expense" and increased comfort of communal living, women "would then all have a chance to develop themselves" through reading and other improving leisure activities (272). Gillies thus makes an important link between women's domestic living arrangements and their social and intellectual progress. Women are produced by their domestic environments, Gillies contends, but they also have the power to change them. Indeed, she envisions her "associated homes" as being run primarily by women, including "one superintending matron" and a "house committee of three ladies" (40). Gillies suggests that women can be liberated from an oppressive historical legacy by envisioning new domestic spaces and arrangements created and managed by women.

Women's involvement in building projects expressed their desire to create new kinds of domestic spaces that would allow them to develop more socially useful vocations as writers, reformers, and philanthropists. It also enabled them to question the class- and gender-based hierarchies that historically had governed domestic relations. If in the past domestic space had been perceived as a kind of patriarchal inheritance, for reformist women of the 1830s and 1840s, it was a new sphere of agency that promised to empower women and bring about progressive social change. This sense of agency in reforming domestic space extended to activities both inside and outside the home, from the design of middle-class living quarters to the development of philanthropic building projects in the local community.

A fascinating case study in this regard is Harriet Martineau. As noted in chapter 3, Martineau built her own home in the Lake District in 1845, carefully designing its floor plan to suit her activities as a professional journalist. She described the building of her home and strategies for domestic management in a variety of publications, including *Household Education* (1849), *Health, Husbandry and Handicraft* (1861), and *Autobiography* (1877).[20] Of course, "A Year at Ambleside" (1850), discussed extensively in chapter 3, also detailed her life in the Lake District and was crucial in establishing her own status as a literary celebrity. In this chapter, I will return briefly to this series, focusing specifically on the ways Martineau was engaged in the discourse on architectural reform. In "A Year at Ambleside," she describes the process of moving to the Lake District after a long illness.[21] Single and successful, she saw no impediment to her desire to build a home of her own. She soon purchased land and began designing the floor plan (57). When Martineau finally moved into her house, she reported that "it was an occasion never to be forgotten— the first entrance upon a home of my own" (71). "Long after others were asleep," she notes, "I sat in the light of the fire, feeling what it was to have entered upon the home in which I hoped to live and die; to work while I could, and rest when I could work no more, if I should indeed live so long. The next sweetest thing was the morning's waking—the rousing up to the first business of a new life" (72). Thus, Martineau imagines building her home as a regenerative act that effaces the historical restrictions faced by women and introduces a brighter future.

In "A Year at Ambleside," Martineau indirectly contrasts her new home to the abodes of the local laborers, which are "undrained, ill supplied with water, close and unwholesome" (51). Because their homes are so degraded, the men assume the "old-fashioned" habit of frequenting the public houses (51). As a result, she argues, "intemperance and all sensual vice" infect local communities (133). For

Martineau, the degraded working-class home was a symbol of the past: "My thoughts being turned on the health of the district, it is natural to observe how entirely all conditions of health were over-looked, while those modes of living grew up which are still followed by the country people." (132). "I saw that something should be done about this" (51), she remarks, and goes on to describe her plans for building homes for the laborers in her neighborhood:

> From the Sanitary Commission in London it was easy to obtain re-ports and other documents which would teach us the best methods of draining and constructing new houses. When these had arrived and been well studied, our builder, John Newton, and our house car-penter, T. C., and his wife, came to tea with me, to talk matters over. It makes my heart ache now to think of that evening; to think how, all unknowing of the future, we sat in happy consultation, perceiving hope and encouragement whichever way we looked, and trusting that in a few years we might see the place regenerated. (134)

This concept of "regeneration" infuses Martineau's narrative, renew-ing and rebuilding her community to take advantage of the natural purity of the Lakeland environment. She writes, "Those of us who live according to her [Nature's] laws find this the healthiest place we have ever dwelt in" (135). Martineau's Building Society, founded in 1848, eventually constructed thirteen modern dwellings for local laborers (136–37).

By contrasting her own modern home with the substandard homes of the workers in her neighborhood, Martineau establishes a sense of her relationship to history. The traditional domestic practices of the local populace, passed down from generation to generation, have a degrading effect on family and community morality. The past must be wiped away and the working classes reeducated in order for public health to be improved. Martineau's own personal renaissance, like the renovation of the community as a whole, is premised on con-structing a new kind of domestic space based on the best scientific and natural laws. Thus, Martineau presents herself as a case study of how involvement in architectural improvement efforts can empower women and the working classes whose interests they represent.

Throughout the century, women continued to become involved in the field of architecture, primarily in an amateur capacity. The Royal Institute of British Architects was closed to women until 1898, and major British architecture schools did not admit women until the beginning of the twentieth century. However, even though women were excluded from professional involvement in the field of architecture, they were nevertheless seen as having an important nonprofessional role to play in revitalizing architectural taste. An article by F. W. Fitzpatrick published in an American periodical, the *Midland Monthly*, reinforces women's roles in bringing about this change.[22] Written in 1897 amid debates over women's suffrage, the article suggests ways that women's engagement in the discourse on architectural improvement can have far-reaching effects on society as a whole. Co-opting rhetoric from the antisuffrage movement, Fitzpatrick suggests ways that women can "influence" public taste rather than having a direct role in the construction of domestic buildings. He begins by reminding each woman of her duty "as a good citizen, to help beautify our streets and contribute to the general good by elevating the general taste" (563) and then proceeds to suggest a "great national movement" to improve architectural aesthetics (565). By exercising "potent influence," he argues, women can change society (565). Fitzpatrick concludes with the following call to action: "Let her urge us to make war upon and destroy vulgarism in buildings; may she spur us on to idealized designs, and may she build up beautiful homes and beautiful cities, thus adding jewels to the crown she will surely wear someday for the noble part she has played in the upbuilding of our nation" (565).

In this way, women's participation in the field of architecture was associated with national progress, with a "war" against the vulgarity of the historical past. Although Fitzpatrick denies women any direct role in the study and practice of architecture as a profession, instead emphasizing their power as consumers, he nonetheless suggests ways that women can be empowered to bring about change within the broader community. The passionate energy with which Fitzpatrick defined women's ancillary roles in the field of architecture is not surprising considering how much was at stake in debates over the control and design of domestic spaces. As Lynne Walker has pointed out, "The debates which surround women's participation in architecture are highly charged both emotionally and politically, because architecture physically defines the public and private spheres: to allow women access to the design of architecture therefore threatens patriarchal control of spatial definitions, which are essential to maintain the social, economic and cultural *status quo*."[23] These debates not only were premised on defining the gender relations of the present but

also were instrumental in defining women's relationship to history—
their desire to correct the errors of the past and bring about new,
more enlightened, social practices.

PRESERVING THE PAST:
WOMEN AND HISTORIC PRESERVATION

The rebuilding and renovation of domestic space expressed one way
that women envisioned their historical role: as change agents who
could reform domestic arrangements and bring about social progress. In the next part of this chapter, I will examine another way
that women used architectural study as a means of expressing their
relationship to history: through the preservation and interpretation
of literary homes. In addition to rebuilding the homes of the past,
Victorian women imagined ways that they could empower themselves
through historical recovery. By retelling history, they highlighted aspects of women's experience that would provide the foundation for
new, modern definitions of womanhood. At the same time, by involving themselves in the growing culture industries, they charted new
paths for women's professional activity.

The impulse to interpret and recover domestic space was expressed
in the historic preservation movement that swept Great Britain at the
end of the nineteenth century.[24] The desire to fix cultural meanings on architectural landmarks was expressed in myriad ways within
Victorian culture, including the establishment of the blue plaque
system in 1867, the formation of the National Trust in 1895, and the
growth of literary societies. As Campbell, Labbe, and Shuttleworth
point out, during the nineteenth century, "Memory became a necessary tool, allowing the collective act of memorializing, encouraging
and bolstering social progression and the transformation of the past
into the future."[25] In this way, these "collective acts" served the purpose of establishing a sense of a cohesive national identity in an era
characterized by "war, revolution, change, and loss."[26]

For women involved in the historic preservation movement, the
impulse to preserve the domestic spaces of the past also expressed
their relationship to history—their belief that domestic spaces and
practices were significant historically and their conviction that the
identities of "great women" of the past were inseparable from the domestic spaces that produced/were produced by them.[27] At the same

time, the discourse on historic preservation enabled women to define themselves as interpreters of historical relics and spaces. Although few had academic training in historiography, they nonetheless used the quasiprofessional activity of historic preservation to "change the subject" of historical inquiry, focusing public interest on women's stories and issues. An important facet of women's participation in the historic preservation movement was their contribution to the discourse on literary tourism in the popular press. Earlier in the century, women's contributions to the discourse on domestic renovation were inherently literary in the sense that they were dependent on the expansion of the periodical press as a venue for women's writing. Later in the century, the connection between literary and architectural study became more explicit as women journalists explored the domestic and professional barriers faced by their literary predecessors. For late-nineteenth-century women journalists, there was a great deal at stake in retelling literary history and reinterpreting domestic spaces from a woman's perspective. Their efforts would justify their work as literary historians and would provide a motivating cause for reforming gender inequities within the domestic sphere.

The discourse surrounding the establishment of Carlyle's House as a London tourist destination in 1895 is an interesting case in point. Although the house was acquired by men and the board of trustees was initially composed entirely of men, women were intimately involved in the process of restoring the home and reconstructing the memory of both Thomas and Jane Carlyle as a product of its domestic environment. Carlyle's niece, Mary Aitken (Mrs. Alexander Carlyle), provided a large share of the relics on display in the house.[28] After Carlyle's death, Helen Allingham created a number of watercolor paintings of the interior that were used as sources for accurately reconstructing its décor (24). Both women went on to pursue careers as memorialists, and Allingham later illustrated books on domestic architecture.[29] Thus, the quasi-professional activities of women in the establishment of Carlyle's House as a tourist destination provided a springboard for more specifically professional literary activity.

To some extent, the opening of Carlyle's House on Cheyne Row would have been unthinkable without the scandal produced by the publication of James Froude's *Reminiscences* (1881), *Letters and Memorials of Jane Welsh Carlyle* (1883), and *Life of Thomas Carlyle* (1882–84).[30] Rather than simply being interpreted as the site where Carlyle entertained Emerson and wrote *The French Revolution*, the house came to

be seen as the location of the most celebrated and conflicted marriage in literary history: the tempestuous union between the "sage of
Chelsea" and his brilliant wife, Jane Welsh Carlyle. Indeed, as journalist Reginald Blunt points out, it was the scandal associated with
the revelation of the Carlyles' domestic discord that proved to be its
greatest attraction to tourists: "Apathy, disapproval, opposition, were
freely encountered. All the fusty threadbare fallacies and heresies
about the life at Cheyne Row were dragged out once more, and stuck
up as scarecrows to warn off the unenlightened citizen whose guinea
might be captured unawares."[31]

The story of Carlyle's House is the story of competing histories.
On one hand, the establishment of the shrine was a reaction against
the salacious narratives being written about Carlyle's domestic life,
stories that threatened to overshadow his accomplishments and genius.[32] As Bill Bell has pointed out, "If the house was to be rescued
for posterity then Carlyle's advocates, it was felt, would be vindicated
against gossip-mongers who in recent years had sought to detract
from his blessed memory."[33] The attempt to supplant gossip with hero
worship is evident in an article soliciting support for purchase of the
Carlyle House published in the *Academy* in 1895. The article makes
no mention of the *Reminiscences, Letters,* or *Life,* instead reinforcing
the idea that there is "no house in London possessing such unique
interest to all who care for literary associations."[34] Likewise, in the
introduction to the *Illustrated Memorial Volume of the Carlyle's House
Purchase Fund* (1896), George Lumsden notes that when he first saw
the house, it "repelled" him because of its dilapidated condition.[35]
The house's condition, he remarks, is a "fitting accompaniment of
all the malevolent abuse that has been heaped upon Carlyle since
his death" (2). He then defines his goal as saving the house from
destruction and, by extension, Carlyle from infamy. The rest of the
introduction reads as a heroic narrative in which Lumsden and his
collaborators raise funds, defend Carlyle against his detractors, and
ultimately purchase the house for posterity.

While some journalists interpreted Carlyle's House as a symbol
of the great author's genius, others preferred to "read" the Carlyle
House as a signifier of another history: the story of Jane Carlyle's emotional and physical suffering. Journalist Marion Harland remarks,
"We have asked to see the kitchen, first of all. For the thought of Jane
Welsh Carlyle, more than the fame of her husband, has brought us to
No. 24—formerly No. 5—Cheyne Row."[36] Indeed, in many accounts,

the Carlyles' difficult marriage is interpreted as a kind of melodrama. For example, an article published in the American newspaper the *Nation* includes the following caveat: "Into the domestic drama of the Carlyle household it is now impossible to intrude, that drama having been made public property, once and for all, when the 'Reminiscences' and 'Letters' were published."[37] However, it soon becomes clear that the author does indeed intend to "intrude" on the private history of the house. This intrusion is justified by the fact that the Carlyle story, through frequent retelling and publication, had become a commodified object similar to the literary relics collected in the house and further "property" for public consumption.

Rather than being interpreted as a factual recounting of the literary events that took place in the house, the article fashions a melodrama wherein an innocent woman suffers at the hands of a tyrannical husband. After recounting one or two instances of marital kindness, the article continues, "Of his tenderness, in so trivial a matter, to his wife after her mother's death, one likes to have the reminder in the room where, for all its distinguished associations, one remembers best the long, bitter days of her loneliness and jealousy, the long, sad evenings when he sat solitary over his dreary Prussian books" (286–87). Such representations of suffering womanhood were ubiquitous within the fin de siècle discourse on the Woman Question. As Judith Walkowitz has pointed out, melodramatic narratives focused on the victimization of women were a staple of the social purity campaigns during the later years of the nineteenth century.[38] Walkowitz contends that "melodrama particularly appealed to female audiences, writers, and performers, precisely because it foregrounded issues of gender and power and highlighted the role of the heroine, however passive and suffering she might be."[39] Located within this broader field of discourse, journalistic representations of Jane Carlyle's suffering thus drew on melodramatic traditions within the women's movement and were central to the definition of the Carlyle House as a tourist destination.

For women journalists, the "opening up" of both the letters and the homes of the Carlyles provided an opportunity to address women's issues. Women journalists first became involved in telling the history of the Carlyles' marriage in 1866, just after Jane Carlyle's death. Geraldine Jewsbury and other women journalists published a collection of anecdotes about Jane in a memorial volume. As Anne Skabarnicki has shown, these memorials depicted an "intelligent, tough-minded and independent [woman], far more sturdy and even more threatening than the 'little' Jane whom Carlyle so often patronized as he commended."[40] In response, Thomas Carlyle began writing his highly sentimentalized counternarrative, *Reminiscences*, which he hoped would correct the inaccuracies of the Jewsbury volume. Later, after the posthumous publication of *Reminiscences* and *Letters*, other women journalists provided their own politicized interpretations of Jane Carlyle's life and marriage. Jane MacNeil, for example, writing for *Munsey's Magazine* in 1901, concludes that "somehow, when all is said of the homes that Carlyle made famous, only one thought remains; not of the genius and the upright man and the thunderer, but of the two troubled, lifelong lovers, who managed to achieve so much misery when they might have had peace, and who were so lonely, so true at heart, so brave, and so unhappy."[41] Although in this passage MacNeil seems to focus on the unhappiness of both Carlyles, the article as a whole highlights Jane's unhappiness, jealousies, and unfulfilled ambitions. MacNeil notes that it was not until Thomas posthumously read his wife's letters and journals that he realized that the "vast longing of her heart had never been satisfied" (639).

The correspondence between the emergence of biographical criticism and the growth of the field of historic preservation thus provided women with the opportunity to "change the subject" of literary history from memorializing the contributions of the great sage to exposing the complex unhappiness of his marriage with the brilliant Jane Welsh Carlyle. For some, Thomas Carlyle is reduced to a tyrannical, misanthropic figure in literary history. For example, Mary Krout, writing in 1899, concludes her visit to Carlyle's House with this comment: "Why Carlyle should have been held in such reverent memory passes comprehension, for no man ever lived who had greater and more out-spoken contempt for the race—'most of them fools,' according to his own estimation."[42]

Perhaps it was Thomas Carlyle's notoriety that led Virginia Woolf to choose an ironic title for one of her most important essays on the Carlyles: "Great Men's Houses" (1932). Like her predecessors, Woolf interprets the house "not so much [as] a dwelling-place as a battlefield."[43] Yet Woolf's attention is not focused on the emotional struggles of the tortured genius, Jane Carlyle; rather, she emphasizes the material conditions that affected her day-to-day life. After a short visit to the Carlyle House, she writes, "One is made acquainted with a fact that escaped the attention of Froude, and yet was of incalculable importance—they had no water laid on" (23). The lack of running water causes Woolf to reflect on the arduous labor of the Carlyles' maids, who pumped water "from a well in the kitchen" and carried it "up three flights of stairs from the basement" (23–24). "The stairs," she notes, "seem worn by the feet of harassed women carrying tin cans" (24). And Jane, for her part, must have been obsessed with the "many problems of the incessant battle, against dirt, against cold" (24). Looking at Jane's portrait, Woolf notes that "her cheeks are hollow; bitterness and suffering mingle in the half-tender, half-tortured expression of the eyes. Such is the effect of a pump in the basement and a yellow tin bath up three pairs of stairs" (25). Foreshadowing her treatment of the material conditions that impede women's artistic expression in *A Room of One's Own*, Woolf "changes the subject" of the Carlyle House story once again, emphasizing the material barriers to genius, rather than retelling the melodramatic narrative of marital suffering inspired by Froude.

The opening of Carlyle's House provided women with the opportunity to view literary history through a new lens. Clearly, for most women journalists, the "Carlyle House" was more accurately titled the "Carlyles' House." Jane Carlyle's story, which had been hidden from view, lost in the shadow of her husband's fame, was now brought to light. This kind of historical and literary recovery prompted by the discourse on historic preservation was an important precursor to the more explicitly feminist literary and historical activities of the late twentieth century. Equally important to the early development of women's historical and literary scholarship was the establishment of literary societies in the late nineteenth and early twentieth centuries.[44] As women became involved in the quasischolarly activities associated with literary societies, they began to develop important skills as managers of historic relics and interpreters of literary history.

The formation of the Brontë Society and the establishment of the Brontë Museum provide a fascinating case study for tracing this progression. Formed in 1893, the society involved many prominent women as key players in the establishment of the Brontë Museum (1895), the purchase of the Brontë Parsonage (1928), and the administration of the society's annual meetings. In the early days of the society, the president and vice-president positions were primarily held by men. However, Agnes Mary Duclaux (née Robinson and later Mrs. Darmesteter, 1857–1944) served as one of the founding vice presidents. Duclaux was author of the Emily Brontë volume in the

Eminent Women series published by W. H. Allen in 1883. She was also a noted poet and scholar of French literature. Throughout the early years of the society, a number of other women served as members of the governing council, including Miss Cockshott, Mrs. F. C. Galloway, Lady Morrison, Miss Lumb, and Mrs. C. E. Sugden. Likewise, from the beginning, a large number of women were counted as members of the society. An informal analysis of the Brontë Society's annual reports reveals that 22 percent of the membership was made up of women in 1899 as compared to 37 percent in 1906.[45]

At the same time that women were becoming more involved as members of the governing council, they increasingly took on leadership roles in the administration of the organization. In 1912, a woman assumed the presidency of the society for the first time, novelist Mary Augusta Ward (Mrs. Humphry Ward).[46] By the time she assumed the helm of the Brontë Society, Ward was a well-known philanthropist[47] and author of several popular novels, including the bestseller *Robert Elsmere* (1888). She had also written critical introductions to the Haworth editions of the Brontë novels (1899–90). Her other memorials to the Brontë sisters included a poem titled "Charlotte and Emily Brontë" published in *Cornhill Magazine* in 1900 and an address to the Brontë Society on the occasion of the centenary of Charlotte Brontë's birth (1916).[48]

In her centenary address, Ward is careful to make a personal connection between her own biography and that of the celebrated author.[49] She reminds readers that Brontë visited her relatives, the Arnolds, during a trip to the Lake District. She also notes that George Smith, Brontë's publisher, was her own "constant and generous friend."[50] But what is most remarkable about Ward's address is the way that she highlights aspects of the Brontës' experiences as women, retelling their stories from a woman's perspective.[51] She situates their achievement as women writers in the Romantic tradition of Goethe and Sand. She also highlights their imaginative genius: "With Charlotte, imagination was a cradle gift no less than with Emily; and Anne, in frailer, feebler measure, was played upon by the same power."[52] Writing at the same time that university scholars were beginning to formulate the literary canon,[53] Ward was careful to make an argument for the canonization of the Brontë sisters: "It is indeed this quality of poetry, sometimes piercingly plaintive and touching, at others grim and fiery, with interludes of extravagance or grotesque, that establishes the claim of Charlotte and Emily Brontë to their high place in literature."[54] Indeed, as Lucasta Miller has recently argued, Ward "was one of the first critics to treat it [*Wuthering Heights*] as a purely literary text rather than regarding it as the freakish consequence of biographical circumstances."[55] Yet Ward premises the canonization of the Brontës not only on their achievements as writers but on their life stories as women struggling in imperfect domestic conditions. She writes of Charlotte, "It is one of the strongest grounds of her immortality that she was also a loving, faithful, suffering woman, with a personal story which, thanks to Mrs. Gaskell's *Life*, will never cease to touch the hearts of English folk while literature lasts."[56]

Though Ward was a well-known antisuffragist,[57] her writings on the Brontë sisters seem protofeminist in the sense that they are focused on canonizing the artistic achievements of Victorian women. In her critical introduction to the Brontë novels, she writes, "As women's life and culture widen, as the points of contact between them and the manifold world multiply and develop, will Parnassus open before them."[58] Through her efforts as a critic, society president, and custodian of Brontë relics, Ward engaged in a specific form of protofeminist activity that incorporated literary, touristic, managerial, and architectural realms of discourse. Ward, like other literary critics of her day, viewed criticism as being infused by the physical and biographical details of everyday life. When a Brontë shrine, Thornton Rectory, came up for auction in 1912 during the first year of Ward's incumbency, a committee was appointed to acquire the property but was unsuccessful.[59] Still, this attempt illustrates the multidimensional nature of Ward's engagement in the discourse on the Brontës, which occurred at the intersection of literary criticism and the material context of historic preservation.

The Brontë Society provided opportunities for women on a number of different levels: as novelists, literary critics, memorial writers, and society administrators. Indeed, the Brontë Society *Transactions*, first published in 1895, provided an important venue for women as they began developing careers as caretakers of literary relics, literary geographers, and, ultimately, professional scholars. By the second decade of the twentieth century, women were listed as scholarly presenters at annual meetings. For example, Esther Chadwick, author of *Mrs. Gaskell: Haunts, Homes, and Stories* (1910) and *In the Footsteps of the Brontës* (1914), was the keynote speaker at the 1911 meeting of the society.[60] Meanwhile, Ellen Nussey and Frances Wheelwright, friends of Charlotte Brontë, were frequent consultants as the society shaped its understanding of the family's history. The *Centenary History of the Brontë Society* notes that "Miss Nussey had attained an advanced age before the Society was formed and could never be persuaded to take an active part in its affairs, but she had manifested the keenest interest in its work."[61]

Other women played instrumental roles in the early years of the Brontë Society as well. When the Brontë Parsonage Museum first opened its doors to the public, it was a woman, Lady Roberts, who turned the front door key. A 1978 guide to the parsonage notes that Lady Roberts had convinced her husband, Sir James Roberts, to purchase the parsonage in order "to do something for his native Haworth."[62] This comment is interesting in that it identifies a possible financial motivation for purchasing the parsonage, which (when developed as a tourist site) would bring economic development to the community. In 1929, Dr. Mabel Edgerley became the first woman to serve as honorary secretary of the society and as a founding member of the Parsonage Museum Committee, a position she held until 1946. Born Catherine Mabel Blackwood, grandniece to William Blackwood, founder of *Blackwood's Magazine,* she became a licensed doctor in 1894. Her eulogist, Donald Hopewell, noted that as secretary to the Brontë Society, Edgerley "husbanded its resources, set her face firmly against extravagance, laid firm foundations; and at her death left it in a strong, healthy and sound financial position. She made contacts all over the world, and her correspondence . . . was voluminous."[63] Interestingly, her involvement in the Brontë Society provided her not only with a venue for demonstrating her administrative skills but also an opportunity to merge her medical and literary interests. She published articles on the physical and psychological state of the Brontë family and the sanitary condition of the parsonage. She also published a number of fascinating articles in the *Transactions,* including a brief historical and architectural survey of the parsonage, published in 1936 along with architectural drawings by F. Mitchell.[64] Her writings on the Brontës were collected in a memorial edition, edited by Donald Hopewell, which was published posthumously by the Brontë Society in 1951.[65] Edgerley's career, like Ward's, illustrates the multifaceted nature of women's involvement with literary societies as managers, historians, and literary scholars. The celebrity writer's home, far from serving merely as a shrine, was a springboard for women's involvement in a variety of quasiprofessional activities, but it was also a means for women to theorize their own relationship to the past and to foreground their experiences in the domestic realm as historically significant and worthy of preservation.

Yet the historic preservation movement was not just about interpreting and preserving the past; it was also about reconstructing it to serve the political concerns of the present. For some feminists, most notably Virginia Woolf, there were dangers inherent in women's obsessive emphasis on historical relics and domestic spaces. In "Haworth, November, 1904," Woolf noted, "I do not know whether pilgrimages to the shrines of famous men ought not to be condemned as sentimental journeys."[66] Inevitably, she argues, the achievement of the woman writer is reduced by the touristic gaze: "But the most touching case—so touching that one hardly feels reverent in one's gaze—is that which contains the little personal relics, the dresses and shoes of the dead woman. The natural fate of such things is to die before the body that wore them, and because these, trifling and transient though they are, have survived, Charlotte Brontë the woman comes to life, and one forgets the chiefly memorable fact that she was a great writer. Her shoes and her thin muslin dress have outlived her" (1:7). Reduced to material objects, the historical remnants of domesticity, Charlotte Brontë the writer is lost. Instead of feeling "reverent," Woolf is "touched" by the objects on display. Brontë's domestic life, rather than her work, is foremost in the literary tourist's mind. The relics on display become a replacement for other, more important, objects—Charlotte Brontë's books—which more rightly should "outlive her." The study of domestic relics is thus reductive in the sense that it replaces the value of an author's literary remains with the value of the author's domestic ephemera.

Indeed, concern over the cultural obsession with women's domestic history continues into our own time. Gail Lee Dubrow, for example, writes, "The ubiquitous presence of historic houses as locations for the public interpretation of women's history inadvertently may buttress the myth of women's confinement in the domestic sphere while missing vital opportunities for marking women's history in the more public arenas of the paid labor force and the community."[67] The home logically became the focus of women's literary and extraliterary activity due to its designation as the feminine sphere, but such an approach nevertheless had the effect of reinforcing and essentializing women's roles as keepers of the domestic hearth. In addition, by focusing on the material relics associated with great women writers, the literary tourism industry interpreted the life story of the woman writer as being more important than her textual contributions to literary history.

Yet even if the discourse on historic preservation, then and now, was premised on "placing" women in domestic spaces and reducing their lives to a collection of domestic relics, it undoubtedly still empowered those who enshrined their memories. It provided opportunities to retain certain values associated with Victorian womanhood while at the same time imagining a more enlightened future, where women would create and manage homes rather than being simply circumscribed by them. As David Lowenthal has pointed out, preservationist impulse is premised on the idea that the "past as we know it is partly a product of the present; we continually reshape memory, rewrite history, refashion relics."[68] Thus, women involved in the historic preservation movement used the process of "saving" literary homes as a means of setting out their own definitions of modern womanhood and laying the foundation for careers as historians, curators, librarians, and managers of the emerging cultural heritage industry. Indeed, in our own time, women scholars have been deeply engaged in exploring the intersection between the practice of women's history and the historic preservation movement.[69] As Heather Huyck has observed, this field of feminist inquiry seeks to construct a "tangible history" that enables the public to "understand the relationships between women's experiences and extant tangible resources."[70] In doing so, it merges interest in the "story" of women's history and its material "remains."[71] In other words, it occurs at intersection of textual narrative and the tangible relics of the past.

As we have seen, the discourse on "literary architecture" or "architectural literature" begins early in the nineteenth century as a major field of inquiry and activity for middle-class women. Women were able to use emerging literary media, especially journalism, as a means of imagining and creating new spaces of agency and meaning. At the same time, they used the reconstruction and preservation of domestic space as subject matter for their literary texts. Thus, the home, far from being a private realm, separate sphere, or gilded cage, was a space that was the focus of ever expanding fields of discourse that collapsed the public/private dichotomy and enabled women to speak out on issues of social concern, especially the status of women and the working classes in Victorian society. The intersecting discourses on literature and architecture provided two metaphors for women's relationship to history: reform and preservation. Although in some ways women's engagement in the discourse on domestic architecture was essentializing and reductive, it undoubtedly still provided women with new spheres of social activism and new ways of asserting a woman's perspective on the historical past.

III
Celebrity and
Fin de Siècle Print Culture

6

Women Writers and
Celebrity News at the Fin de Siècle

THE DEVELOPMENT OF THE LITERARY TOURISM AND HISTORIC PRES-
ervation movements at the end of the nineteenth century corresponded with a rapid expansion in celebrity print media. Of course
gallery portraits, court circulars, and profiles of famous writers were
a staple of periodical print culture throughout the century; however,
it was not until the 1870s that celebrity news became a ubiquitous
feature of the popular press. Six-penny weekly newspapers founded
in the 1870s, such as the *World* (1874–1922) and the *Whitehall Review*
(1876–1912), included gossip pages, interviews, illustrations, and
other features designed to provide intimate knowledge of the lives of
Victorian celebrities. How did women writers negotiate the demands
of the celebrity news media that emerged at the end of the nineteenth
century? In what ways did the publication of time-sensitive celebrity
news in newspapers and periodicals affect the sorts of domestic arrangements, sexual identities, and professional opportunities women
could pursue? In this chapter, I address these questions by examining
a selection of celebrity features published in newspapers and periodicals at the end of the nineteenth century.

CELEBRITY JOURNALISM AND
THE WOMAN AUTHOR

It was during the second half of the nineteenth century that the term
celebrity came into common usage in the press, to a large extent replacing terms such as *hero, lion,* or *notable person.* According to the
Oxford English Dictionary, the use of the term *celebrity* to refer to a

person, rather than the state of being celebrated, was first introduced in 1849.[1] By the 1880s and 1890s, the term was widely employed in the periodical press, particularly in illustrated monthlies such as the *Strand* (1891–1950) and *Windsor Magazine* (1895–1939) as well as in weeklies such as *Truth* (1877–1957) and *Sketch* (1893–1959). At the same time, periodicals focused exclusively on celebrity culture were published, including the *Weekly Gallery of Celebrities* (1891) and monthlies such as *Our Celebrities* (1888–95) and *Celebrities of the Day* (1881–82). Equally significant was the development of specialist monthlies focused on the "news" associated with authorial lives and the publishing industry, such as the *Bookman* (1891–1934).[2]

Within the expanding discourse on celebrity in the newspaper and periodical press, women writers were increasingly the subject of articles and profiles. Featured as "news," the woman author seized the public limelight in ways that would have been unimaginable earlier in the century. The depiction of her domestic life and writing habits, revealed to the public through photographs and personal interviews, promised to demystify the life of the woman author and illustrate the compatibility of work and domestic responsibilities. However, at the same time, representations of the woman author mystified and sensationalized her private life by referencing unmentionable "secrets" that could only be addressed through innuendo. The celebrity female body, increasingly represented in visual terms in illustrated periodicals, became the focus of heightened, if ephemeral, consumer interest. As W. Robertson Nicoll pointed out in an 1894 interview published in *Sketch*, "Freshness is essential. It's no good to try to deceive the public. Old matter won't do."[3] As commodities, writers and their work supplied the ever-changing demand for newness in the literary marketplace. Value was defined as being of the moment rather than for all time. The woman author was especially prone to such commodification given the perception that women writers were the "rage" and images of women's bodies were becoming ubiquitous marketing devices in the popular press.

A dominant characteristic of celebrity newspapers was their active incorporation of male and female readers. As one of the most important papers of the 1870s to feature celebrity gossip,[4] Edmund Yates's the *World* identified this dual audience in its subtitle, *A Journal for Men and Women*. In his 1874 prospectus, Yates writes that the "*World* will recognise women as a reasonable class of the community, whose interests should be equitably considered, and their errors explained without levity or hysterics."[5] Later he attributed the newspaper's success in part to its ability to "interpret the real wants" of modern women, who "were hitherto obliged to be content with recipes for cookery, hints for illness, precepts for the nurture and training of infants, patterns for needlework, and mild facetiae culled from the columns of would-be comic prints."[6]

As an innovator in the field of celebrity journalism, Yates owed a great deal to women's newspapers, particularly the *Queen*, a six-penny weekly founded by Samuel Beeton in 1861. As Margaret Beetham has pointed out, the *Queen* was the first of the illustrated papers to bring the "concept of the lady, the techniques of illustration and the category of news into dynamic relationship with each other."[7] Writing under the pseudonym "Mrs. Seaton," Yates wrote a society gossip column for the *Queen* from February 1872 to March 1873.[8] During this period, he no doubt became familiar with the *Queen's* use of society news, short articles, profiles of famous women, and "answers" to correspondents—just the sort of features that would characterize the new celebrity media. The *Queen*, like the *World*, specifically catered to women readers who would be "insulted by a collection of mere trivialities."[9] The commonalities between the two newspapers thus draw attention to the important interdependence between journalism specifically aimed at women and the new "society" journalism aimed at a mixed-gender audience. Consequently, the word *men* in the subtitle of Yates's newspaper was just as likely a marketing add-on as the phrase *and women*.

Nothing better served the common interests of the modern man and the modern woman, in Yates's view, than the celebrity profile, which would detail the "exact social surroundings and daily lives and labours, the habits and manners, the dress and appearance, of the men of mark in the present day."[10] Perhaps the most popular feature in the *World* was its "Celebrities at Home" series of interviews.[11] By 1885, nearly 400 celebrities had been interviewed as part of the series, and several articles had been republished in book form.[12] Subjects included politicians, aristocrats, sports heroes, attorneys, actors, and writers. The narrator-interviewer of each profile—most likely Yates—refers to himself in the second person. Such intrusions of the personal pronoun *you* were justified in some degree by the presence of women readers, who were expected to take an active interest in domestic life. However, the fact that most of the celebrities profiled in the series were men suggests that an interest in celebrity lifestyles crossed expected gender lines. "Historian[s] of the future," Yates later wrote in his *Recollections,* will turn away from dry histories of famous men and instead examine the author's "daily life and personal habits, the strange household nourished by his charity, his tricks of post-touching and tea-drinking, his general method of tossing and goring all those differing from him in opinion."[13] As Joel Wiener has pointed out, Yates's emphasis on gossip anticipated the development of the New Journalism, which highlighted the "newsy" aspects of popular culture and established "shared confidences" between editor and reader.[14]

Rather than providing an overview of a celebrity's life and works, as in a conventional "gallery portrait," the "Celebrities at Home" articles provided a slice of life, a depiction of a particular moment in the daily experience of the celebrity subject. Such a snapshot approach suggests the spontaneity of photography, which captures the evanescence of the momentary gaze. Writers were not often the topic of the "Celebrities at Home" feature, but their profiles nevertheless reveal the ways that domestic space was being reconceived as both a scene of professional activity and a location for the display of literary taste. Each article provides the details of home décor: furniture, drapes, carpets, color schemes, books, paintings, and other accoutrements of domestic life. Such details, Richard Salmon points out, were interpreted as "revelatory signs" of the celebrity's "sanctified personality" and "worldly success."[15] The interest in material culture is reinforced by the inclusion of advertisements footnoted at the bottom of each page hawking hotels, china, and other commercial interests. In this way, Yates solidified the connection between commercial enterprise and celebrity worship. As Margaret Beetham has pointed out, the link between "news," taste, and commercial culture via the "advertorial" was a crucial feature of women's magazines during the 1880s and 1890s.[16] This is likewise true of publications such as the *World,* which, as previously noted, owed a great deal to women's newspapers. The inclusion of advertorials was premised on constructing a new model of insatiable consumer desire. Indeed, as Chris Rojek has argued, "The logic of capitalist accumulation requires consumers to constantly change their wants. The restlessness and friction in industrial culture partly derives from the capitalist requirement to initiate perpetual commodity and brand innovation. In such circumstances desire is *alienable,* transferable, since wants must be perpetually switched in response to market developments."[17] The focus on the domestic "fashion of the moment" thus serves to spark consumer desire in response to stimulation that changes from week to week.

The emphasis on commodity culture in celebrity profiles was of significant concern to women writers because so much was at stake in their visibility as professionals. Depictions of the woman writer's domestic life had the potential of illustrating new ways of living and working for middle-class women. The career of the woman author, after all, had been a test case of women's suitability for professional activity throughout the century. Thus, her celebrity profile had a kind of "currency"—in both senses of the term—within the broader discourse on the Woman Question. Yet the focus on women authors' homes and texts as fashionable obsessions had the effect of locating their work, along with their possessions, in the realm of ephemeral, and sometimes sensational, consumer interest.

CHARLOTTE ROBINSON

The 1890 "Celebrities at Home" profile of journalist and interior designer Charlotte Robinson offers a compelling case study of the complex ways celebrity news features depicted the woman writer. In this article, Robinson's home is depicted as the location and the product of her professional activity and sexual identity. Charlotte Robinson (1859–?) was a prominent home decorator, socialite, and Manchester shop owner who had studied at Queen's College and shared her home in a domestic partnership with Emily Faithfull (1835–95). In 1887, she was appointed home decorator to Queen Victoria and shortly thereafter began writing a home decoration column for the *Queen*, a post she held from 1888 to 1901.[18] She was an unusual choice for Yates's series given that she only marginally fit the category of "celebrity." Although well known in Manchester and to readers of the *Queen*, she was hardly a household name in British society. In profiling Robinson, Yates was most likely attempting to capitalize on the sensationalism of Robinson's success as a professional decorator and her close association with Emily Faithfull, whose fame was well established by the 1880s. Yates might also have been indirectly puffing the *Queen*, which, as Arlene Young has shown, was becoming increasingly known for its progressive advocacy of professional opportunities for women.[19]

The 1890 article begins by asserting, "To bring within 'the home' the beautiful in form and colour, and to brighten by every available influence the prosaic details of ordinary existence, is distinctly feminine work."[20] What at first seems to be an essentializing comment about a woman's sphere soon becomes clearly identified as a plug for women's professional activity in the fields of journalism and home decoration. Yates refers to Robinson's extensive collection of scrapbooks, drawings, textile samples, and letters from the readers of the *Queen* in order to reinforce her identity as a domestic professional. At the end of the interview, Robinson remarks, "These letters are full of plans, patterns, and questions, which would overwhelm me if I allowed them to accumulate" (13). The implication is that she will set to work the minute the interviewer departs. Just as the "Celebrities at Home" series identifies the home as a suitable field of interest for historians as well as homemakers, it also defines the home as a quasi-professional space that should be of interest to both men and women. The reader is just as likely to leave the article admiring Robinson's décor as her business acumen. The publicity surrounding her interior designs, which the article notes are favored by Queen Victoria, serves as a kind of advertisement set alongside other ads for domestic goods on the paper's cover and at the foot of each page.

But the Charlotte Robinson profile was not only an advertisement for the *Queen* and for Robinson's home decoration business. It was quite possibly also an advertisement for an alternative women's domestic culture. Early on, the article notes that Robinson shares her abode with "Miss Emily Faithfull—who has been her guide, philosopher, and friend ever since she left Queen's College" (12). It further states that their "modest" home has been "skillfully adapted to their mutual literary and artistic avocations" (12). What at first seems like an insignificant reference to Robinson's domestic life actually offers an important clue for understanding how the celebrity home was politicized. As noted earlier, the home is depicted as hybrid space, a location of private and professional activity, even if the term *professional* is studiously avoided. By mentioning Faithfull, Yates evokes her widely publicized efforts to promote women's employment, and Robinson thus becomes an exemplar of Faithfull's lifework.

Of course, for many Victorians, there was a deeper layer of reference: the scandal associated with Faithfull's involvement in the

Codrington divorce case of 1864, during which her "romantic friendship" with Helen Codrington had come to light.[21] As Maria Frawley has pointed out, the sexual scandal surrounding the Codrington trial had little impact on the stunning success of the Victoria Press, *Victoria Magazine,* or Faithfull's prolific career as a writer and activist.[22] However, the ongoing gossip surrounding Faithfull's sexuality was premised on what Martha Vicinus has called the "silence at the heart of the Codrington trial – the unnamable thing," in other words, "lesbian sex."[23] The same could be said of the "friendship" between Robinson and Faithfull as depicted in the *World.* On one hand, Yates attempts to protect Robinson from accusations of sexual transgression by suggesting that Robinson's liaison with Faithfull is temporary. "An extensive *ménage*," he writes, "would just now represent more trouble and responsibility than Miss Robinson would care to tolerate."[24] Likewise, he mentions that her house is overseen by a maid with the "snowiest of caps and aprons," and there is no sign of "lilies lank and wan" or other trappings of the "high-art craze" associated with Aestheticism (12). At the same time, however, he titillates readers with sexual innuendo. Yates may be alluding to Faithfull's scandalous past when he writes of Robinson,

> Women are said to love best those who cause them the most trouble. Perhaps this hypothesis explains Miss Robinson's sentiments for "the little den" you learn that she once regarded as "hopeless." While she recounts, with the peaceful smile of one who has endured and conquered, the task of adapting it to the purpose she had in view, you are thinking how completely all "the difficulties" complained of have disappeared under her magical touches, and that nothing better could have been evolved for what may perhaps be described as "a boudoir workshop." (12)

This passage suggests that it is not only the house but Faithfull herself that may be defined as Robinson's reformatory project. Likewise, the concept of a "boudoir workshop" merges suggestions of gentility, professionalism, and intimacy. If the boudoir is a shared workshop, Emily Faithfull herself is a kind of absence who is always present—a gap that produces gossip. In this way, the seemingly straightforward profile of a professional woman becomes a titillating view into a home that is simultaneously a progressive example of the modern abode and a sensationalized site of voyeuristic interest.

MARY BRADDON

Yates's profile of Mary Braddon (1837–1915), also published in the *World*, depicts an image of the woman author that blends the specifics of her writing life with the details of her domestic habits, while at the same time alluding to Braddon's scandalous sexual past. The title of the essay, "Miss M. E. Braddon (Mrs. Maxwell) at Richmond," immediately signals the indeterminacy surrounding her marital status. The fact that Mary Braddon had lived with John Maxwell in an adulterous relationship from 1861 to 1874 is alluded to by the use of "Miss" to refer to a writer who for many years posed as a single woman while living with a married man. Yates notes that Braddon's work "was quickly appreciated by the Gaul," even when her own countrymen derided her work as "sensational."[25] In this way, he suggests that only the French are capable of appreciating such a free-thinking woman.

After riding through the forest on horseback, Yates and Braddon arrive at her estate, Lichfield House. She leads him to a "blue chamber, from which the profane are rigidly excluded," her "literary workshop" (319). Yates depicts her in militaristic terms, noting that she wears a "riding-dress of the severest order" (317), presides over a "regiment of drawers opening and shutting simultaneously" (319), and has handwriting similar to that of an "adjutant of a cavalry regiment" (320). Yet she also wears a thimble on her middle finger to prevent the "brand of ink" on her hands, which would mark her as a literary woman (320). In this way, Yates links conventional symbols of domesticity with images of masculine militancy as a way of characterizing Braddon's unconventional fusion of masculine and feminine characteristics.

The article does not depict many interactions between Yates and Braddon. In fact, Yates spends most of his time simply watching Braddon at work in her study. He notes that there is "copy" everywhere, just as "there are pictures, as there are books, as there are receipted bills and housekeeping accounts" (320). By making reference to both the implements of writing and housekeeping, he once again suggests the difficulty of separating the writer from the domestic woman. Yet for Yates, these are just the "outward expression" of her identity (320). To access the "hidden spring" of her personality, he resorts to Gothic metaphor, suggesting that her "skeletons" are hidden in a "carefully locked" drawer (320).[26] On one hand, these "skeletons" refer to the outlines of future novels produced in the privacy of Braddon's imagination; however, they simultaneously allude to her own domestic indiscretions, which secretly inform the sensationalist content of her novels. A few sentences later, one hidden "skeleton" of a future novel takes on a life of its own: "As the work goes on and the creature breathes and moves, it displays an irrepressible instinct either to break out of bounds, to multiply the number of its vertebrae, or to abandon the higher form altogether and dwindle into an invertebrate of one volume" (321). The novel, like the writer's own past, resists containment, thus morphing, like Frankenstein's creature, into a force beyond the "author's" control. The use of Darwinist metaphor is significant because it associates authorship with natural processes of de/evolution and thus further reinforces the author's helplessness in determining the "creature's" outcome. Indeed, Yates notes that *Lady Audley's Secret* was an "unmitigated misery to its author, who misdoubted the well incident, and trembled at the fire with Robert locked up in his room" (322). This passage seems to associate Braddon with the title character of her novel, whose hands are "clenched" nervously as she remembers setting fire to the Castle Inn.[27] In this way, Yates raises the question of whether Braddon, like Lady Audley, was truly culpable for her actions.

Yates concludes his visit with a double entendre, remarking that Braddon "lives, like a true artist, entirely in her art" (324). This remark suggests that she lives to create great fiction, but at the same time it suggests that she lives the same sort of sensational life she writes about in her novels. Of course, in alluding to Braddon's sexual past, Yates echoes more direct criticism Braddon had received from reviewers such as Margaret Oliphant, who noted that Lady Audley was an "invention which could only have been possible to an Englishwoman knowing the attraction of impropriety, and yet loving the shelter of law."[28] However, as Braddon's longtime friend and professional associate,[29] Yates most likely believed his profile was a useful advertisement that would stimulate sensational interest in Braddon and her novels while simultaneously sparking higher sales of the *World*.

MARIE CORELLI

It is important to note that the profiles published in the *World* were not accompanied by photographs or other images. The imagery associated with the interviewer's visit, like the imagery associated with

LIX. — MISS MARIE CORELLI.

By Arthur H. Lawrence.

Illustrated by Photographs specially taken for this article.

IN beginning the exceedingly pleasurable task of recording the only "interview" yet published with Miss Marie Corelli, I confess that, for one special reason above all others, I could wish that it may be read by every one of the hundreds of thousands who form her great reading public all the world over, and who, like myself, have felt indebted to her for so many happy hours by reason of the brilliancy and magic power of her work.

It is a perfectly natural thing that those of us who are interested in any fine work should feel an ever-increasing interest in the personality of the worker, and it was on this basis, and on no other, that, after receiving a very courteously worded refusal, I ventured to urge my request on the gifted authoress. The fame which Miss Marie Corelli has earned has been entirely gained by the public recognition of her work. If, at any time, the "advertisement" of reviews, paragraphs, interviews, and the like could have been of the slightest assistance to her, that time has long since gone by ; and while I feel that this statement applies in no less degree to this

article, I confess that I am animated by the hope—and this is the "special reason" to which I have already alluded—that it will be possible for me to do something to negative the extraordinary caricatures of the charming novelist which so many of my "friends" on the Press have so industriously circulated.

Prior to the publication of this "interview," one or two biographical articles concerning Miss Marie Corelli have been written by those who have met her, and countless other articles have been written by those who have known nothing about her, a statement which also applies to those who have written innumerable paragraphs emanating from certain journalists, who have made up in rudeness and vulgarity for what has been lacking in knowledge and wit. I have read the criticisms— and have been the personal recipient of verbal criticisms — of her work by professional critics, whose main qualification has confessedly been that they have carefully abstained from reading the work which they have pretended to criticise.

I shall feel happy indeed with the countless pleasant memories which are associated with my visit to the country retreat of Miss

A Snap-shot of Marie Corelli and her pet dog 'Czar' in 'The Lounge' at The 'Royal'.

[*Miss Corelli is the right-hand figure.*]

Figure 8. Arthur Lawrence, "Illustrated Interviews: Miss Marie Corelli," *Strand Magazine* 16 (July 1898): 17.

gossip, must be recreated and embellished in the reader's mind. Of course, during the 1890s, celebrity newspapers and periodicals often depicted writers' bodies and lives in visual terms.[30] The increasingly visual, sensational nature of celebrity profiles featuring women writers highlighted the "embodiment" of the woman author as a visual commodity. For example, the *Strand Magazine* (1891–1950), edited by George Newnes, published more than 500 portraits of celebrities between 1891 and 1917, including more than 100 portraits of women.[31] An illustrated interview with Marie Corelli (1855–1924) published in the *Strand* in 1898 includes photographs of the author's home, the Royal Hotel, Woodhall Spa. Most of the images in the article depict the hotel itself, which makes the single image of Corelli stand out. The fact that Corelli calls it a "snap shot," rather than a portrait, draws attention to the ephemerality of the moment. However, the photo is taken at such a distance so as to make Corelli's features indistinguishable, and Corelli's companion, Bertha Vyver, is not identified in the caption. This distance creates a sense of mystery surrounding Corelli's identity and domestic life.

As in the Robinson and Braddon interviews, the author's unconventional domestic arrangements incite speculation and thus serve as a marketing device.[32] Yet the article also emphasizes Corelli's resistance to being interviewed and her outright hostility toward male reviewers. The article begins by claiming that it features the "only 'interview' yet published with Miss Marie Corelli."[33] The article's author, Arthur Lawrence, explains why Corelli has hitherto resisted interviews. Her novels are so popular, he notes, that the "advertisement" provided by "reviews, paragraphs, interviews, and the like" is unnecessary (17). Lawrence justifies his own "advertisement" of Corelli by stating that his mission is to counteract the "rudeness and vulgarity" of his fellow reviewers and biographers (17).[34] He quotes Corelli as saying, "And in certain parts of the world you may still see carts drawn by a woman and an ox yoked together, while the man-driver sits aloft and curls his whip round with a stinging blow on woman and ox equally. This is just the sort of attitude some men assume towards women in art" (20–21). Corelli depicts her "contest" with these critics as an epic struggle on behalf of her sex (21).[35] Meanwhile, the public acts as umpire, settling the question of value by purchasing more than one hundred thousand copies of her latest novel.[36] "Miss Marie Corelli has certainly committed one great crime," Lawrence notes ironically later in the article, "she has attained popularity!" (24). Indeed, it would not be long before the *Manchester Chronicle* would refer to Corelli as "this most popular novelist of the hour."[37]

Elsewhere in the press, the public was far from being perceived as a fair arbiter of literary value. Grant Richards, writing for the *Weekly Gallery of Celebrities* in 1891, quotes an anonymous male novelist as saying that the "public's taste was as fickle and as variable as a woman's."[38] Likewise, an article on Julia Margaret Cameron's celebrity photographs quotes Tennyson as saying that the female passion for authorial "autographs and anecdotes and records" made him fear being "ripped open like a pig."[39] The emphasis on the male victim of a feminized, fickle public is noteworthy considering that women writers were so often the *objects* of celebrity journalism at the fin de siècle. Such a shift reflects the tendency toward depicting male writers as the victims of a feminized mass reading public during this time period.[40]

For Corelli, as for Robinson and Braddon, the home was a place of work, where papers and letters are defined as the necessary accoutrements of a literary life. Lawrence notes that Corelli receives a "huge" pile of letters from literary fans on a daily basis.[41] This includes "desperate love-letters" as well as communications from "would-be translators," "dramatists," and "autograph-hunters" (22). This crowd of fans serves as a stand-in for the popular reading public, the stalkers and persistent admirers who ensure the transformation of writers' works and personalities into high-demand commodities. But the home of the celebrity becomes a site of popular desire in another way as well: as a marker of economic prosperity. The photographs detailing the interior of Corelli's home illustrate how her literary success has enabled her to amass a collection of beautiful objects. One of Corelli's fans writes, "Dear Miss Corelli,—Please send me one of your old violins. I want so much, and my mother cannot afford to buy one. I saw in a book a picture of one of your rooms, and in it I saw a beautiful violin and harp, so I thought I would ask you for one. Please don't be cross" (23). The image of Corelli's domestic space becomes a stimulus to consumer desire, not only for the author's books but also for the accumulated wealth they have produced. If Corelli has one violin, she must have others, just as one book presupposes another. The illustrated interview thus serves as an advertisement not only for the "authentic" Marie Corelli, who is inaccessible to most members of the "vulgar" press, but also for a domestic culture that is both mysterious and sensational. The article incites desire not only for knowledge of the author's private life and her books but also for the material wealth resulting from a successful career.

THE CELEBRITY NEWS FEATURE

Part of the reason for women's association with commodity culture was the increasing ubiquitousness of images of women *in general* in the popular press. The publication of portraits of the woman author was concomitant with the proliferation of images of "professional beauties" in journals and newspapers. These images were further consumed through the sale of celebrity photographs in London stationary shops. The *Weekly Gallery of Celebrities*, for example, not only included profiles of famous people of the day but also a regular feature, "The Latest: New Photos and Where to Get Them," which listed available photographs and shop addresses.[42] The proliferation of images of famous women in popular print culture had the effect of constructing beauty as "news." The editors of *Sketch* drew attention to the time sensitivity of beauty by periodically featuring the image of a beautiful woman on the cover of the newspaper, a photograph that would serve as an eye-catching marketing device on increasingly crowded newspaper stalls.[43] In the first anniversary edition of *Sketch*, for example, the editors assert that "unemployed loveliness has proved one of our greatest trials, for at times the staircase leading to this office has been turned into a kind of Tower Hill by resolute ladies, armed with photographs, and demanding instant publication."[44] Likewise, *Sketch* prints a letter from an "emancipated curate" who exclaims against the "narrow teaching which cuts off religion from the amusements of the people" (1). "I never see the high kick of the skirt dancer," he writes, "without a feeling of thankfulness for the wonders of Nature" (1). The desire to gaze and be gazed upon thus became the focus of the celebrity profiles at century's end. In the mass-market publications aimed at a mixed-gender audience, such as *Sketch*, the objects and subjects of the consuming gaze were both male and female, leading to a compelling sexual indeterminacy that was a crucial component of the marketing appeal of celebrity journalism.

As images of women became a visual commodity and the subject of "advertorials," the image of the woman writer, by association, became "news" as well, a time-sensitive commodity that seized intensive,

THE SKETCH

o. 58.—VOL. V.   WEDNESDAY, MARCH 7, 1894.   SIXPENCE.
By Post, 6½d.

Figure 9. Hills and Saunders, "Miss Lily Hanbury," *Sketch* **5 (March 7, 1894).**

if temporary, readerly attention. For example, a feature on novelist Edna Lyall (1857–1903), published in *Windsor Magazine* in 1895, remarks that Lyall "holds her own" in the company of other "quickly made names," who create a "temporary *furore*."[45] The author, Ellen Velvin, follows this backhanded compliment with a description of Lyall's family background and appearance, noting her "slight and fragile" figure (19). Yet this seemingly conventional woman, who is "full of sympathy and cheery encouragement, and ever ready to give practical help and advice," is also comfortable with the latest technology, symbolized by a typewriter, which is the focal point of one of the photos in the article (19, 22). Lyall also demonstrates keen business acumen by allowing her publishers to select the title of her next novel from a list of six possibilities, choosing the "one they consider most saleable" (23). Lyall's attention to the latest technologies of publishing—typewriters and consumer relations—thus defines her as a specimen of newness, the best of the "quickly made names."

The focus on the relationship between authorship and time is also vividly illustrated in the popular "Celebrities at Different Times of Their Lives" series published in the *Strand*.[46] This series provided time-stamped portraits of popular authors and other celebrities, setting them in chronological order. The feature on Charlotte Yonge, for example, draws attention to the extent of her career, noting that at twenty-one she was already a published author and that today she is "editor of *The Monthly Packet*."[47] Rather than focusing on domestic spaces associated with the present moment, however, the series represents Yonge's development from young lady author to woman of letters. That such a progression should be depicted in visual terms—a series of sequential portraits—suggests that the image of the author has changed to reflect her changing professional status and that her portraits, as much as her books, should be of interest to readers and consumers. Has she aged well? Does her appearance reflect her authorial persona? To what extent are her talents and successes "written on the body"? By prompting such questions, the "Celebrities at Different Times of Their Lives" feature creates "news" from what would otherwise be a series of disparate images. To be able to see the aging process—and consequent loss of beauty—creates readerly pleasure by providing "new" information on an "old" author that is enabled by the time stamping of authorial images. For women, the visual narrative of women's achievement of professional success could only be seen simultaneously as a narrative of decline because female

From a Drawing by] AGE 21. [W. B. Richmond.

From a] AGE 35. [Photograph.

From a] AGE 40. [Photograph.

From a Photo. by] PRESENT DAY. [Elliott & Fry.

MISS CHARLOTTE M. YONGE.

AT the age of twenty-one, Miss Yonge had already written "Abbeychurch," the first of the long series of novels which have made her name familiar to innumerable readers. Miss Yonge's books have done good, not only by their healthy moral teaching, but by the generous use which she has made of the proceeds of their sale.

The profits of "The Heir of Redclyffe," which was written at the age of thirty, she devoted chiefly to the fitting-out of the missionary schooner, *The Southern Cross*, for the use of Bishop Selwyn ; and the sum of £2,000, which resulted from the sale of "The Daisy Chain," to the erection of a missionary college at Auckland. Miss Yonge is at present editor of *The Monthly Packet.*

Figure 10. "Portraits of Celebrities: Miss Charlotte M. Yonge," *Strand Magazine* **2 (November 1891): 479.**

beauty was associated with cultural power. As Annette Federico has pointed out, "Hostile stereotypes of the woman writer's physical unattractiveness or sexual abnormality circulated during the 1880s and 1890s, usually in illustrations caricaturing her 'masculinity' or her neglect of domestic responsibilities."[48] Images of the aging Charlotte Yonge, then, established her respectability as a "feminine" author and woman of letters while drawing attention to the decreasing sense of visual capital associated with her commodified public image. Clearly, she was no longer a "new" writer and thus was only "news" when viewed retrospectively.

In addition to including celebrity news focused on particular women writers, articles featured profiles of celebrities focused on a specific theme. The *Strand* published an especially rich array of such articles, including "Celebrities at Play," "The Dogs of Celebrities," and "Celebrities in Caricature."[49] In one such feature, "Distinguished Women and Their Dolls," published in 1894, author Frances Low asked several celebrity women to write letters to the *Strand* recalling their favorite childhood dolls. At the outset, Low states her hypothesis: that women's love of dolls is evidence of the "instinct" of "maternal love."[50] By reproducing the handwriting and signatures of celebrity contributors, the article evokes the female genre of the autograph book, thus underscoring its focus on conventional femininity. Yet the celebrity letters Low features in the article would seem to contradict her purpose. She refers to Anne Thackeray Ritchie (1837–1919) as the "most exquisitely *feminine* woman writer of the day" (251; her emphasis) but then quotes from Ritchie's letter, which indicates that her childhood dolls "all came to violent ends" and that she consequently gave them up at the "age of four" (252).[51] Low further reports that Frances Power Cobbe (1822–1904) "loved the woods and living things" more than dolls, thus suggesting her later avoidance of conventional domestic life (257).

Perhaps most striking is the profile of New Woman novelist Mona Caird (1854–1932), who played with dolls as a child but used them to act out the dysfunctional habits of her neighbors: the "pompous parents" and the "ambitious elder daughters" (253) who discussed marriage proposals in a "business spirit" (252). Caird identifies this play as a form of "unconscious satire," which "photographed pretty exactly the impressions which the work of grown-up people was making upon my mind at the time" (253). "The picture was not very flattering," she concludes (253). Low notes that Caird's letter reveals how her "tastes and thoughts inclined to the subject of marriage," thus alluding to Caird's searing critiques of the marriage institution in her essays and novels (252). Low's selection of celebrities, then, complicates her own thesis about dolls as mediums for the expression of maternal instinct. Indeed, dolls seem more useful as tools for foretelling women's complex—and often conflicted—stance toward marriage and family institutions. Celebrities' possessions and memories thus become clues for uncovering their "secret" motivations and life choices. For example, in her letter to Low, Millicent Garrett Fawcett (1847–1929) recalls breaking her sister's doll and offering her own as a replacement: "I don't think this was maternal; but I well remember the anguish of making the offer, and the wild, incredulous joy with which I heard my sister decline it. I thought her the most nobly generous creature in the world, and could not picture myself being offered my doll and saying 'No'" (254). In this way, Fawcett denies that dolls express an essentializing "maternal instinct" and validates women's choice to say "no" to the offer of a doll and, by extension, to childbearing.

The Low essay, like other articles in the celebrity news genre, relied on notions of conventional femininity to justify its intrusion into women's domestic spaces and lives, yet at the same time, it provided a series of narratives, partly voiced by celebrities themselves, that undercut any notion of "correct" feminine behavior. As Gerry Beegan has recently pointed out, "Late-Victorian magazines were sites for multiple, sometimes contradictory, cultural messages that readers could draw on to make sense of the conflicts in their own lives."[52] The image of the home and the image of the woman celebrity thus together mobilized a series of interrelated cultural concerns and enticements related to women's domestic lives, professional aspirations, and increasing independence within the economic realm. Could a woman with a scandalous sexual past achieve respectability in the professional realm? What alternatives to marriage and childbearing were suggested by their often unconventional domestic lives? Such provocative questions sparked consumer interest in the "newness" and "newsworthiness" of women authors, whose careers and homes illustrated the compatibility of professional and domestic life, while at the same time alluding to mysterious "secrets" that lay just beneath the surface of a seemingly innocuous interview.

Journalists such as Edmund Yates, Arthur Lawrence, and Frances Low knew the power of gossip and innuendo and capitalized on the public thirst for private knowledge as a way of succeeding in an increasingly competitive field. As a writer for the *Strand* put it, "Everybody knows, or wants to know, everybody else's little weaknesses. . . . The demand for such information is insatiable, and the competition in the journalistic world so keen that the demand is supplied with as much detail as possible."[53] For women writers, such competition provided unprecedented opportunities for self-promotion as they, too, attempted to seize a share of an increasingly crowded literary marketplace. Yet such publicity located women within a culture of commodities focused on the new, the beautiful, and the sensational. Along with the feminization of mass-market publishing came the increasing marginalization of women within the emerging canon of British literature. Even though male writers were just as often the subject of celebrity profiles as women authors and male readers were just as often identified as major consumers of celebrity gossip as female readers, there was more at stake in the celebrity game for women than for men. As time-sensitive images of women became ubiquitous in popular print culture, women writers and artists were increasingly stereotyped as the primary consumers and subject matter of celebrity news. Consequently, their works were often viewed as fads of the moment rather than legacies for all time. The association with material culture was viewed as a necessary prerequisite for a successful literary career, yet such popularity had the effect of ensuring women's invisibility in literary history for most of the twentieth century.

7

Representations of the Authorial Body in the *British Medical Journal*

THE CELEBRITY BODY WAS NOT ONLY AN OBJECT OF KEEN INTEREST IN mass-market newspapers and periodicals but in specialist journals as well. This chapter examines the use of Victorian authors as case studies in the field of medical journalism. The sensationalist treatment of authorial ailments and symptoms served an instrumental role in the professionalization of medicine. After the passage of the 1858 Medical Act and the consequent reform of medical education, British medicine became increasingly specialized. One of the most immediate results of this specialization was the proliferation of medical periodicals. As Bynum and Wilson have pointed out, approximately "479 medical periodicals [were] established in nineteenth-century Britain, an average of one about every seventy-seven days."[1] By the end of the century, medical periodicals increasingly employed technical jargon in clinical case studies. Indeed, as Lisa Kochanek has observed, medical journals were intent on "representing the medical gaze as distinct from every other form of looking," a form of viewing that was analytic rather than sensationalized or entertaining.[2] Even with increased specialization, however, most nineteenth-century medical journals were written in such a way as to be accessible to a general educated audience. By including book reviews, medical curiosities, sensational narratives, and editorials on hot-button medical issues, late-nineteenth-century medical journals had a great deal in common with mainstream literary reviews and magazines of the time period.

As Jane Wood has pointed out, Victorian "medicine and literature looked to each other for elucidation and illustration," resulting in a conflicted, ambivalent exchange.[3] Certainly recent studies have confirmed the richness and complexity of the relationship between medical discourse and the novel during the nineteenth century.[4] However, recent scholarship has thus far neglected to examine the connection between celebrity biography and medical discourse in late Victorian print culture. The cultural obsession with the psychological and physiological health of the Victorian author can be seen as a subset of a broader interest in celebrity culture during the latter years of the nineteenth century.[5] As noted in previous chapters, the dominance of biographical criticism in late-nineteenth-century reviews and the corresponding growth in the industry of literary tourism provided a backdrop for the burgeoning cultural fascination with the life of the author. This interest became increasingly invasive as the century progressed, which makes the growing interest in the bodies of Victorian authors less than surprising. If the domestic novel, the biographical review, and the literary tour authorized the minute examination of daily life, then the body of the author provided a similarly rich vein of investigation.

In this chapter, I will argue that the body of the author played a crucial role in linking medical journalism to other forms of literary discourse while at the same time demarcating medical analysis from other forms of textual exegesis. The *British Medical Journal* (*BMJ*) participated in and, in some cases, instigated medical controversies over a variety of topics, including baby farming, the Contagious Diseases Acts, vaccination, vivisection, and medical education for women. The *BMJ* was also involved in a number of controversies over the medical histories of Victorian authors. In the following pages, I highlight three of these controversies: the debate over Harriet Martineau's alleged cure by mesmerism in 1844, the dispute over the causes of infertility and discord in the marriage of Thomas and Jane Carlyle, and the controversy over the supposed criminality of Ernest Hart. These case studies illustrate the ways that the *BMJ* used the trope of the authorial body for contradictory purposes, on one hand establishing a self-consciously literary identity while at the same time demarcating medical analysis from more literary forms of viewing and reading.

MEDICAL JOURNALISM AND THE VICTORIAN AUTHOR

In medical journals of the fin de siècle, literary content intersects with medical subject matter in fascinating ways. For example, during the last two decades of the nineteenth century, the *Boston Medical and Surgical Journal* and other periodicals published articles on representations of doctors in Dickens's novels as examples of good and bad medical practice.[6] Another article published in the *Journal of Mental Science* focuses on Tennyson's portrayal of the "psychopathic origin of insanity" in the poem *Maud*.[7] That literary texts could be used to illustrate patterns of professional behavior or symptoms of mental disease is interesting in that it melds literary and extraliterary realms of meaning. Medical periodicals make reference to literary subject matter in a seemingly self-conscious way, as if to present a high-culture rather than a strictly professional perspective on medical science.

In addition to using literary texts to illustrate medical practices and ailments, journalists focused increasingly on the psychology and physiology of Victorian authors as a way of illuminating various medical conditions. Generalist literary journals such as the *Nineteenth Century* and the *Fortnightly Review* as well as specialist medical journals such as the *Lancet* and the *Journal of Psychology* published a diverse array of articles on the ailments and infirmities of great writers past. Walter Scott, George Eliot, the Brownings, and the Brontës were frequently used as case studies in these literary postmortems. Interestingly, diagnoses of these literary "cases"—whether focused on their nearsightedness, monomania, or dyspepsia—were conducted in lay terms in both medical and mainstream periodicals. Were writers more prone to illness and madness than other members of society? To what extent was the infirmity of writers produced by sex, heredity, or environment? These questions were to some extent prompted by the appearance of a number of book-length studies on the insanity and infirmity of genius that were published midcentury and subsequently reviewed widely in medical and mainstream literary periodicals. This included Warren Babcock's *On the Morbid Heredity and Predisposition to Insanity of the Man of Genius* (1895), J. F. Nisbet's *The Insanity of Genius* (1891), and Cesare Lombroso's *The Man of Genius* (1888, trans. 1891).[8] Of course, debates over the infirmity of genius predated the late Victorian era.[9] What made the discussion unique at the fin de siècle was the way in which it brought together two seemingly unrelated literary genres: authorial biography and the medical case study.

As the organ of the British Medical Association, the *BMJ* played an instrumental role in the professionalization of medicine during the second half of the nineteenth century. The *BMJ* was founded as the *Provincial Medical and Surgical Journal* (*PMSJ*) in 1840 by Dr. Hennis

Green. After two decades of struggle and a title change,[10] the *BMJ* found its footing in 1867 when Ernest Hart (1835–1898) assumed the editorship and transformed the journal into the leading medical periodical of the day. Under his editorship, the *BMJ* increased its circulation from 2,500 in 1867 to 20,500 in 1897.[11] In the pages of the *BMJ*, short articles, medical anecdotes, case studies, and lectures by eminent physicians were juxtaposed with editorial campaigns in support of sanitation reform and a variety of other public health issues. The miscellaneous nature of the *BMJ* supported its role as a clearing house of information for members of the British Medical Association (BMA). That the *BMJ* became an organ of the BMA soon after its founding attests to its importance to the emerging medical profession, especially its efforts toward autonomy and self-regulation. As Hart once said, the medical journalist's first principle was the "government of the profession by the profession for the profession."[12] During Hart's tenure, the reach of the BMA extended to professional branches throughout the Empire. And it was one of the first scientific journals to employ the process of peer review.[13]

The medical gazes inscribed in the *BMJ* were gendered masculine in the sense that they were defined in opposition to what were perceived as hysterical, sentimental, and otherwise non-objective assessments of health by women authors and their biographers. Early on, the *PMSJ* had promised to display a "hale and vigorous manhood."[14] Yet by the fin de siècle, the emergence of the figure of the woman doctor suggested ways that the confident masculinity of the medical gaze was becoming increasingly destabilized.[15] Thus, while medical journals such as the *BMJ* certainly used the body of the woman author to define the difference between professional and unprofessional forms of medical narrative, they also provided opportunities for the subtle redefinition of the investigatory gaze. Likewise, while medical journals attempted to establish a sense of exclusivity and professional privilege, they simultaneously enabled the diffusion and popularization of medical knowledge by sensationalizing the case studies of famous authors. Thus, my reading of medical journalism counters interpretations of fin de siècle medical culture where women are interpreted as the passive objects of an increasingly invasive and exclusive masculine medical establishment.[16] Following recent feminist scholarship,[17] I elucidate the complex, historically contingent ways that female authority was both asserted and undermined at the intersection of literary and medical discourses. However, by focusing on the connection between medical journalism and authorial biography, I illuminate the crucial link between the formation of the medical profession and the rise of biographical literary criticism, where the author and the doctor, as interlinking tropes, were used to delimit and extend the boundaries of scientific inquiry.

HARRIET MARTINEAU

The controversy over the case of Harriet Martineau began in 1844 when, after a long convalescence due to an ovarian tumor, Martineau publicly claimed to have been cured by mesmerism. By the 1840s, Martineau was a well-known woman of letters who had published several influential texts, including *Illustrations of Political Economy* (1832–34).[18] Consequently, the publication of the details of her cure in *Letters on Mesmerism* (1845) caused a stir in the medical community.[19] In response to these claims, Martineau's brother-in-law and physician, Thomas Greenhow (1791–1881), published a refutation of her interpretation in a pamphlet titled *Medical Report of the Case of Miss H—M—* (1845).[20] In this report, Greenhow disputes Martineau's interpretation of her cure, arguing that it resulted from the natural progression of the disease rather than from the effects of external stimuli. In doing so, he publicized the details of her gynecological symptoms in grotesquely graphic terms.[21] As a result of this publication and the publicity that ensued, Martineau refused any further contact with him, personal or professional.

The controversy soon made its way into the pages of the *PMSJ*, where it served as a test case for defining the early medical profession. In June of 1844, an editorial described mesmerism as a "so called science" that had become a cultural obsession, making "fresh converts, in spite of the efforts of reason against it."[22] Soon concerns about the popularity of mesmerism escalated as the controversy over Martineau's miraculous cure hit the press. An editorial published in the January 29, 1845, edition of the *PMSJ* begins by expressing regret that "members of the medical profession are called upon to devote their valuable time, to the exposure of every silly conceit or impudent imposture."[23] The use of the term *profession*, like the use of the term *reason* in the previous article, is interesting in the way that it attempts to define medicine as scientific practice, a way of seeing and knowing that is accessible to an elite group of practitioners. Although it is impossible for the editor of the *PMSJ* to define Martineau as unlearned, given her prominence as a journalist and political economist, he still attempts to define her as an "incompetent witness" due to her lack of medical training (70). This serves as a springboard for defining just what a "competent witness" within the medical profession might be: "The first (honesty, sincerity, and such moral qualities being assumed) is intellectual competency. This competency is not a general competency, but *special*, with reference to the particular subject. It necessarily presupposes a special education. . . . Ignorant people, indeed, talk familiarly of the evidence of their senses'; but the uneducated senses are the most delusive of witnesses, as is known to every inquirer, and may be proved by a thousand familiar examples" (70–71; his emphasis). The use of the term *incompetent witness* to describe Martineau suggests that she is incapable of adducing "facts" due to the limitation of her training and presumably also due to her inability to see her own body dispassionately through a scientific lens. The effect of this assessment was to throw Martineau's reputation for objectivity[24] into question while at the same time discrediting her as a source of medical knowledge.

Interestingly, the 1845 editorial is followed by a letter to the editor outlining a proposal for establishing a college for training unregistered physicians and surgeons in London. The letter alludes to legislation under consideration in the House of Commons: Sir James Graham's 1844 Medical Reform Bill, which proposed instituting centralized licensing of physicians.[25] The article recommended more consistent practical training of practitioners who would not be licensed under Graham's plan and to "send forth to the country, a large class of individuals sufficiently educated for all practical purposes" (72). Thus, in the *PMSJ*, the case of the unregistered practitioner, like the case of Harriet Martineau, became a means of defining educational standards and certifying levels of professional competence within the medical profession.

After Martineau's death in 1876, the controversy over mesmerism reemerged, this time in the pages of the *British Medical Journal*. In response to Martineau's self-written obituary published in the *Daily News* on June 29, the *BMJ* published an editorial notice retelling the story of her incorrect diagnosis with degenerative heart disease, which had been disproved by the cessation of symptoms in 1844.[26] The article laments that "there can be no doubt that Harriet Martineau's case is not one of the triumphs of the profession, and that the public attention attracted to the case did not add to the confidence of many persons in medical skill as to the diagnosis and prognosis of affections of the heart" (21).[27] The article concludes that Martineau's incorrect diagnosis would be "scarcely likely to be given now" (21). Thus, Martineau's story, spanning the most critical years of the profession's development—1844 to 1876—is defined as a test case for measuring the progress of medical science.

In response to Hart's editorial statement, one of Martineau's physicians, Thomas Watson, published a letter on July 8 defending himself against the charge of misdiagnosing her heart condition, and a week later, James Martin published a letter defending the medical profession's diagnosis, instead placing the blame on Martineau herself, claiming she was "led astray by the *post hoc* argument" that her symptoms were alleviated by mesmerism.[28] He writes, "Where Miss Martineau failed was in at once adopting the idea that her cure was the result of the mesmerism because she happened to obtain relief just at the period she adopted its use, whereas her medical attendant knew that just at that period the real *fons mali* was being gradually removed" (99). In this way, Martin distinguishes between what he sees as the logical basis of scientific thought and the irrational basis of Martineau's self-assessment.

The publication of Martineau's *Autobiography* in 1877 reinvigorated debates in the *BMJ* over professional standards. On April 14, Thomas Greenhow, Martineau's estranged brother-in-law, once again appeared in print to defend his own professional behavior during the early years of Martineau's ailment and to provide a defense of the profession more generally.[29] Greenhow begins by asserting that her account of her own health "contains *little fact* and *much imagination*" (449).[30] The "*post mortem* examination," he argues, illustrates that "instead of her being cured by mesmerism or any other agency . . . no *cure* was effected, but temporary suspension of suffering took place from natural causes connected with local disease" (449; his emphasis). After excerpting notes from the autopsy performed by Martineau's physician, Dr. W. Moore King, and her brother-in-law, Alfred Higginson, Greenhow summarizes the case. He recounts the discovery of a "vast tumor," thirty inches in circumference, attached to one of Martineau's ovaries (449). The temporary cessation of Martineau's abdominal symptoms, he argues, was due to the growth of the cyst, which gradually "raise[d] the uterus from its imprisonment in the lower part of the pelvis" (450). He concludes by noting that hers was an "interesting case" and a "remarkable example" that would not only provide useful diagnostic information about ovarian cysts but also explain her "peculiarities of character" (450).

A few weeks after the publication of Greenhow's article, the *BMJ* published a speech made by gynecological surgeon T. Spencer Wells (1818–97) at the Clinical Society of London on April 27, 1877.[31] The focal point of the speech and the article is the cyst itself, which had been preserved in fluid by Alfred Higginson. It is "by the desire of a brother-in-law" that Wells "exhibits" the tumor before the assembly (543). Her body is further "exhibited" in an excerpt from Thomas Watson's case notes, which gives the details of her weight gain and urination (543). For the most part, Wells agrees with Greenhow's assessment of Martineau's case, although he laments that the cyst had not been surgically removed (543). Wells justifies his presentation of her case based on the presence of Martineau's brother-in-law, who is designated as the "owner" of her body and medical history, disseminating it in anatomized parts for public viewing, both in a glass jar and in the pages of the *BMJ*. Wells concludes by quoting Greenhow's cryptic reference to Martineau's "peculiarities of character" (543). Her contested medical history consequently becomes a lens through which to view her writing and her career, emphasizing her "peculiarities" as a medical oddity rather than her achievements as an influential woman of letters. What is interesting about this exchange is the way that doctors cite a variety of medical narratives—autopsy reports and case analyses—as more truthful versions of Martineau's case than those she herself provided in her *Autobiography* and *Letters on Mesmerism*. Literary texts and their textual bodies are depicted as a necessary foundation for medical writing but are also discounted as the product of imagination, which is seen as having less validity than science. Thus, the authorial body is useful for demarcating the medical profession from mainstream literary texts and gazes, which are seen as lacking the observational rigor of science.[32]

That Hart should choose to publish a series of articles on mesmerism is not surprising considering his own long-standing interest in hypnotism.[33] In the late 1850s, during his early career as house surgeon at St. Mary's Hospital, London, Hart first experimented with mesmerism and subsequently published articles on the topic in a variety of journals, including the *BMJ*.[34] In this series of articles, Hart uncovers what he calls the "humbug" associated with mesmerism, spiritualism, and telepathy through a series of control experiments.

However, he simultaneously develops his own theory for what causes the hypnotic trance, attributing it to the dynamics of blood flow in the brain. Thus, the case of Harriet Martineau fit within the journal's emphasis on debunking the spiritualist aspects of mesmerism as well as explaining the causes and effects of hypnosis within the realm of rational medical discourse. In defining the medical profession, Hart and Greenhow used mesmerism as a test case for determining what professional medicine was *not*. They also were motivated by the desire to refute a story that seemed focused on highlighting the failure of the medical profession. After all, in her *Autobiography*, Martineau claimed that she resorted to mesmerism only after "every thing that medical skill and family care could do for me had been tried, without any avail."[35] Likewise, in her introduction to *Letters on Mesmerism*, she had called for an alternative professional organization of mesmerists that would be promoted via its own professional journal, *Zoist*.[36] The controversy over Martineau and mesmerism in the *BMJ* thus highlighted ways that the authorial body became the focus of competing interpretations. The *BMJ* opposed Martineau's story on two levels: its depiction of mesmerism as a valid professional science and its depiction of Martineau's "imaginative" interpretation of her own bodily cure.

THOMAS AND JANE CARLYLE

The controversy over the marriage of Thomas Carlyle (1795–1881) and Jane Carlyle (1801–66), like the debate over Martineau's cure by mesmerism, employed literary analysis as a means of disproving popular narratives about the medical condition of Victorian authors. The debate over allegations of impotence and abuse in the Carlyles' marriage was instigated by the publication of James Froude's *Reminiscences* (1881), *Letters and Memorials of Jane Welsh Carlyle* (1883), *Life of Thomas Carlyle* (1882–84), and *My Relations with Carlyle* (1903).[37] As literary journalists reviewed these texts, speculating on the causes of discord in the Carlyles' marriage, medical journalists offered their own interpretations of the case. One of the most interesting of these articles is Dr. James Crichton-Browne's "Froude and Carlyle: The Imputation Considered Medically," published in the *BMJ* in 1903.[38] Crichton-Browne (1840–1938) was an alienist by training who came into prominence as an expert on the psychology of lunatics and children.[39] He was also a devotee of fellow Scotsman Thomas Carlyle and was author (with Alexander Carlyle) of the *New Letters and Memorials of Jane Welsh Carlyle* (1903) and *The Nemesis of Froude: A Rejoinder to James Anthony Froude's "My Relations with Carlyle"* (1903).[40]

In his article published in the *BMJ*, Crichton-Browne claims that his goal is to disprove Froude's theory outlined in *My Relations with Carlyle*: that Thomas Carlyle "had some physical defect which prevented the consummation of his marriage, and which was the cause of his failings and aberrations of temper and character, and of his wife's misery."[41] Such a topic, he asserts, should not be addressed in a "frank biography" when it is more appropriately left "to the judgment of the medical profession" (1498). In this way, Crichton-Browne attempts to delimit what kinds of medical information should be communicated to specialist and nonspecialist audiences.

In making his case against Froude in the *BMJ*, Crichton-Browne first attempted to discredit his sources of information. He points out that Froude's main informant was novelist Geraldine Jewsbury. Using evidence from Jane Carlyle's letters, Crichton-Browne concludes that Jewsbury was a "morbid, unstable, excitable woman" who had inappropriately "erotic" feelings toward Jane Carlyle (1499). He writes, "Purely in the interests of the frank biography this unmarried woman came to Froude, who was not a medical man, and discussed with him the marital inefficiency of the man for whom she had professed undying gratitude, and the causes of the barrenness of the woman whom she called her dearest friend" (1499). Further, Jewsbury could produce no evidence from her "confidential correspondence" with Jane to substantiate her claims (1500). Crichton-Browne concludes that Froude and Jewsbury could not produce sufficient literary evidence to support their medical diagnosis and thus resorted to gossip and slander.

Putting the Froude-Jewsbury narrative aside, Crichton-Browne then attempts to debunk the rumor that Jane Carlyle's body had been examined by a doctor postmortem and was found to be "*virgo intacta*" (1501). According to gossip, the examination had taken place at St. George's Hospital, where Jane Carlyle's body had been taken after her sudden death in 1866. For Crichton-Browne, this rumor provides an opportunity to reinforce the professional standards of medical practice. He asks, "Now, does any one conceive that in one of our great public hospitals such an outrage would be committed as the examination of the body of a lady temporarily deposited there on the question of her virginity? What could suggest such a gratu-itous outrage?" (1501). However, on the outside chance that some "blackguard young medical man or student" had in fact succeeded in examining Jane Carlyle's corpse, Crichton-Browne suggests that there is a reasonable explanation for why her hymen might have re-mained intact: "I believe no gynaecologist will contradict me when I say that, in the case of a woman of 65 years of age who had never had a child, contraction to an extreme degree may have taken place as a result of changes occurring after the menopause, and yet the subject may have had complete sexual relations for many years" (1501). In discounting the rumor of Jane Carlyle's alleged virginity, Crichton-Browne makes the claim that the medical profession ensures the inviolability of the body, yet he premises his authority upon the expe-rience of having penetrated the body's most intimate regions. Thus the autopsy, like the case study, provides the ground on which licit and illicit—professional and prurient—investigatory procedures can be distinguished.

After disposing of the alleged medical evidence of Thomas Car-lyle's impotency, Crichton-Browne offers his own judgment of Car-lyle's writings as a replacement for the gossip and calumny circu-lating in London society. He writes, "Is the splendid virility of his writings to count for nothing? Was there in his style, his manner, his voice, his appearance, his conduct, one of the traits which we as-sociate with maimed manhood?" (1501). Crichton-Browne provides few examples from Carlyle's writing as proof of this "virile" writing style; instead, he assumes that the predominately male readers of the *BMJ* will be "literary" enough to be familiar with Carlyle's works and sophisticated enough to distinguish between "potent" and "im-potent" writing. The literary evidence Crichton-Browne does pro-vide is primarily selected from Jane Carlyle's letters and journals. He uses these sources to support his claim that Jane, not Thomas, was the source of childlessness and discord in the marriage. She was a "highly neurotic woman," Crichton-Browne's asserts, due to her inherited sterility, her grief over losing her father, and her studious lifestyle as a young girl (1502).[42] Thomas Carlyle, for his part, suf-fered his wife's bouts of depression and illness "with noble patience and forgiveness" (1502).

What is most fascinating about this article is the way that it pres-ents the physician, Crichton-Browne himself, as the most authorita-tive judge of the case. Just as literary biographers, due to their taste for sensation, cannot be trusted to tell the medical histories of others, neither can authors be competent judges of their own symptoms. In the absence of autopsy, written and verbal testimony is the only available source of information, and the medical examiner becomes the most authoritative critic. "Bold, filthy, scurrilous assertions like Froude's," Crichton-Browne concludes, "may mislead the unwary and the ignorant, . . . but they will scarcely deceive the elect who have been admitted into the communion of medical science" (1502).

Like other doctor-critics writing for the *BMJ*, Crichton-Browne argued that nonspecialist readers, particularly women, could not be trusted to interpret medical case studies. However, at the same time, his attempt to limit interpretive authority had the effect of stimulating a variety of nonspecialist responses. Just three years before publishing his article in the *BMJ*, Crichton-Browne had given an address focused on countering Froude's imputations and diagnosing Jane Carlyle's "climacteric melancholia" and "cerebral neurasthenia."[43] The fact that he initially delivered the lecture to the Edinburgh University, Dumfriesshire, and Galloway Literary Society and then later published it in the *Journal of Mental Science* (*JMS*) suggests a specialist and non-specialist audience for his work on the Carlyles. Following the publication of the *BMJ* and *JMS* articles, Crichton-Browne's books *The Nemesis of Froude* and *The New Letters and Memorials of Jane Welsh Carlyle* made frequent references to the health of the Carlyles that were clearly directed at a nonspecialist audience, thus further fanning the flames of public interest in the case.[44] In *The Nemesis of Froude*, for example, Crichton-Browne refuses to discuss the specific imputations of Carlyle's alleged impotency, reminding readers that these allegations "have been fully examined in the pages of a medical journal, where alone they could be properly considered."[45] But the rest of the chapter reads like an expanded version of the *BMJ* article with generous excerpts from the original source. Indeed, the debate over Carlyle's alleged impotency in the literary and medical press continued into the first few decades of the twentieth century.[46] The desire to contain discussion of authorial health issues within the medical community thus corresponded with, and in many ways depended on, the proliferation of medical case studies in the popular press.

In the *BMJ*, doctors also used medical theory to "change the subject" of the Carlyle controversy, using their case to address other national concerns. Just three months after the publication of Crichton-

Browne's *BMJ* essay, George Gould (1848–1922), an American oph-
thalmologist and medical writer, put forward his own analysis of the
case. In a two-part article, "The Role of Eyestrain in Civilization,"
published in the *BMJ* in 1903,[47] Gould analyzes the Carlyles along
with nine other "patients" whose cases form the basis of his study,
including Robert Browning, George Eliot, and George Henry Lewes.
After a review of their medical symptoms (nervousness, dyspepsia,
headaches, and so on), Gould asserts that their "miseries were consequent directly and quickly upon use of their eyes in writing or
reading."[48] As evidence for his theory, Gould relies on what he calls
"biographic clinics," or summaries of accounts in letters and other
biographical source materials, which provide evidence of the causes
and effects of eyestrain in individual cases (663).

Like Crichton-Browne, Gould is particularly interested in the case
of Jane Carlyle. However, he provides an alternative explanation for
her symptoms. Gould analyzes Jane Carlyle's case as one piece of
evidence supporting the need for better diagnostic procedures for
identifying and curing eyestrain among the general populace, which
includes needle workers and other industrial laborers. However, his
diagnosis is intended to solve another problem as well: the controversy over the alleged abusiveness of Thomas Carlyle. He writes, "Mrs.
Carlyle's life was spent in thirty-hour or sixty-hour continuous vomit-
ing and in suffering, and if this could have been avoided, the time
and much good white paper, spoiled by critics and biographers concerning her and her husband, would have added greatly to the national income—especially in the saving of paper!" (664). Gould enters into contemporary debates on the nature of the Carlyle marriage
by providing yet another medical solution to the problem of Thomas
Carlyle's alleged cruelty. He reinforces his claim in his second article
by asserting that the "over-critical sharpness and acidity of Mrs. Carlyle's letters, and possibly of her conduct, were the cry of her suffering
brain" (759). Women such as Carlyle are especially susceptible to the
malady, he argues, because of their "unstable" constitutions and their
excessive sewing, reading, and other indoor pursuits (758).

One of the most interesting moves Gould makes in his article is
to connect the cure of eyestrain on an individual basis, as illustrated
in literary case studies, to the health of the nation more generally.
"Eye strain," he asserts, "is wholly a disease of civilization" brought
on by occupational activities requiring "near-range work" (759). The
effect is that eyestrain "morbidizes character, doubles suffering and

personal burdens, lessens all productive capacity, depreciates the national valor, and validity, and wealth, and delays the advance of civilization" (760). The misdiagnosis of eyestrain, he argues, also results in the spread of quackery—so-called doctors who peddle "powders" and "patent medicine" to unsuspecting consumers who seek relief from the symptoms without understanding the underlying cause (760). The health of the nation thus simultaneously depends on the spread of professional medicine and the suppression of "spectacle-peddlers" (760). But perhaps most importantly, attention to the ocular health of the nation will liberate writers from debilitating illness, thus enabling them to be better facilitators of national progress. He writes, "Geniuses, the instruments and makers of civilization, depend at last on the medical profession" (760). Thus, for Gould, the health of the author is inextricably linked to the health of the nation. Presumably, because women are particularly susceptible to eyestrain, they are included in the category of geniuses, and thus, to some extent, Gould provides a counterpoint to Crichton-Browne's reading of gender relations. Jane Carlyle, in Gould's estimation, was the victim of a curable malady, not deep-rooted psychological neurosis. Better diagnostics, he argues, will prevent the spread of misinformation and will prevent lost opportunities of the past from being replicated in the present.

For both Gould and Crichton-Browne, diagnostic studies of the health of dead Victorian writers were literary in the sense that they were based on close reading of biographical texts—the examination of words in place of the absent authorial body. These diagnostic readings were medical in the sense that they suggested a scientific gaze alone could produce the truth of the past and hope for social progress. Such a diagnostic gaze authorized the medical profession by positioning it as a key facilitator of national health in both the moral and physical senses of the term.

ERNEST HART

The greatest literary scandal involving the *BMJ* was never directly addressed in its pages: the controversy over the alleged criminality of the journal's editor, Ernest Hart himself. During his long tenure as editor, Hart was accused of having murdered his first wife in 1861 and of embezzling funds from the BMA in 1869. His irascible temperament made him "difficult" in the minds of many of his contemporaries, a view that may have been the result of anti-Semitism since Hart was Jewish.[49] "A man so 'pushful,'" wrote one contemporary, "could not fail to have many enemies."[50] The causes of what some considered to be Hart's "unscrupulous" or "odd" personality were not addressed in the journal until Hart's death in 1898, when the medical gaze finally turned toward the body of the editor himself.[51] The long obituary published in January of that year is, for the most part, laudatory, enumerating his many successes as a doctor, humanitarian, and medical journalist. However, at the end of the obituary is an extended account of his decline in health, including his diagnosis with diabetes in 1883, the amputation of his leg in 1897, and his subsequent battle with nervous depression and dyspepsia. His blisters and boils are described in minute detail, as is his final "cold, deathly sweat."[52] The account of Hart's final illness and death can be explained by the Victorian fascination with rituals of death and dying, but it can also be seen as one more analysis of a celebrity body that could be used as a case study for illustrating a particular medical condition. However, perhaps most significantly, the postmortem analysis of Hart's medical history can be seen as a meta-journalistic moment where the gaze of the journal is turned on itself through the editorial investigation of its own editor.

The postmortem analysis of Ernest Hart served as a means of explaining the presumed pathology of the man of letters. Because Hart had a reputation for irascibility and was rumored to have engaged in criminal activity, the focus on his dyspeptic and nervous troubles serves as a way to explain and, to some degree, excuse his difficult personality, if not his alleged criminality. For many doctors at the fin de siècle, genius was associated with insanity and degeneracy. Warren Babcock, for example, writes in the *Journal of Nervous and Mental Disease,* "If the exuberant, fertile soil of his [the genius's] mentality is not cultivated by education and early training, or modified by the civilizing influences of society, it develops along the crooked lines of degeneracy with which it started at birth."[53] Hart's body and story were converted into an interesting case study used to illustrate the fine line between literary genius, madman, and criminal. However, unlike the controversies over Martineau and Carlyle, the analysis of Hart's medical history was not used to disprove his autobiographical self-representations. Rather, it was used to smooth over a troubled past and to create a narrative of success that would authorize further professional expansion and development of the BMA and the *BMJ.*

If Hart's death provided an occasion for softening his combative personality, it also served as an opportunity for reconfiguring the gender politics associated with the medical gaze. While in the cases of Harriet Martineau and Jane Carlyle the medical gaze had been defined as a masculine alternative to "imaginative" female interpretations of the body, in the case of Hart's literary postmortem, the medical gaze is in places curiously feminized. The obituary begins with a statement that "some details of this [Hart's last] illness and of the courage with which he bore it are given on another page by a hand which ministered to him at the last."[54] The suggestion here is that this "hand" belongs to Alice Hart, Ernest Hart's widow, who was trained as a doctor in France and was known to be her husband's literary collaborator.[55] A tribute to Hart published by Elizabeth Garrett Anderson, M.D., attributed his support of women's medical education to "Mrs. Hart, who studied medicine in Paris, helped him to a wider and more sympathetic view of women's lives than he had had as a younger man."[56] This reference to Hart's reform perhaps alludes to the controversy over the death of his first wife, which had exposed him to charges of spousal neglect and possible homicide.[57] Masculine maturity is thus defined as an acceptance of women's authority within the medical profession and perhaps increased respect for them at home as well.

Although the detailed account of Hart's final illness is signed only by "a correspondent" and refers to his wife in the third person, it can be assumed that Alice Hart was the source due to the intimate nature of the detail provided. On one hand, the account reads as a melodramatic tale recounting Hart's heroic work ethic: "Despite the internal misery and the nervous depression the diabetes frequently caused, he went bravely on, dealing with public questions with a *verve* and grasp which were amazing."[58] His deathbed scene reads like an excerpt from a domestic novel: "About 6 o'clock he asked to be turned on the right side, and calling his wife to his side he spoke with her, gave a few sighs, and fell calmly asleep like a weary child in her arms. The indomitable spirit had fled" (185). Yet the sentimentalized portions of this account are countered by medical interpretation of Hart's case. When defining the conditions that preceded the amputation of Hart's leg, the account states, "In June a crop of herpetic spots on the right leg and foot ulcerated. Slowly ulceration took on a necrotic character. Under careful and patient treatment all the ulcers healed, excepting one above the first metatarsal bone, which slowly spread till a patch of dry gangrene was produced" (185). Thus, the account of Hart's struggle is at once medical and personal, dispassionate and sentimental. The woman doctor, the half-concealed "I" of Alice Hart herself, is defined as being capable of sympathetic care and expert medical testimony.

Throughout the account, references to the actions of Alice Hart further reinforce this image of female medical competence. The article mentions that she conducted a "careful and special study of diabetic dietaries," which she then implemented (184). This may have indirectly served as a plug for her book *Diet in Sickness and in Health,* published just two years before, which provided the details of her dietary scheme.[59] Thus, even though the account of Ernest Hart's illnesses may or may not have been written by Alice Hart, the allusion to her signed book publication reinforces her authority as a writer and doctor.[60] The compatibility of her roles as helpmeet and physician is reinforced by Henry Thompson's introduction to her book, which states that the "accomplished authoress has the advantage of possessing not only a remarkable acquaintance with the various branches of medical knowledge, after many years devoted to their study, but also in no less degree that which has been conferred by long culinary and housewifery experience."[61]

The account of Ernest Hart's final days as editor of the *BMJ* also reinforces the importance of Alice Hart as her husband's editorial assistant and intellectual collaborator. The article states that, on the way to his amputation operation, the "last thing he did before being carried to the operating table was to dictate to his wife some notes for a leader in the Journal."[62] And even on the day of his death, "he sat down to read the evening papers with the old keen interest in public affairs of the world, discussing them with his wife" (185). In this way, the female doctor-wife is revealed to be a key interpreter of the great man of letters. As writer, wife, and doctor, she brings a multifaceted lens to her analysis of the authorial body that is undeniably authoritative because it is based on both sentimental and scientific knowledge. Interestingly, these (self) depictions of Alice Hart also shed a positive light on Ernest Hart's difficult personality, addressing concerns about his misogyny and violent tendencies by providing an image of a driven, heroic man who had a softer side as well. To balance out his reputation for harshness, the article often places Hart at home, in nature, and among friends. For example, the article references "large garden parties" given by the Harts. Indeed, even when "he could not stand, and had to be carried everywhere" he engaged in "vivacious conversation" and "present[ed] his guests with bouquets of roses" (185). If, as an obituary in the *Jewish Chronicle* suggested, Hart had a "complex temperament," then his combative, violent tendencies could be easily explained by his heroic struggle with disease.[63]

The use of Victorian authors as medical case studies in the *BMJ* and many other journals of the period performed a key function in the professionalization of medicine. On one hand, the *BMJ* employed the conventions of mainstream literary journalism, highlighted literary controversies, and cited auto/biographical narratives to attract general interest readers and to authorize itself in the realm of mainstream literary discourse. The health of the genius, contributors argued, was inseparable from the health of the nation. However, at the same time, the authorial body was used as a site for distinguishing between the subjective interpretations of literary authors and the more objective interpretations of medical analysts. The controversies over Martineau and Carlyle illustrate the ways that this medical gaze was defined in opposition to what was perceived as the overheated imagination or hysteria of women's auto/biographical texts. They cannot know their own bodies, and thus they must rely on the medical specialist to interpret their texts in order for the correct diagnosis to be produced. The "correct" objective interpretation of the authorial body would limit the circulation of subjective information, which would, in turn, authorize the medical gaze as a more reliable source of knowledge. The case study, like a speculum, allowed medical journalists to view the interior of the authorial body, even if only as it was represented in written texts, defining it as a space that only they could rightly interpret.

Yet the attempt to contain discussion of the authorial body within medical journals was concomitant with a tendency to extend discussion of medical subject matter into the popular press: biographies, pamphlets, literary journals, and other mainstream publishing media. As writers, doctors such as Thomas Greenhow, Spencer Wells, James Crichton-Browne, George Gould, and Ernest Hart played a key role in the simultaneous specialization and popularization of medical discourse at the fin de siècle. Whether writing for literary periodicals or medical journals, the authors of literary postmortems often relied on the image of the unreliable female author as a figure against which the reliability of the male doctor could be defined. By the end of the century, however, the emergence of the woman doctor as a professional figure and literary trope suggested that the subject-object relations within medical discourse were due for change.

8

The Celebrity Cause:
Octavia Hill, Virtual Landscapes,
and the Press

In the winter of 1875, Octavia Hill (1838–1912) sat in the gallery of the House of Commons listening to Ughtred Kay-Shuttleworth's speech on the Artisans' Dwellings Bill. She was listening quietly when suddenly she heard her own name resounding though the chamber. Kay-Shuttleworth was reading from her article "The Homes of the London Poor," which had been published in *Macmillan's Magazine* the previous year.[1] "Instead of quoting dry facts and figures," she later told a friend, "he read aloud from it the description of the wonderful delight it gave me to see the courts [outside working-class homes] laid open to the light and air."[2] It was a key moment in Hill's career—both as a housing reformer and a journalist—because it highlighted the power of the press and the power of personality to bring about social change.[3] The *Macmillan's* article was just one of many short essays Hill published in periodicals as part of her campaigns for working-class housing reform and the preservation of open spaces. Between 1866 and 1905, she published more than twenty-six articles in the periodical press, most notably in the *Fortnightly Review, Macmillan's Magazine,* and the *Nineteenth Century.* At the same time, she published letters to the editor of the *Times* as a way of reaching an even broader audience.

In this chapter, I demonstrate how Octavia Hill used the press in a strategic way to garner popular support for her campaigns, particularly the open space movement. As a founding member of the Kyrle Society and cofounder of the National Trust, Hill attempted to establish a sense of common national culture by preserving and marking geographical landscapes, constructing their social significance through the mediating influence of journalistic texts. Hill's success was premised on her ability to use the press to popularize her own name as celebrity advocate. Like Harriet Martineau, Jane Carlyle, and many other women before her, Hill was to some degree constrained by media representations of the woman author. However, by capitalizing on the convention of signed publication and the advertisement of celebrity contributors in the *Fortnightly, Macmillan's,* and the *Nineteenth Century,* Hill was able to forge a positive connection between her name and the open space movement. The tendency of these journals, particularly *Macmillan's,* to publish women writers made them ideal venues for Hill's public relations campaign.[4] Her frequent letters to the editor of the *Times* also had the effect of associating her name and celebrity identity with the emergence of the open space movement. Consequently, although there were many activists involved in the effort, including H. D. Rawnsley and Robert Hunter, it was Octavia Hill's name that became most closely associated with its public identity. As Sydney C. Cockerell[5] wrote in 1935, "Of those who called the National Trust into being in 1895 Octavia Hill occupies the central place, with Canon Rawnsley and Sir Robert Hunter on either side."[6] Indeed, by the early twentieth century, Arthur Greenwood, MP, would confess that he was wearied by frequent invocations of the "sainted name of Octavia Hill."[7] So how did Hill become the "sainted name" associated with the open space movements of the late nineteenth and early twentieth centuries?

As I demonstrate in this chapter, Octavia Hill pioneered the idea of the mass-media "celebrity cause," which today remains a significant preoccupation within popular print culture. Hill established her own celebrity name in emerging mass media as a way of furthering her efforts to raise public and private funds for the acquisition of rural and urban open spaces for the people. Yet as a middle-class woman, she was careful to enforce a boundary between Octavia Hill the biographical individual and "Octavia Hill" the celebrity in order to maintain middle-class respectability. At the same time that Hill was careful to manage her own celebrity, she capitalized on the discourse on celebrity as a way of promoting the acquisition of open space for the general public. The best way to immortalize loved ones, she argued, was to donate land that represented their most beloved scenes or texts. Although Hill and her collaborators were eager to mark the land with names and other personal signifiers of meaning, they simultaneously acknowledged the necessity of effacing these private associations as a way of creating "national landscapes" that would be the communal property of all Britons. The tension between public and private identities as well as between public and private landscapes is a crucial feature of the open space movement as it emerged during the second half of the nineteenth century.

ESTABLISHING A NAME

Octavia Hill published her first periodical essay in 1866 as a way of publicizing the success of her housing projects. With the assistance of John Ruskin, she purchased two working-class tenement courts in Marylebone and transformed them from squalid slums into model housing yielding a 5 percent return on investment. In September 1866, when Hill consulted Ruskin about publishing an article on her work in the *Fortnightly Review,* he responded, "State your own views in beginning this thing; say that I furnished you with the means in order to prove and practise one of the first principles of my political economy: that proper use of money would give proper interest, and that no one could otherwise than *criminally* take more. Make the thing short, but put in *some* distinct and interesting stories about your tenants, and I doubt not the immense good you will do, and probably induce others to do."[8] Clearly, Ruskin imagined his own celebrity as a determining factor in the success of Octavia's Hill's journalistic campaign, yet soon she would establish a celebrity identity quite distinct from her mentor's. In this passage, Ruskin nevertheless sets out a strategy that Hill would use throughout her various campaigns: constructing short didactic articles woven with sentimentalized stories from working-class life intended to attract volunteers and financial support. The *Fortnightly Review* was an ideal choice for her first periodical appeal because George Henry Lewes, Hill's distant relation, was editor at the time.[9] The liberal slant of the journal also made it an appropriate location for her article because she was a strong opponent of the "dole" and promoted a self-help approach to philanthropic activism.[10]

Hill's articles advocating investment in working-class housing were indeed successful in terms of attracting a large number of investors and volunteers. By 1877, Hill and her collaborators managed housing for 3,500 tenants in buildings worth as much as £40,000.[11] However, Hill's legacy as a housing reformer was probably less significant than her influence as an advocate for the open space movement. As Diana Maltz notes, "Even as her methods of house management met with obsolescence under the welfare state, Hill's aestheticizing mission survived into twentieth-century British town planning."[12] Hill was by no means the first activist to advocate for open space; in fact, the movement to preserve suburban greenways from the encroachment of railways and other development had been underway for many years.[13] However, as Barbara Gates points out, Octavia Hill, in collaboration with the other members of the Kyrle Society, "introduced a new concentration of attention on the metropolitan spaces of London," particularly the need for green space in the impoverished neighborhoods of Marylebone, Southwark, and the East End.[14]

It was while working as a landlady in urban neighborhoods during the 1860s and 1870s that Hill first became aware of the need for urban parks. She began by developing playgrounds in association with her housing projects. Her interest in acquiring land for urban open spaces did not begin in earnest, though, until 1873 when she first learned that the Swiss Cottage Fields were due to be sold to housing developers. "I think of little else but my Fields day and night," she wrote to her friend Jane Nassau Senior.[15] The imminent development of the fields prompted her to write her first essay on the open space movement, "Space for the People," which was published in *Macmillan's Magazine* in 1875. In this essay, she extols the "healing gift of space" and proposes three types of green space needed in the urban environment: "places to sit in," "playgrounds," and "places to stroll in."[16] After illustrating the need for these spaces, she turns her attention specifically to Swiss Cottage Fields. The rest of the article reads as a series of sophisticated marketing maneuvers, culminating in a plea for financial contributions for the purchase fund. She begins in a sentimental vein, writing "They are the nearest fields on our side of London; and there on a summer Sunday or Saturday evening you might see hundreds of working people . . . Fathers, with a little girl by each hand, the mother with the baby, sturdy little boys, and merry little girls—as they entered the small, white gate, you might see them spread over the green open space like a stream that has just escaped from between rocks" (330). The repetition of the phrase "you might see" in this passage invites readers into a scene they would be unlikely to experience firsthand, encouraging them to visualize and thus empathize with those who depend on the fields for solace and recreation. She concludes the idyll with an exclamation, "Acres of villas!

Yes, at last, the fields will be built over, if they cannot be saved" (330). She follows this passionate exclamation with a reference to her own personal experience, writing, "I knew them many years ago, when I used to walk out of London alone" (330). On the next page she adds, "I happen to know the special beauties of these, and their value to our side of London, and to be personally very fond of them" (331). This "I," so characteristic of Hill's periodical writing, reinforces her importance as the source of knowledge about working-class needs and as a "personality" whose viewpoints can serve as a stand-in for those of middle-class readers of the journal.

The essay continues with a paragraph designed to ignite Christian feeling: "When God made the world, He made it very beautiful, and meant that we should live amongst its beauties, and that they should speak peace to us in our daily lives" (332). This appeal to religious feeling is followed by a more practically minded postscript, where she notes that "influential people have taken up the scheme, and several thousand pounds have already been subscribed. But many thousands more are wanted, and I hope that some of those who read this paper may see their way to helping forward a plan which to my mind promises a large and lasting benefit to our London poor" (332). Hill's direct appeal to readers, when combined with a personalized "I," creates a sense of intimacy between writer and reader, a bond designed to produce support from the general public. No address is provided, presumably because writers would contact Hill via the Macmillan's offices, where the editorial staff would field public inquiries.

At the same time that Hill was enlisting the support of the editors of *Macmillan's*, she was also attempting to reach a broader audience by writing letters to the *Times*. At first she doubted whether she could interest the editors of a national newspaper in her cause. In July 1875, when the development of the Swiss Cottage Fields seemed imminent, she described her struggles in a letter to Sydney J. Cockerell: "Thanks for [your] offer about the *Times*, the sub-editor himself has promised to 'look after' my letter which I sent yesterday, but I never have believed in *any* succeeding in the *Times*, it isn't my line, they wouldn't like me, nor I them, we all incline to thinking the letter was too 'emotional' or else the *Times* thinks it still—or that the public think it still too local."[17] Her task was to make what seemed like a local issue—or an emotional "feminine" concern—into a national priority. In fact, her letter *was* published in the *Times* on July 20, just four days after her anxious message to Cockerell. In the short letter, she pleads for "promises of support" for purchase of the fields, calling them a "perpetual blessing while London lasts."[18]

Although Hill's letter and essay did facilitate the collection of more than £9,000 in donations for the purchase of the Swiss Cottage Fields, her efforts ultimately did not meet with success.[19] In an August 23 letter to the *Times*, Edward Bond announced that negotiations for the fields had failed, and an editorial note published on October 5 reported that the parcel was "already laid out for building purposes."[20] However, this early campaign nonetheless provided Hill with the opportunity to develop a set of highly effective rhetorical strategies that she would employ in many campaigns to come. Late in 1875, after the failure of the Swiss Cottage Fields campaign, she began working closely with the Commons Preservation Society. The following year, her sister Miranda founded the Kyrle Society, which was dedicated to the beautification of urban neighborhoods.[21] When the Open Spaces Subcommittee of the Kyrle Society was founded in 1879, Octavia Hill was appointed treasurer—and rightly so, because she had already proven herself an exemplary fund-raiser and publicist during the Swiss Cottage Fields campaign.

Although Hill was initially unsure of her ability to appeal to a national audience, she later learned that there was a direct relationship between her letter-writing campaigns and the success of her projects. For example, in 1887 after the land for the Red Cross housing project was secured, she sent a letter to the *Times* requesting £2,500 for a tract of land adjoining the parcel to build six cottages and a hall.[22] Sydney C. Cockerell noted that Hill received £2,105 the same day the letter appeared and an additional £200 by the end of the month.[23] Because a national newspaper had a broader circulation than a literary journal and appeared on a daily basis, it was an ideal medium for Hill's public relations efforts. The success of the Red Cross fund-raising effort demonstrates Hill's mastery of the epistolary genre and testifies to the increasing cachet associated with her authorial signature. By the late 1880s, she was well known as a successful activist and environmentalist; thus, her signature on a short letter to the editor was enough to inspire public confidence.

One of the ways Hill created an aura of trust was to publicize her properties once they had been purchased and developed. When planning a celebration marking the 1888 opening of the Red Cross project, for example, Hill made a point of asking Sydney C. Cockerell to "invite the Press" and "prepare to hand them a short paragraph."[24]

Indeed, on June 4, just two days after the opening ceremony, a celebratory notice appeared in the *Times*.[25] In this way, Hill not only used the newspaper press to solicit funding for her projects but also to publicize the successful realization of her efforts. The letter to the editor was an ideal medium for these campaigns because it enabled Hill to reach a national audience and thus to redefine her open spaces projects as national, rather than local, concerns. In addition, the opportunity to reach the public on a day-to-day basis enabled Hill to solicit and collect funds in an efficient and timely way. Hill's use of the epistolary genre likewise enhanced her efforts by suggesting the immediacy and intimacy of a personal communication.

Indeed, Hill's letter-writing campaigns were wildly successful. During the next few years, Hill and her collaborators secured Parliament Hill Fields, Vauxhall Park, Deptford Park, and a variety of other properties, including several reclaimed urban graveyards. These achievements were not only made possible by letter-writing campaigns but also by the publication of persuasive essays in the periodical press. Although the monthly or biweekly periodicals were published less frequently and commanded smaller audiences than a national newspaper, they nonetheless provided greater opportunities to deepen the public's understanding of the problem at hand. As an essayist, Hill employed increasingly sophisticated techniques in her periodical writing that were intended to help readers "picture" the devastating effects of urbanization in new ways. For example, her article "More Air for London," published in the *Nineteenth Century* in 1888, includes the same references to firsthand experience and sentimental narrative that characterized her earlier articles. She begins, "It is one thing to know theoretically and scientifically that they [open spaces] are needed, and it is another to live, as it were, side by side with those who need them."[26] "This is different from reason and science," she writes, "this is life, and this is pain. This urges me to speak, making it my duty to speak, and that before it is too late" (181). Hill, as a kind of prophet who is "urged to speak," reports what she sees as a way of enabling middle-class readers to experience these spaces, if only in a virtual way.

Accompanying the article is a foldout map with open spaces printed in green. With this illustration, she hoped to provide a "bird's eye view of the condition of things." In other words, she illustrated that the amount of green space per capita in the West End was greater than in the east and that the areas outside the central core were greener

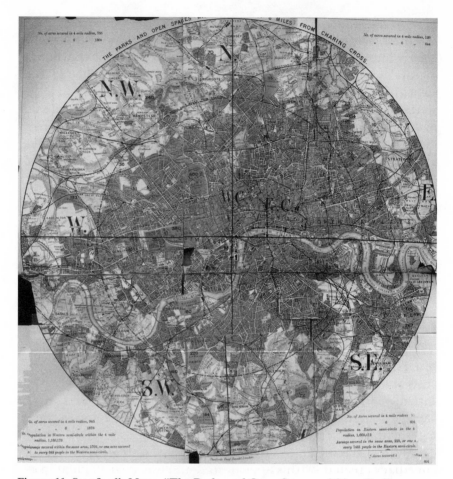

Figure 11. Stanford's Maps, "The Parks and Open Spaces within a Radius of 6 Miles from Charing Cross," in "More Air for London," by Octavia Hill, *Nineteenth Century* 23 (1888): 184–85.

than those in the inner city (182). Later in the article, she coins the term *green belt* to describe her plan for developing a system of pedestrian paths that would provide "pleasant walking ways" through the city (185). She concludes with a specific appeal to the "rich people of London," asking them to donate private funds for the purchase of Parliament Hill as an extension to Hampstead Heath (187). In this article, then, the visuality of Octavia Hill's rhetoric is particularly apparent. She includes eyewitness testimony written from the perspective of a first-person narrator to an audience addressed familiarly as "you." She also uses a color foldout map that enables Londoners to view their city from a new perspective. The readers of the *Nineteenth Century* thus need not walk to the East End to receive a convincing "picture" of the problem at hand: the lack of parks and open spaces, particularly for those living in the poorest neighborhoods.

Another rhetorical strategy Hill used to sharpen her campaign for urban space was to suggest a sense of impending doom caused by the encroachment of urban sprawl. For example, in a plea for purchase of the Deptford Hilly Fields published in the *Graphic* in 1892, Hill writes,

> Take a map of London, and look at the dense black mass which shows how far the houses have spread over the quiet fields; look at the sudden space of white just on its edge marked "Loam Pit Hill" or "Hilly Fields," or, better still, find your own way to the spot itself, and ask yourself whether this breathing space shall be absorbed into the waste of building, or shall, partly by your effort, be retained a breezy holiday ground for ever. One of my fellow-workers said, "Tell people it is 'Now if ever; now for ever.'" And this is literally true, for the time when we have the option of purchase is just expiring.[27]

Here Hill uses visual imagery as a way of illustrating the apocalyptic sense of change in the urban environment. The foreboding "dense black mass" is opposed to the "white" purity of the open spaces on the map. The encroachment of black onto white suggests a loss of purity that is irretrievable; due to the imminent threat posed by the "waste of building," the hills must be purchased "now if ever." The sense of immediacy created by this appeal no doubt was instrumental in its success. Indeed, in her 1893 *Letter to Fellow-Workers*, Hill was finally able to proclaim, "Hilly Fields is won!"[28]

Hill attempted to heighten the effect of her written appeals by giving speeches to various groups within the philanthropic community. She then published these speeches in the periodical press as a way of expanding the reach of her orations. For example, the essay "A Few Words to Fresh Workers," published in the *Nineteenth Century* in 1889, was first "read at the summer meeting of University Extension students at Oxford,"[29] and the essay "A More Excellent Way of Charity," published in *Macmillan's Magazine* in 1876, was initially "read at a meeting held in a suburban district."[30] In addition, her speech "Open Spaces," presented to the National Health Society in 1877, was republished in *Our Common Land* the same year.[31] The lecture, like the letter to the editor, mediates the speech of the author by suggesting a more "private" audience for communication even at the same time that it justifies a broader public readership. The authority of the writer is underscored by the cachet of the name associated with the letter and the significance of being invited to speak at a prestigious professional gathering. Yet the modesty of the writer is enhanced via the suggestion that the letter or lecture was originally intended for a private audience.

Another technique Hill used to expand the audience for her work was to include cross-references in her articles, thus linking individual essays into a coherent body of work.[32] For example, in an 1876 article on the need for training charity workers, she writes, "I have, in the July number of *Good Words*, given a sketch of a practical scheme for securing this end."[33] This effort to link her periodical essays into an oeuvre was reinforced by the republication of her periodical essays in book form: *Homes of the London Poor* (1875) and *Our Common Land* (1877).[34] That both books were published by Macmillan is significant because many of the essays collected in these volumes originally appeared in *Macmillan's Magazine*. As Ann Parry points out, it was a conscious strategy of the periodical's editor, George Grove, to "extend the cultural interests of the reader . . . and thereby, prepare a market for the books the House was to publish."[35] In the case of *Homes of the London Poor*, such marketing efforts clearly succeeded. Soon after the book was published, Hill boasted to Sydney J. Cockerell, "My book has been so well reviewed, fourteen reviews in all, and all favorable!"[36]

As a result of her speeches, letter-writing campaigns, and essay publications, Octavia Hill soon became a recognizable "name" in British society. In an 1877 letter, Ruskin acknowledged Hill's rising celebrity: "You will find yourself, without working for it, taking a position in the literary, no less than in the philanthropic, world. It seems to me not improbable that the great powers and interests you are now exciting in so many minds, will indeed go on from the remedial to the radical cure of social evils."[37] However, beyond her attempt to republish some of her essays in book form, there is no evidence to suggest that Hill viewed her essays as anything more than ephemeral writing—in other words, as necessary publicity for her philanthropic projects. As a grassroots activist, she viewed writing as way to influence public opinion and to solicit volunteer contributions. In "More Air for London," she writes, "let me point out that each of us can in a measure influence public opinion, and that much will depend on public opinion in the next few months with regard to any schemes for saving or purchasing."[38]

Curiously, although Hill was eager to associate her name with her periodical and book publications, she was somewhat reticent about linking her name to the details of her personal life. When Princess Alice was preparing a German translation of *Homes of the London Poor*, she asked Hill if she would mind the inclusion of a biographical preface. Hill protested, saying she hoped to keep the focus on the "work itself quite without any impression of *me*."[39] Similarly, she refused to allow publication of her *Letters to Fellow-Workers*, which were privately printed and distributed annually to those involved in the cause.[40] She explained, "When I sit down as I shall do next Sunday to write my annual letter, I feel that I am writing not to the world but to my own friends . . . to those who I may dare to trust."[41] For Octavia Hill, there was a clear separation between letters written for private and public purposes. When in 1892 Sydney C. Cockerell asked permission to print quotes from her letters, she agreed to do so only reluctantly, saying "no private matters should be made public."[42]

Hill's construction and careful management of her own literary celebrity was reinforced by representations of her work in the periodical press. For example, in a signed article published in *Fraser's Magazine* in 1873, Florence Nightingale suggests that Hill is a modern-day Dorothea Brooke. Nightingale points out that in *Middlemarch*, George Eliot "can find no better outlet for the heroine . . . *because* she cannot be a 'St. Teresa' or an 'Antigone' . . . Yet close at hand, in actual life, was a woman . . . who has managed to make her ideal very real indeed."[43] That a fictional heroine is the best touchstone for understanding Hill's persona is interesting in that it draws attention to the construction of her identity as another kind of literary persona.

Of course, representations of Hill's idealism were not always positive. In a short notice published in *Punch* in 1885, the editors compare her efforts to Tennyson's "Charge of the Light Brigade." Responding to Hill's appeal for £500 to purchase an open space at Deptford, the editors write, "That admirable lady, Octavia Hill, will gladly receive donations at 14, Nottingham Place, W. Who will 'tip' this particular *Hill* with gold, or even silver? Five hundred donors at a pound apiece would do it. Now, then, 'Noble Five Hundred,' here is a 'charge' for you worth undertaking, and, duly done, perhaps as well worth celebrating in Tennysonian numbers and many themes to which the Poet-Laureate has put his silver pen."[44] On one hand, the article seems to promote Hill's campaign by providing her address and by suggesting that the preservation of open space is a "noble" enterprise worthy of great poetry. However, the fact that the charge of the light brigade was a senseless slaughter of soldiers due to mis-construed orders suggests that the open space campaign is similarly founded on poor leadership and promises a devastating outcome for the "noble five hundred" who put themselves at her command.[45] The article, like Tennyson's poem, is at once a celebration of noble purpose and a reminder of the tragedy that results from the poor execution of lofty goals.

Although the name *Octavia Hill* loomed large in periodicals dur-ing the final decades of the nineteenth century, there are few pub-lished images of her. Indeed, Hill seems to have been very careful to control the circulation of her portraits. In 1899, Hill gave Frederick Hollyer permission to photograph the portrait of her painted by John Singer Sargent and to display his photo at the Royal Photographic Society Exhibition. However, as she wrote in an 1899 letter to Sydney C. Cockerell, she did so only with the proviso that "after July 1901 the entire and exclusive copyright is in my hands."[46] "He also assures me," she notes, "that he certainly would not allow reproduction of it without my written authority." Clearly, although Hill was eager for the publicity of signed publication, she was careful to enforce a boundary between Octavia Hill the biographical individual and "Octavia Hill" the celebrity.

Although there were apparently no portraits of Hill published in the press during her lifetime,[47] there is one illustration from an 1883 issue of *Punch* that at least attempts to depict the open space move-ment and its proponents via illustration. The cartoon begins with a quote by Octavia Hill from the *Times*: "The value of small open spaces in densely-populated districts, near the homes of working people, is increasingly recognized year by year."[48] The caption at the bottom of the image responds to this quote with "'Recognised!' Ay, but by whom? The wise of heart and the kindly! / Scarce by the Kings of Gold, the Lords of the Rail and Mart" (266). Thus, once again *Punch* seems to promote Hill's efforts by publicizing her article in the *Times* and by making its own plea for the "wise of heart and kindly" to con-tribute to the open space movement. However, there is clearly a sense of parody at work here as well. After all, the stand-in for Octavia Hill is a scantily clad embodiment of spring who leaves children in her shadow. *Punch* illustrator Linley Sambourne thus on one hand pres-

OUR PLEA FOR OPEN SPACES.

The Rhymester, musing in City Slums, indulges in Elegiacs concerning possible Elysia for the City Children.

"The value of small open spaces in densely-populated districts, near the homes of working people, is increasingly recognised year by year."
Mrs. Octavia Hill, in the "Times."

"RECOGNISED!" Ay, but by whom? The wise of heart and the
    kindly!
Scarce by the Kings of Gold, the Lords of the Rail and Mart.
Little by *Bumble* the bumptious, blundering coldly, blindly,
On in the olden ways, stolid and tough of heart.

Then, whilst the Springtide burst of rejuvenescent beauty
    Breaks upon holt and hedgerow, quickens the pulse like
    wine,
Where are the souls will list to the bidding of citizen duty,
To claims of the City children considerate ear incline?

Figure 12. Linley Sambourne, "Our Plea for Open Spaces," *Punch* 84
(June 9, 1883): 266.

ents Hill as a powerful symbol of regeneration while at the same time suggesting she may be oblivious to the serious obstacles presented by the squalor that surrounds her and by developers who refuse to hear her pleas. Yet such a complex representation of Hill and her movement is hardly on the surface of this text. For the most part, Octavia Hill remains a name, rather than an image, whose celebrity signature, more than her likeness, is linked to the open space movement.

NATIONAL AND PERSONAL MEMORIALS

Octavia Hill's apparent reluctance to being represented visually in the press is interesting considering the open space movement itself was so intensely visual. In a sense, the spaces Hill "created" visually through her writings and open space projects served as stand-ins for her own image. The desire to "see" Hill was converted into a desire to "see" Freshwater Place or Deptford Park, even if only by reading one of Hill's essays. Hill reinforced the connection between virtual and literal landscapes in innovative ways. In the discourse on open spaces in Octavia Hill's work, there is a fascinating attempt to "write" or "mark" the land through language, not only by publishing essays about specific locations (Swiss Cottage Fields or Parliament Hill) but also by literally marking these spaces with the written word. For example, after building a park near Freshwater Place, one of her first tenement houses, Hill raised funds for an inscription in tiles to be placed along the length of the building facing the playground.[49] The tiles, designed by William de Morgan, read, "Every house is builded by some man; but He that built all things is God."[50] She wrote letters to her nearest supporters soliciting their financial assistance for her project. She pleaded, "If any of you will give a letter, you may like to feel that you have helped to write a sentence that will speak when you are far away, and after you are dead" (294).[51] In a sense, the project of creating gardens was about communal writing, inscribing the landscape with language that would commemorate the collective activity of Hill and her supporters. Thus, the inscription had a public meaning, a moral to be read by those who used the park, but it also had a private meaning for those who had "written" it into existence.[52]

In a sense, Octavia Hill's project was to use her own writing as a way of changing the way that the land was "named," thus shifting its associations along with its use patterns. This was especially true of the Kyrle Society's campaign to reclaim urban graveyards as public parks.[53] In *Our Common Land*, Hill writes, "There are, all over London, little spots unbuilt over, still strangely preserved among the sea of houses—our graveyards. They are capable of being made into beautiful out-door sitting rooms."[54] With grants from the vestry and the Metropolitan Board of Works, she notes, the incumbent of a parish can have the tombstones removed and an "authorised plan made of the ground, showing precisely the place of every grave" (115–17). In this way, they can preserve the names of those buried but still erase the written record on the visible surface of the land, replacing tombstones with benches, fountains, and flower beds. The area then becomes a "park" that can be used by the poor in the local neighborhood. Just as the inscription on Freshwater Place was a "quiet memorial" to the insiders who had paid subscriptions to have it built, the reclaimed graveyard represses the "secret" names of the dead. The result is the creation of new public meanings on the surface of the urban landscape that are intended to bring life and health.

In *Our Common Land*, Hill is careful to distinguish her plan for reclaiming urban graveyards from outright acts of desecration. For example, she contrasts her own work to the actions of the Society of Friends, who in 1876 refused to sell their burial ground at Whitecross Street to the Kyrle Society. Hill notes that the Quakers instead sold the parcel for a housing development after first "uprooting five thousand bodies" and reburying them in a "large hole at the other end of the ground" to make way for the construction project (125, 127).[55] "That which was once the form which embodied any human soul, named or unnamed," she writes, "would have seemed to me worth a little gentler care" (127). In Hill's view, a garden would have been a more suitable memorial to the dead, even if their names were no longer written in stone.

Hill's campaign for converting disused churchyards was remarkable in the way that it reconceived of the national landscape as a memorial to the dead, while at the same time serving as a depersonalized "common ground" accessible to the general population. That national landscapes should perform both functions suggests a new conception of heritage as the simultaneous invocation and effacement of the names of the dead. The Gothicism of this notion of national landscape recalls the "homes and haunts" approach to literary tourism discussed in chapter 2, where readers and tourists were invited to commune with the spirits of dead authors.

During the early years of the National Trust, lands associated with famous authors were interpreted differently than other property acquisitions. While the names of the anonymous thousands buried in graveyards must be suppressed to make way for "common ground," the names of dead celebrities must be preserved in association with the landscapes they loved. As H. D. Rawnsley wrote in the early days of the National Trust, "Go to, let us remember the greatest writers, poets, and thinkers of the Victorian time; and if it be possible let us obtain for posterity one or other of the scenes most associated with their life's work; and let the National Trust hold it as a memorial of her Most Gracious Majesty's long reign."[56] By affixing the name of a celebrity to a parcel of land, its value was determined at the intersection of land and text, the virtual landscapes of literature and the actual landscapes that must be "saved." It then became a national memorial to the greatness of the age, a marker of Victorian achievement at the vanishing point of a long century.

The memorialization of John Ruskin is a particularly fascinating case study for investigating the ways that the acquisition of land and the memorialization of celebrities worked in tandem. After Ruskin's death in 1900, his relatives and supporters spearheaded a movement to construct a memorial in Westminster Abbey. In a letter to the *Times*, Hill responded with an alternate proposal: "Ruskin needs no memorial. If in memory of him we can preserve some ancient building in untouched loveliness, or save the top of some mountain, a sea cliff, lake shore, or wooded glade to be kept in natural loveliness unspoilt for ever, we should be not so much erecting a memorial as realizing a hope, carrying out a desire of the great spirit which lived with us and taught us. Surely the continuance of the work of a friend and teacher is better than a monument."[57] Hill's letter sparked a lively exchange in the *Times* over the suitability of her scheme. Arthur Severn, Ruskin's cousin, wrote a letter proclaiming, "The suggestion of buying some headland or beautiful place and preserving it to John Ruskin's memory is all very well, and, of course, the kind of monument most of us would wish; but such a scheme is beset with difficulties, and, even if carried out, might be very unsatisfactory."[58] Indeed, an outdoor memorial to Ruskin was erected by the National Trust at Friar's Crag, Keswick, in October 1900.[59] The memorial, a single block of Borrowdale stone, is inscribed with a quote from Ruskin: "The first thing that I remember as an event in life was being taken by my nurse to the brow of Friars' Crag, Derwentwater."[60] The memorial, one of the first erected by the National Trust, thus invites spectators to view the lake and the surrounding countryside from Ruskin's perspective.[61] In addition, it forges a link between the land and Ruskin's oeuvre—the very texts that had inspired Octavia Hill and her collaborators to found the open space movement.

If land could be used to memorialize celebrities, forging a connection between their names and the landscapes they loved, it could also be used to *create* celebrity. That is, it could be used to make private identities public by converting private homes and lands into national landmarks. Early on, Hill and other founders of the National Trust used the concept of perpetual fame to promote the acquisition of property. H. D. Rawnsley, writing for *Cornhill Magazine* in 1897, notes, "Rather than be content with some dreary monument upon a grave, let me bequeath, to the perpetual joy, and thought, and health, and life of future generations, some fair scene such as my friend delighted in, some ruin which he loved to ramble in, the birthplace or the home of one of the thinkers of the past he held in honour."[62]

Yet as much as the development of the National Trust relied on the donation of lands as memorials, it was also premised on the notion that the process of memorialization must go beyond the local, situating individual memorials and gifts within a broader network of national holdings. In "Natural Beauty as a National Asset," a 1905 article published in the *Nineteenth Century*, Hill asks, "Is it not important for national as well as for family life that they [open spaces] should be as far as possible preserved?"[63] The donation of land, she notes, provides the "added satisfaction of knowing that long after they have passed away such possessions will remain to be a blessing to succeeding generations" (938). Here and elsewhere in her works promoting the National Trust, Hill exhorts readers to imagine nation as a common interest in national buildings and landscapes, the heritage that situates the individual life (and death) within a broader historical narrative. National landscapes thus are reconceived as "memorial[s] to those we have lost, more abiding and surely as beautiful as stained-glass window or costly tomb" (939).

Indeed, the Hill family donated substantial acreage in Kent to the National Trust during the late nineteenth and early twentieth centuries. In 1907, a memorial to Octavia's mother Caroline was constructed on Mariner's Hill, and in 1911, Octavia's niece and nephew purchased thirty-four acres at One Tree Hill, Kent, in memory of Octavia's half-brother, Arthur Hill.[64] The High Weald region of Kent thus came to be marked with multiple references to the Hill family.[65] Of course, Hill's country home, which she shared with Harriet Yorke after 1884, was located at Crockham Hill and was situated within this network of family shrines. Virtually until the day she died, Hill worked to extend National Trust holdings in the region. In fact, the day before her death, she received the final £500 she needed to extend the Mariner's Hill parcel by fourteen acres.[66]

When Octavia Hill died in 1912, her name became literally associated with the open spaces she had constructed and "saved" via her published writings. A stone memorial to Octavia Hill was erected on the peak of Mariner's Hill, thus literalizing an association between land and name that had been so essential to the success of her preservationist projects. "The preservation of Mariner's Hill as an open space," it reads, "was due to the efforts of Octavia Hill."[67] As the locus of private and public meanings, the lands surrounding Octavia Hill's former home are at once public memorials to her celebrity and private markers of family memories. In her 1903 *Letter to Fellow-Workers*, Hill notes that the first parcel of the Mariner's Hill property was in part purchased from the Kyrle Society's "In Memoriam Fund" and consequently served as an "offering and dedication" for all bereaved relatives who contributed to the fundraising effort.[68] In a later letter, Hill imagines the public viewpoints of Mariner's Hill as belonging to an even broader national constituency: "Those who have no country house, but who need, from time to time, this outlook over the fair land which is their inheritance as Englishmen" (579).[69] Thus, in addition to serving as a location of private associations, Mariner's Hill becomes a site of nationalist pride and communal ownership. Central to the idea of Mariner's Hill as a national open space is "Octavia Hill," who is identified as the landscape's "savior" and to some degree its claim to fame. However, at the same time, the name is peripheral in the greater scheme of national heritage, which effaces individual identity, clearing the land of its private meanings and associations.

OCTAVIA HILL AND
THE WOMEN'S MOVEMENT

The appearance and disappearance of "Octavia Hill" as a celebrity name associated with the preservation of national landscapes is to some degree a product of domestic ideology. Hill realized that celebrity must be managed carefully to construct the kind of morally virtuous public persona that would not threaten conventional notions of feminine decency. Like Harriet Martineau before her, she did so by constructing herself as a morally upright single woman whose work was informed by a sense of righteous duty. Yet at the same time, Octavia Hill's larger than life persona, marked so overtly with the personal pronoun "I," seemed intent on promoting not only the expansion of space available to inner-city workers but also the extension of the space available for middle-class women to work in the public realm. "Customs have altered in a marked manner," she notes in "A Few Words to Fresh Workers," an essay published in the *Nineteenth Century* in 1889.[70] "It used to be difficult for a girl to walk alone, and it was considered almost impossible for her to travel in omnibuses or third-class trains. The changes in custom with regard to such matters have opened out fresh possibilities of work" (454). A few years later, in "Trained Workers for the Poor," she detailed the sorts of training and preparation women would need to serve as professional social workers. "The more volunteer work increases," she notes, "the more need there is of a certain proportion of paid work to keep it together."[71] A course of training would show the "way to a moderate income for many women who have the care of the poor as much on their hearts as any volunteer" (40–41).

Given her support of women's employment and her own high-profile career as a celebrity activist, it is difficult to understand Hill's opposition to women's suffrage. In a 1910 letter to the *Times*, she explains her position this way: "I believe that men and women help one another because they are different, have different gifts and different spheres—one is the complement of the other."[72] Engaging in the political life of the country would "militate against their [women's] usefulness in the large field of public work in which so many are now doing noble and helpful service" by distracting them from their real work as caretakers of the "sick, the old, the young, and the erring, as guardians of the poor" (9A). Although she conceptualizes these activities as "public" actions that benefit the country as a whole, they nonetheless constitute "out-of-sight, silent work" (9A).[73] Yet clearly there was nothing "silent" about Octavia Hill's own career; as a spokesperson for several causes, she was one of the most visible social activists of the second half of the nineteenth century. An anecdote included in the letter suggests the contradictory nature of Hill's attitude toward her own visibility. She writes, "I remember a great actress, performing before a somewhat untrained audience, telling me that when they were somewhat noisy they called out to her to speak louder; 'then,' she said, 'I always drop my voice, and they become quiet and listen" (9A). By comparing women workers to actresses, Hill inadvertently draws attention to their performative identities in the public realm, on the stage, as it were, before an "untrained" national audience. She lowers her voice to be heard, yet she is still the focus of attention as a theatrical performer. There is perhaps no better metaphor for Hill's own work in the public realm. She must "train" her audience through strategic appearances, speaking softly in the role of an exemplary single woman activist, yet her overall goal is to be heard.

For Hill, as for many Victorian women writers, the ability to manage her own level of exposure in the press was instrumental in her professional success. It enabled her to pioneer housing reform and radically expand the number of public parks and open spaces available to the British public. That Hill did not see this as political power per se is surprising but understandable given the amount of influence she was able to exert without direct political representation. Although Hill was opposed to female suffrage, she nonetheless imagined a variety of new roles and spaces for women as well as for workers. By constructing a variety of compelling texts that incorporated maps, vividly drawn examples, and first-person accounts, Octavia Hill constructed landscapes that would be accessible to the middle classes in a virtual way via the periodical press. This literary effort was inseparable from her goal of marking the land in a literal way: redefining empty lots and disused churchyards as "open space" and converting these ephemeral landscapes into permanent memorials on a rapidly changing landscape. Such landscapes, as Hill envisioned them, served as "quiet" memorials to private individuals or celebrated national heroes while at the same time erasing the markers of human agency, including her own.

Coda:
Literary Celebrity, Gender,
and Canon Formation

"I BEGAN WITH THE DESIRE TO SPEAK WITH THE DEAD," STEPHEN Greenblatt writes at the beginning of *Shakespearean Negotiations*.[1] He continues, "This desire is a familiar, if unvoiced, motive in literary studies, a motive organized, professionalized, buried beneath thick layers of bureaucratic decorum."[2] Literary study, for Greenblatt, is a process of attempting to revivify the past, accessing what he calls "social energy" or the "capacity of certain verbal, aural, and visual traces to produce, shape, and organize collective physical and mental experiences."[3] Literary texts shape and distort cultural knowledges and practices, thus circulating "power, charisma, sexual excitement, collective dreams, wonder, desire, anxiety, religious awe, free-floating intensities of experience."[4] Through textual encounters, we experience this energy "long after both the death of the author and the death of the culture for which the author wrote."[5] Literary study thus becomes a kind of necromancy, a desire to converse with the "many voices of the dead."[6]

Such a desire, I would argue, characterizes much recent literary criticism in the field of Victorian studies, where literary analysis addresses an increasingly diverse array of texts, revivifying the spirits of authors and their associated contexts. This approach is rooted in the second half of the nineteenth century, when the cult of literary celebrity prompted journalists, tourists, and general readers to imagine they could understand the past on intimate terms. The practice of reading texts, mapping cultural landmarks, retelling literary history, and visiting/renovating authorial homes was premised on the idea that there was a kind of magic associated with literary texts produced by their ability to synthesize and distort national ideals and cultural

195

anxieties. Literary study and its associated practices of celebrity worship gave the impression of immortal life at the same time that they celebrated a past that was beyond recovery. The fact that the past, like the dead author, could never be fully known or understood fueled the emerging culture industries, leading to a variety of textual and geographical investigations.

The desire to commune with the spirits of dead writers is linked to the efforts of Victorian writers to memorialize their own lives and careers. Authors and their supporters attempted to erect permanent memorials on the landscape of Great Britain, material markers that would link their literary texts to specific spatial locations. Yet, such efforts, as I have shown, were always partial or incomplete. Literary value, like the land itself, was continually subject to alteration and change. The resonance of a text could dissipate just as easily as it could be re/generated. The pleasure of reading, like the pleasure of literary travel, was just as often a process of exploring places and texts with enduring collective appeal as it was resurrecting authors and works that had been forgotten or misunderstood. Literary celebrities of the past could be found as well as made—continually discovered, forgotten, and rediscovered in the ongoing process of national identity formation.

As complementary cultural practices, literary study and celebrity worship were premised on the notion that reading was an expression of national fidelity. The period associated with the rise of English studies in the academy roughly corresponds to the time period addressed in preceding chapters: 1850–1914. The development of the cult of literary celebrity is inseparable from the institutionalization of English studies during the same time period. In the following pages, I will briefly examine the link between celebrity worship and canon formation, highlighting the ways that women's literature came to be marginalized within these intersecting fields of discourse. The rise of New Criticism in the 1930s was preceded by earlier efforts to create a more objective critical practice, one that marginalized the work of women authors on aesthetic grounds while at the same time emphasizing a decontextualized approach to literary study in the academy. Yet as I will demonstrate, such attempts at defining a "masculine" national literature and culture divorced from historical context were partial and unsure, leading inevitably toward fractured and indeterminate definitions of literary value.

As Terry Eagleton and others have noted, the study of English literature began in women's colleges and mechanics' institutes, where it was imagined as a tool for fostering national values.[7] Charles Kingsley, in an 1848 lecture at Queen's College, argued that the systematic study of English literature would lead to the "spread of healthy historic views" and would provide a "record of its doubts and its faith, its sorrows and its triumphs, at each era of its existence."[8] Such a course of study would cure women of the "un-English" tendencies promoted by the study of foreign literatures and thus "give them a better chance of seeing things from that side from which God intended English women to see them" (60, 62). In the 1853 edition of *Chambers's Cyclopaedia of English Literature*, Robert Chambers declared his intention to address the "deficiency in the Literature addressed at the present time to the great body of the People."[9] The systemized study of "national authors," Chambers argues, would cultivate a "social and uniting sentiment" and would enhance "our national character, and the very scenery and artificial objects which mark our soil" (i). Here Chambers highlights the connection of land and literary heritage as two interconnected components of national identity. Indeed, he writes, it is "our common reverence for a Shakespeare, a Milton, a Scott" that "counteracts influences that tend to set us in division" (i). Such divisions are both literal and figurative: Britons must traverse the same national landscapes and texts to discover a common culture. Reading British literature thus provides an antidote to "un-English" forms of social unrest based on class and gender inequities.

By the 1880s, the study of English literature was a curricular requirement in most British colleges and universities and for civil service exams. Meanwhile, English literature as a field of study slowly gained acceptance at Oxford, where the English school was founded in 1894, and at Cambridge, where the English tripos was established in 1919.[10] The expansion of literary study at all levels of the British education system was concomitant with the publication of a variety of anthologies and histories of English literature. Thus, at the same time that "literary Britain" was being mapped in journals and tourist guides, "English literature" was being imagined as a coherent body of work that could be taught and studied. Likewise, at the same time that authors were being divided into major and minor figures in literary history, their bodies, homes, texts, and legacies were being investigated and evaluated in the popular press. The increasing focus on identifying "great" British authors—those who best embodied national ideals—inevitably led to the marginalization of women authors and texts in the emerging English studies academy. As Brian Doyle has pointed out, in the first decades of the twentieth century, English was "transformed into a 'masculine' academic discipline."[11]

Yet before 1890, the canon of English literature was decidedly unformed. This was especially true where contemporary literature was concerned. Most literary histories and anthologies of the period included current literature and attempted to formulate "Victorian literature" as an emerging literary field. In these early days, anthology editors were rather eclectic in their choice of contemporary authors and texts. For example, the third edition of *Chambers's Cyclopaedia of English Literature*, published in 1885, included a diverse array of literary genres, including travel writing and biography, as well as a variety of what today would be considered obscure authors, including working-class writer David Vedder and dramatist Douglas Jerrold.[12] *Chambers's* is remarkable for its inclusion of contemporary women writers, including Mary Braddon, Charlotte Yonge, and Eliza Cook. This sense of inclusivity was in keeping with the mission of the *Cyclopaedia*, which aimed to reach a popular audience. The same can be said of Henry Morley's *A First Sketch of English Literature*,[13] which from 1873 to 1898 sold more than 30,000 copies.[14] The first section of his survey of early Victorian literature is dominated by discussion of women writers, including Frances Trollope, Mary Howitt, Elizabeth Barrett Browning, and Harriet Martineau. The second section of the survey begins with Charles Dickens and William Makepeace Thackeray but includes a wide variety of women authors, including the Brontës, George Eliot, Elizabeth Gaskell, and Christina Rossetti as well as lesser known figures such as Elizabeth Sewell and Charlotte Yonge. Morley also includes the work of natural scientists, journalists, theologians, and historians in his expansive definition of "Victorian literature."

When writing surveys of contemporary literature, literary historians of the period had difficulty determining the boundaries of an emergent field. H. A. Dobson, in his *Civil Service Handbook of English Literature*, first published in 1874, confines his survey of Victorian authors to those who are deceased due to the fact that there is a "poverty of biographical material" on living writers.[15] Yet even with this limitation, Dobson, like Morley and Chambers, is decidedly comprehensive in his vision of the English canon, including a variety of contemporary poets, novelists, and nonfiction writers in his narrative of literary history. Dobson includes the names and brief biographies of a wide variety of women writers without defining "female literature" as a separate tradition; likewise, he includes working-class writers such as Ebenezer Elliott and William Cobbett in his survey of nineteenth-century literature.

In George Craik's *Compendious History of English Literature*, first published in 1861, a narrower definition of "Victorian literature" is asserted.[16] He includes Charlotte Brontë and George Eliot in the list of distinguished contemporary authors, while at the same time defining women's literature as a "distinct school" separate from male literary tradition (534–35). Craik explains, "Perhaps the kind of writing for which the female genius is best adapted is that of narrative —especially of such narrative as does not demand a rigid adherence either to any particular series of facts or to any particular form of composition, but in its entire freedom from all rules and shackles of every description comes nearest of all writing to ordinary conversation" (533–34). In poetry, however, women achieve a higher degree of excellence, according to Craik. Elizabeth Barrett Browning is identified as one of the first poets of the age, and *Aurora Leigh* is singled out as the only great Victorian poem to achieve "extensive popularity" (532). Yet compared to other literary histories of the period, Craik's *History* is less inclusive and comprehensive in its review of contemporary English literary history.

The increasingly unsure position of women writers in literary histories was linked to debates in the periodical press over the future of English studies. Henry Craik, writing for the *Quarterly Review* in 1883, asks, "Of our verse, our essays, our history, how much will float down upon the surface of the stream of time? In short, if we ask ourselves what are the bounds of the storehouse which we are to search for the treasures of English literature, the question is one which only a very rash man will attempt with any confidence to answer."[17] Literary anthologies, societies, and histories, he argues, have not helped Victorian readers understand the achievements of individual authors. "How much more real has he become to them," he laments, "how much has he spoken to them in his own words?" (190). Greek and Latin texts, on the other hand, are "dead, yet speaketh" (194). Ironically, for literature to "speak" to readers, it must be written in a dead language; remoteness in time and culture promotes intelligibility. A more rigorous critical practice will be needed, according to Craik, for English literature to "speak" to a modern audience. It must defamiliarize and decontextualize national authors and texts, locating them in the category of "dead" literary traditions.

During the 1880s, the academic study of English literature was perceived by many as the latest educational fad. John Churton Collins, writing for the *Nineteenth Century* in 1887, remarks, "In spite of its great vogue, and in spite of the time and energy lavished in teaching it, no fact is more certain than that from an educational point of view it is, and from the very first has been, an utter failure."[18] Henry Craik likewise quips, "It can scarcely be a matter of surprise that a domain of intellectual interest, whose promise is so wide and access to which is so easy, should count its students by thousands, and should find itself popularized in every provincial lecture-room, and in every young ladies' school."[19] For John Churton Collins and Henry Craik, the solution is the creation of a more systematic approach to literary study that employs rigorous historical and critical apparatus. Meanwhile, they argued, a canon of suitable English authors and texts must be established. Collins laments that there is "no good general history [of English literature] in existence."[20] In *A Compendious History of English Literature*, George Craik proposes defining classic English texts in opposition to the fashionable novel of the present because "in literature mere novelty cannot be admitted to have any legitimate attractiveness whatever."[21] Craik's analogy is telling: "In some things, indeed, novelty is almost all in all; in some, as for instance, in a fashionable article of dress, it is at least absolutely indispensible; the coat or bonnet may have all the other recommendations that could be desired, but without novelty, according to our modern notions, it cannot be fashionable" (540).[22] Here Craik explicitly identifies women as the consumers of fashion—and by extension, the consumers of literary novelties as well. The fashionable literary text, like the latest bonnet, is defined as a feminine object of exchange. These commodities possess popular appeal rather than lasting value.

For English studies to gain acceptance as a field of university study, then, it needed to distance itself from its association with popular reading and women's education. Alfred Ainger, in an 1889 article in *Macmillan's Magazine*, distinguishes between texts that produce "high and noble pleasure" and "ephemeral works that are no part of literature at all."[23] He continues, "Better to read 'Ivanhoe' on the sofa—to find the merest amusement in the genuine romantic vein of Sir Walter, than in the pinchbeck-romantic of —, and —, and — (for I dare name no names!), whose books seem to be hardly in existence a month before they are in their two hundred and fortieth thousand" (107). Here popularity is clearly associated with a lack of literary quality, and *Ivanhoe* is enthroned as "genuine" literature. Because Ainger names no names, it is difficult to know whether he specifically means to exclude women's writing from his definition of literature. However, the fact that he mentions only one worthy woman author in his article—Jane Austen—suggests that the blanks might be filled with the names of Mary Braddon and other popular woman novelists of the day. The focus on creating a distinctly male literary tradition intensifies in the first years of the twentieth century with the publication of anthologies such as the three-volume *Oxford Treasury of English Literature* (1906–8), which includes just one nineteenth-century woman writer: Jane Austen.[24] This is surprising given the fact that one of the anthology editors was Professor Grace Eleanor Hadow (1875–1940), a tutor at Lady Margaret Hall and pioneer of women's education at Oxford.[25]

Even if nineteenth-century women's literature was increasingly excluded from anthologies and histories of British literature, women were nonetheless still identified as students within the emerging academic discipline. Once English was institutionalized at Oxford, most students in the new field of study were female. In 1897, for example, ten women and four men stood for honors examinations in English; by 1906, the number was twenty-two students and five students, respectively.[26] Yet doubts about the study of English literature, even for women, remained. "Why should I send my daughter to a class to read a book?," Alfred Ainger imagines parents asking about the new field of English studies. His answer follows: "to have got so far towards understanding what literature is, and why certain writings have become classical and certain others have not."[27] Women students, like their male counterparts, were intended to learn the power of discriminating between ephemeral and "classical" texts. Consequently, literary value was increasingly defined as an inherent quality of a text, rather than as a product of discussion and evaluation. As women made inroads at the most distinguished British universities, they were asked to master an increasingly male literary canon of English classics, thus authorizing themselves as "serious" students within a legitimate field of study. As Brian Doyle points out, such a move was concomitant with a "concentration on a specific set of objects (the 'texts') and developing a strict 'scientific' method of understanding these objects."[28] As critics moved away from situating literature within what Leslie Stephen called the "whole social organism," they increasingly focused on a smaller number of literary masterpieces that could be decontextualized as artifacts of a dead language and culture.[29]

Indeed, with the increasing professionalization of English studies in the late nineteenth and early twentieth centuries came increasing focus on the text itself. Even before the New Critics began to theorize a more objective form of textual exegesis, late Victorian critics re-imagined the study of national literature as the exploration of universal themes in timeless literary texts. Alfred Ainger writes, "I have felt more and more that one mistake has been to magnify (as I have put it) the notes above the text, and to teach *round about* the great writers, while all the time the great writers themselves leave the young student, if not wearied and glad to hear the last of them, at least uninspired by them."[30] John Churton Collins likewise advocates the study of the "social, political, moral, [and] intellectual" context of literature but only if "accompanied throughout with illustrations drawn from the constituent elements of typical works."[31] One of the greatest faults of modern criticism, according to Henry Craik, is its biographical tendencies. The critic, he argues, feels obligated "not only to condone but to praise literary faults and eccentricities, on account of some supposed peculiarity of genius of which such eccentricities are the sign."[32] In recent criticism, he notes, the "memory of [Thomas] Carlyle has been covered with obloquy on account of defects of temper and of judgment," yet no critic has had the courage to focus on the "faults and affections of style" in the texts themselves (210). Likewise, George Eliot is venerated not for the greatness of her novels but for her ability to "repeat most exactly the favourite ideas which our age fancies to be its exclusive property" (210). Instead of focusing on authorial biography or social context, according to Craik, the critic must study literary masterpieces as models of taste and style (215).

Matthew Arnold perhaps defined the new approach most succinctly in 1864 when he called literary criticism a "disinterested endeavour to learn and propagate the best that is known and thought in the world."[33] Where contemporary literature was concerned, the critic's job was to "establish a current of fresh and true ideas" (282), but such an aim was complicated by the fact that "not very much" of contemporary English literature qualified as the "best that is known and thought in the world" (282). Arnold's wariness about contemporary literature is particularly evident in his review of Stopford Brooke's *Primer of English Literature* (1876).[34] It is an admirable aim, he notes, to develop a guide that shows the "growth of our literature, its series of productions, and their relative value" (844). However, he objects to Brooke's inclusion of contemporary literature, writing, "No man can trust himself to speak of his own time and his own contemporaries with the same sureness and proportion as of times and men gone by" (851). He then offers a sample passage, entreating Brooke to "make a clean sweep of all of this": "Charlotte Brontë revived in *Jane Eyre* the novel of Passion, and Miss Yonge set on foot the Religious novel in support of a special school of theology. Miss Martineau and Mr. Disraeli carried on the novel of Political opinion and economy, and Charles Kingsley applied the novel to the social and theological problems of our own day" (851). Indeed, in the 1897 revised edition of the primer, retitled *English Literature*, Brooke does briefly mention contemporary poetry, including the work of Christina Rossetti. However, he eliminates discussion of contemporary prose, including the passage cited above.[35] Brontë, Yonge, and Martineau are completely missing from the 1897 edition.

The decanonization of women prose writers, however, was clearly open for reassessment. When Brooke's *English Literature* was revised in 1919, some women writers were restored.[36] Two new chapters by George Carpenter were added detailing the history of English and American literature, 1832–92. In this edition, George Eliot and Elizabeth Gaskell are included, even if afforded only secondary status to Dickens and Thackeray. Likewise, Elizabeth Barrett Browning and Christina Rossetti are mentioned under the category of "other poets" (278). However, even if women authors were afforded secondary status, their reinclusion is significant in that it shows a field of study still subject to renegotiation and change. Indeed, even F. R. Leavis complained in 1932 that the "tradition has dissolved: the centre— Arnold's 'centre of intelligent and urbane spirit' . . . has vanished."[37] The lack of a common literary and intellectual culture, for Leavis and other New Critics, justified developing a more rigorous set of literary practices and aesthetic judgments that would enable criticism to return to an Arnoldian ideal.

Of course, even as English departments strove to authorize themselves in the academy by promoting text-centered, scientific criticism, their efforts were inseparable from nonspecialist literary practices, including the implementation of the blue plaque system, the formation of literary societies, the expansion of the National Trust, and the publication of popular scholarship. Literary study—both inside and outside the academy—aimed to foster a national culture, even if through different means. Such a national culture was formed by designating certain texts, landscapes, and authors as significant. Yet the effort to establish a national canon and an associated network of culturally significant landscapes was contingent and unsure. The Victorian desire to reimagine the past—to speak with the dead, as it were—was premised on both asserting and questioning definitions of literary value. Searching for lost writers and forgotten landscapes was just as gratifying as honoring the authors and spaces validated by cultural institutions. Such a quest enabled critics to reread history in gendered terms, reconsidering domestic arrangements, national landscapes, authorial bodies, and literary canons.

As we have seen, the obsession with literary celebrity not only served the interests of protofeminist criticism and historiography but a variety of other purposes as well: the professionalization of medicine, the formation of the open space movement, and the development of the British culture industries. Taken together, these interrelated developments relied on the trope of the celebrity author as a means of delimiting the appropriate objects and limits of professional inquiry. Which authors and texts should be studied at the university level? How should they be read? Which historic homes and landscapes are nationally significant? Who has the right to discuss the private lives of celebrities and in what context? These questions of course continue to spark lively discussion in the twenty-first century. Our enduring fascination with celebrity culture is rooted in the Victorian era, when the expansion of popular print culture provided opportunities for armchair tourists to experience the landscapes, homes, and lives of celebrities in a virtual way. Fascinated by the sensationalized spaces and personalities featured in newspapers and periodicals, readers were able to imagine new sexualities, gender roles, and domestic arrangements. Yet by reflecting on ephemeral landscapes and the spectral presences of lost writers, they engaged in a form of nostalgia that could be mobilized for a specific political purpose: preserving the landscapes, authors, and buildings threatened by the wheels of progress. The discourse on literary celebrity thus enabled Victorians to reconsider their relationship to history, formulating and challenging definitions of gender, authorship, and national culture.

Notes

Introduction

1. Maria Frawley, ed., *Life in the Sickroom*, by Harriet Martineau (Peterborough, Ontario: Broadview, 2003); Deborah Logan, ed., *Illustrations of Political Economy: Selected Tales*, by Harriet Martineau (Peterborough, Ontario: Broadview, 2004); Deborah Logan, ed., *The Collected Letters of Harriet Martineau*, 5 vols. (London: Pickering and Chatto, 2007).

2. Nicola Watson, ed., *Literary Tourism and Nineteenth-Century Culture* (Basingstoke, UK: Palgrave, 2009); Ann Hawkins and Maura Ives, ed., *Women Writers and the Artifacts of Celebrity in the Long Nineteenth Century* (Aldershot, UK: Ashgate, forthcoming).

3. Nicola Watson, *The Literary Tourist: Readers and Places in Romantic and Victorian Britain* (Basingstoke, UK: Palgrave, 2008); David Lowenthal, *The Past Is a Foreign Country* (Cambridge: Cambridge University Press, 1985); Dean MacCannell, *The Tourist: A New Theory of the Leisure Class* (New York: Schocken, 1976); James Buzard, *The Beaten Track: European Tourism, Literature, and the Ways to Culture, 1800–1918* (Oxford: Clarendon, 1993); John Glendening, *The High Road: Romantic Tourism, Scotland, and Literature, 1720–1820* (New York: St. Martin's, 1997).

4. Alexis Easley, *First-Person Anonymous: Women Writers and Victorian Print Media, 1830–70* (Aldershot, UK: Ashgate, 2004).

5. Mary Poovey, *Uneven Developments: The Ideological Work of Gender in Mid-Victorian England* (Chicago: University of Chicago Press, 1988); Joanne Shattock, ed., *Women and Literature in Britain, 1800–1900* (Cambridge: Cambridge University Press, 2001); Linda Peterson, *Becoming a Woman of Letters: Myths of Authorship and Facts of the Victorian Market* (Princeton, NJ: Princeton University Press, 2009); Marysa Demoor, ed., *Marketing the Author: Author Personae, Narrative Selves, and Self-Fashioning, 1880–1930* (Basingstoke, UK: Palgrave, 2004).

6. Mary Spongberg, *Writing Women's History since the Renaissance* (Basingstoke, UK: Palgrave, 2002); Rohan Maitzen, *Gender, Genre, and Victorian Historical Writing* (New York: Garland, 1998).

Chapter 1. The Virtual City

1. Francis Miltoun, *Dickens' London* (Boston: Page, 1903), 11.

2. There are, of course, many studies of Dickens and London. See, for example, Jeremy Tambling, *Going Astray: Dickens and London* (Harlow, UK: Pearson,

2009); Nicholas Freeman, *Conceiving the City: London, Literature and Art, 1870–1914* (Oxford: Oxford University Press, 2007); Grahame Smith, *Dickens and the Dream of Cinema* (Manchester, UK: Manchester University Press, 2003); Philip Collins, "Dickens and the City," in *Visions of the Modern City: Essays in History, Art, and Literature,* eds. William Sharpe and Leonard Wallock (New York: Columbia University Press, 1983), 97–117; F. S. Schwarzbach, *Dickens and the City* (London: Athlone, 1979); Raymond Williams, *The Country and the City* (New York: Oxford University Press, 1973); and Alexander Welsh, *The City of Dickens* (Oxford: Clarendon Press, 1971). My research builds on these studies by exploring the specific ways "Dickensland" was portrayed in the connected practices of literary tourism and literary criticism at the fin de siècle.

3. Jean Baudrillard, "Symbolic Exchange and Death," in *Selected Writings,* ed. Mark Poster, trans. Charles Levin, 2nd ed. (Stanford, CA: Stanford University Press, 2001), 147–48.

4. Jonathan Crary, *Techniques of the Observer: On Vision and Modernity in the Nineteenth Century* (Cambridge, MA: MIT Press, 1990), 14. See also Grahame Smith's *Dickens and the Dream of Cinema,* which explores how technological innovations such as train travel and photography shaped the visual interpretation of the city, thus pre-figuring the development of film technologies at the end of the century.

5. Freeman, *Conceiving the City,* 162. Freeman also discusses impressionistic and empiricist interpretations of the city in the years following Dickens's death, 1870–1914.

6. Frederic Harrison, "London Improvements," *New Review* 7 (October 1892): 414, 416.

7. Walter Dexter, "Charles Dickens's London," *English Illustrated Magazine* 25 (September 1901): 547. All further references to this article are cited parenthetically by page number in the text. Similarly, Francis Miltoun refers to the "holocaust" caused by urban improvements, which has led to the disappearance of "landmarks and shrines" in London. Miltoun, *Dickens' London,* 18.

8. See also Miltoun, *Dickens' London,* 18, 127.

9. Earlier in the century, Dickens's representations of the city are even less likely to be described as comprehensive or omniscient. In an 1858 article, for example, Walter Bagehot compared Dickens's genius to a newspaper where "every thing is there, and every thing is disconnected." [Walter Bagehot], "Charles Dickens," *National Review* 14 (October 1858): 468. In London, as in the modern newspaper, he writes, "there is every kind of person in some houses; but there is no more connection between the houses than between the neighbours in the lists of 'births, marriages, and deaths'" (468). Similarly, Dickens's "memory is full of instances of old buildings and curious people, and he does not care to piece them together. On the contrary, each scene, to his mind, is a separate scene,—each street a separate street" (468).

10. Ford Madox Hueffer [Ford Madox Ford], *The Soul of London: A Survey of a Modern City* (London: Alston Rivers, 1905), 15.

11. See Caroline Ticknor, "London and Charles Dickens," *The Lamp* 29 (August 1904): 34–36; and Charles Dickens, Jr., "Disappearing Dickensland," *North American Review* 156 (June 1893): 670–84.

12. T. Edgar Pemberton, *Dickens's London: or, London in the Works of Charles Dickens* (London: Tinsley, 1876); Charles Dickens, Jr., *Dickens's Dictionary of London, 1879: An Unconventional Handbook* (1879; repr., London: Howard Baker, 1972); Robert Allbut, *Rambles in Dickens' Land* (1886; repr., New York: Truslove, Hanson and Comba, 1899); Miltoun, *Dickens' London*; H. Snowden Ward and Catherine Ward, *The Real Dickens Land with an Outline of Dickens's Life* (London: Chapman and Hall, 1904); Frank Green, *London Homes of Dickens* (1928; repr., London: Folcroft, 1970). The publication of these guides was linked to actual tour guide services in some cases. For example, an advertisement in the back of Allbut's guide offers the author's services as a "competent escort" for "Dickensian rambles" in the city.

13. "Our '100-Picture' Gallery: Through Dickens-Land," *Strand Magazine* 33 (April 1907): 411–18. See also Ward & Ward, *Real Dickens Land*, which is richly illustrated with photographs. For a more recent example of the photo-tour genre, see Tambling's *Going Astray*.

14. Frank Green, *London Homes of Dickens*.

15. Allbut, *Rambles in Dickens' Land*, xxv. Indeed, even a fairly recent study claims that a Dickens character "can virtually walk off the page, and be treated as a personage with an identity distinct from that of its creator." Schwarzbach, *Dickens and the City*, 4.

16. William Hughes, *A Week's Tramp in Dickens-land; Together with Personal Reminiscences of the "Inimitable Boz" Therein Collected* (London: Chapman and Hall, 1893), xv–xvi.

17. Gerald Brenan, introduction to *Rambles in Dickens' Land*, by Robert Allbut (1886; repr., New York: Truslove, Hanson and Comba, 1899), xiv. All further references to this introduction are cited parenthetically by page number in the text.

18. J. Ashby-Sterry, "Charles Dickens and Southwark," *English Illustrated Magazine* 62 (November 1888): 105. All further references to this article are cited parenthetically by page number in the text.

19. William Sharp, "Literary Geography: The Country of Dickens," *Pall Mall Magazine* 29 (February 1903): 241.

20. "Charles Dickens and London," *Bookman* 41 (February 1912): 241. All further references to this article are cited parenthetically by page number in the text.

21. W. Kent, "The Blind Side of Dickens," *Bookman* 58 (June 1920): 110. All further references to this article are cited parenthetically by page number in the text.

22. "With Dickens in Hatton Garden," *Chambers's Journal* 5 (1902): 382. All further references to this article are cited parenthetically by page number in the text.

23. Brenan, introduction to *Rambles in Dickens' Land*, x.

24. "In the Footsteps of Dickens," *Bookworm* (January 1892): 78. All further references to this article are cited parenthetically by page number in the text.

25. Charles Dickens, Jr., "Disappearing Dickensland," 670. All further references to this article are cited parenthetically by page number in the text.

26. Charles Dickens, Jr., "Notes on Some Dickens Places and People," *Pall Mall Magazine* 9 (July 1896): 344.

27. Charley toured America in 1887, giving readings from his father's novels.

28. This family tradition was continued by several of Dickens's descendents, including Charley's son, also named Charles Dickens, who published his own guide to London in *Munsey's Magazine*. Charles Dickens III, "Relics of Dickens' London," *Munsey's Magazine* 27, no. 6 (September 1902): 833–42. For a later example, see Cedric and Monica Dickens's contributions to Kenneth Baxendale, *Charles Dickens' London, 1812–70* (West Wickham, Kent, UK: Alteridem, 1984).

29. Dickens, Charles, Jr., "Pickwickian Topography," *English Illustrated Magazine* 111 (December 1892): 186–98; Dickens, Jr., "Disappearing Dickensland"; Dickens, Jr., "Notes on Some Dickens Places and People."

30. Joss Lutz Marsh, "Imagining Victorian London, an Entertainment and Itinerary (Chas. Dickens' Guide)," *Stanford Humanities Review* 3, no. 1 (1993): 72.

31. Dickens, Jr., "Notes on Some Dickens Places and People," 352. All further references to this article are cited parenthetically by page number in the text.

32. Charles Dickens, *The Letters of Charles Dickens*, ed. Graham Storey and Kathleen Tillotson (Oxford: Clarendon, 1995), 8:245.

33. Jim Barloon, "The Black Hole of London: Rescuing Oliver Twist," *Dickens Studies Annual* 28 (1999): 8.

34. Crary, *Techniques of the Observer*, 13.

35. *A Dickens Pilgrimage* (New York: Dutton, 1914), 67. Reprinted from the *London Times*. See also the American Moncure Daniel Conway, who writes in his autobiography, "The more I saw of London the more I loved and honoured the London Dante who had invested it with romance, and peopled its streets and alleys with spirits, so that the huge city could never more be seen without his types and shadows." Moncure Daniel Conway, *Autobiography: Memories and Experiences* (Boston: Houghton Mifflin, 1905), 2:7.

36. Henry James, *Autobiography* (New York: Criterion, 1956), 388. All further references to this book are cited parenthetically by page number in the text.

37. By the end of its second year, the fellowship enrolled 6,500 members. See Mazzeno for further discussion of the early activities of the Dickens Fellowship. Laurence Mazzeno, *The Dickens Industry: Critical Perspectives, 1836–2005* (Rochester, NY: Camden House, 2008), 45–47.

38. Dickens Fellowship, *The Dickens House* (London: The Dickens Fellowship, n.d., ca. 1926), 1.

39. Green, *London Homes of Dickens*, 19.

40. Miltoun, *Dickens' London*, 127. All further references to this book are cited parenthetically by page number in the text.

41. Dickens, Jr., "Disappearing Dickensland," 678.

42. Dickens III, "Relics of Dickens' London," 834. All further references to this article are cited parenthetically by page number in the text.

43. Miltoun, *Dickens' London*, 127. See also Harger Ragan, who defends the authenticity of the Old Curiosity Shop by saying that the "novelist could as easily fancy its removal as he could fancy anything else in the story." Harger Ragan, "In the Footsteps of Dickens," *Cosmopolitan* 15 (May 1893): 4.

44. Miltoun, *Dickens' London*, 268. A similar claim is made by Gerald Brenan in his introduction to Allbut's guidebook, where he exclaims, "Let us make real

the scenes we have read of and dreamt of—peopling them with the folk of Dickens, so that familiar faces shall look upon us from familiar windows, familiar voices greet us as we pass." Brenan, introduction to *Rambles in Dickens' Land*, xxi–xxii.

45. John Tosh, *A Man's Place: Masculinity and the Middle-Class Home in Victorian England* (New Haven, CT: Yale University Press, 1999), 33.

46. See also Kitton's depiction of Dickens as a congenial host at Gad's Hill Place. Frederic Kitton, *Charles Dickens: His Life, Writings, and Personality* (London: Jack, 1902), 476–78.

47. Hans Christian Andersen, "A Visit to Charles Dickens," *Temple Bar* 31 (December 1870): 29. All further references to this article are cited parenthetically by page number in the text.

48. "The Late Charles Dickens," *London Journal* 52 (August 1870): 28.

49. After Dickens's death, his household goods were sold at public auction. The house was purchased by his son Charley, who sold the property in 1879. In 1924, the house was converted into a school. The building is slated to be converted into the Dickens Visitor Centre in 2012.

50. Moncure Daniel Conway, "Footprints of Charles Dickens," *Harper's New Monthly Magazine* 41 (September 1870): 614. All further references to this article are cited parenthetically by page number in the text.

51. Caroline Ticknor, "London and Charles Dickens," 34. All further references to this article are cited parenthetically by page number in the text.

52. The Dickens Fellowship, "Charles Dickens Museum," http://www.dickens museum.com.

53. Marsh, "Imagining Victorian London," 70.

54. Dickens World [visitor attraction], http://www.dickensworld.co.uk.

55. Dana Huntley, "Visiting in Dickens World," *British Heritage* (September 2008): 44.

56. Ibid.

57. Judith Flanders, "Great Forebodings about Dickens World," *The Guardian*, April 17, 2007, http://www. guardian.co.uk.

58. Dea Birkett, "Fake Snow and Faux Fun," *New Statesman* 136, nos. 4875–4877 (December 17–January 3, 2008): 25.

59. Dana Huntley notes that today "along Rochester's ancient High Street there is barely a shop, pub or eating place that doesn't play on a Dickensian theme in its name, décor or marketing." Huntley, "Visiting in Dickens World," 44.

CHAPTER 2. THE HAUNTING OF VICTORIAN LONDON

1. William Howitt, *Homes and Haunts of the Most Eminent British Poets* (London: Bentley, 1847); Walter Thornbury, *Haunted London* (London: Hurst and Blackett, 1865); Theodore Wolfe, *A Literary Pilgrimage among the Haunts of Famous British Authors* (Philadelphia: Lippincott, 1895); Marion Harland, *Where Ghosts Walk: The Haunts of Familiar Characters in History and Literature* (1895; repr., New York: Putnam, 1898); H. B. Baildon, *Homes and Haunts of Famous Authors* (London: Wells Gardner, Darton, 1906); E. Beresford Chancellor, *The Literary Ghosts*

of London: Homes and Footprints of Famous Men and Women (London: Richards, 1933).

2. For discussion of the complex relationship between women and public space during the Victorian era, see Judith Walkowitz, *City of Dreadful Delight: Narratives of Sexual Danger in Late-Victorian London* (Chicago: University of Chicago Press, 1992); Deborah Epstein Nord, "The Urban Peripatetic: Spectator, Streetwalker, Woman Writer," *Nineteenth-Century Literature* 46, no. 3 (1991): 351–75; and Lynda Nead, "Mapping the Self: Gender, Space and Modernity in Mid-Victorian London," in *Rewriting the Self: Histories from the Renaissance to the Present*, ed. Roy Porter (New York: Routledge, 1997), 167–85.

3. Lynda Nead, "Mapping the Self," 176.

4. Linda Shires, "The Author as Spectacle and Commodity: Elizabeth Barrett Browning and Thomas Hardy," in *Victorian Literature and the Victorian Visual Imagination,* ed. Carol Christ and John Jordan (Berkeley: University of California Press, 1995), 199.

5. Ibid., 201.

6. Virginia Woolf, "Great Men's Houses," in *The London Scene: Five Essays by Virginia Woolf* (New York: Random House, 1982), 23.

7. Leslie Stephen, *George Eliot* (New York: Macmillan, 1902), 5.

8. W. Robertson Nicoll, preface to *A History of English Literature*, ed. William Francis Collier (London: Nelson, 1910), vi.

9. Peter Mandler, "'The Wand of Fancy': The Historical Imagination of the Victorian Tourist," in *Material Memories*, ed. Marius Kwint, Christopher Breward, and Jeremy Aynsley (Oxford: Berg, 1999), 139.

10. Julian Wolfreys, *Victorian Hauntings: Spectrality, Gothic, the Uncanny and Literature* (London: Palgrave, 2002), 3.

11. Ibid. For further discussion of literary specters, see Dickerson, who examines the literary and social dimensions of Victorian women's spectrality. Vanessa Dickerson, *Victorian Ghosts in the Noontide: Women Writers and the Supernatural* (Columbia: University of Missouri Press, 1996).

12. For useful overviews the notion of the "uncanny" in literary contexts, see Nicolas Royle, *The Uncanny* (New York: Routledge, 2003); and Wolfreys, *Victorian Hauntings*.

13. Royle, *The Uncanny*, 16.

14. Washington Irving, *The Sketch Book of Geoffrey Crayon, Gent* (1819–20; repr., London: Dent, 1963), 268.

15. Sigmund Freud, *The Uncanny*, trans. David McLintock (New York: Penguin, 2003), 150.

16. Chancellor, *Literary Ghosts of London*, 213.

17. See Harold Macfarlane's "The Value of a Dead Celebrity," where he satirizes the habit of "relic collecting" among his contemporaries. He compiles the prices of various relics associated with dead celebrities (locks of hair, etc.) and concludes that the average dead celebrity would gross £5,000 on the open market. Harold Macfarlane, "The Value of a Dead Celebrity," *Cornhill Magazine* 8 (March 1900): 371.

18. For extensive discussion of the development of spiritualism and psychic research as major cultural preoccupations during the second half of the nine-

teenth century, see Janet Oppenheimer, *The Other World: Spiritualism and Psychical Research in England, 1850–1914* (Cambridge: Cambridge University Press, 1985); and Alex Owen, *The Darkened Room: Women, Power and Spiritualism in Late Victorian England* (1989; repr., Chicago: University of Chicago Press, 2004).

19. Lisa Brocklebank, "Psychic Reading," *Victorian Studies* 48, no. 2 (2005): 234.

20. Ibid.

21. For a discussion of Wilde's telepathic writings, see Elana Gomel, "'Spirits in the Material World': Spiritualism and Identity in the *Fin de Siècle*," *Victorian Literature and Culture* 35 (2007): 189–213; and for treatment of Tennyson's post-mortem communications, see "Our Gallery of Borderlanders: Tennyson," *Borderland* 4, no. 4 (1897): 349–59.

22. "Our Gallery of Borderlanders: Tennyson."

23. Sara Underwood, "Our Gallery of Borderlanders: Elizabeth Barrett Browning," *Borderland* 4, no. 4 (1897): 363. All further references to this article are cited parenthetically by page number in the text.

24. Sara Underwood reports that Taylor, an old friend of the Brownings, was cured of a fever after an encounter with Elizabeth Barrett Browning's ghost. Underwood, "Our Gallery of Borderlanders," 366.

25. "Our Gallery of Borderlanders: Tennyson," 349.

26. R. R. Bowker, "London as a Literary Centre," *Harper's New Monthly Magazine* 76 (May 1888): 815.

27. Bowker, "London as a Literary Centre," 842. Likewise, there was a sense in the periodical press that the literary center of the English speaking world was gradually shifting away from London. Brander Matthews, writing for the American *Bookman* in 1900, for example, predicted that by the end of the twentieth century, "most of the leading authors of English literature will be American and not British in their training, in their thought, in their ideals." Brander Matthews, "The Future Literary Centre of the English Language," *Bookman* 12, no. 3 (1900): 239. Due to the growth and expansion of American population and culture, he contends, "London sooner or later will cease to be the literary centre of the English-speaking race" (239).

28. Thornbury, *Haunted London*, v. All further references to this book are cited parenthetically by page number in the text.

29. Chancellor, *Literary Ghosts of London*, 318.

30. Quoted in Alice Corkran, *The Poet's Corner: or, Haunts and Homes of the Poets* (London: Ernest Nister, 1892), 1. Line numbers for this poem are cited parenthetically in the text.

31. Although the blue plaque campaigns began in 1867, most women writers' homes were not marked with plaques until the early to mid-twentieth century.

32. See Lootens for a detailed discussion of the critical construction of Rossetti's posthumous reputation as "sweet lady, and poet, and saint." Tricia Lootens, *Lost Saints: Silence, Gender, and Victorian Literary Canonization* (Charlottesville: University Press of Virginia, 1996), 158–84.

33. Bowker, "London as a Literary Centre," 827.

34. Katharine Tynan Hinkson, "Some Reminiscences of Christina Rossetti," *Bookman* (New York) 1, no. 1 (1895): 28. All further references to this article are cited parenthetically by page number in the text.

35. See Amy Levy, "The Old House"; Mary Coleridge, "The Witch"; E. Nesbit, "Haunted"; and Charlotte Mew, "The Farmer's Bride"—all anthologized in Angela Leighton and Margaret Reynolds, eds., *Victorian Women Poets: An Anthology* (Oxford: Blackwell, 1995).

36. Christina Rossetti, "At Home," in *The Complete Poems of Christina Rossetti*, ed. Betty Flowers and R. W. Crump (London: Penguin, 2001), 22. Line numbers for this poem are cited parenthetically in the text.

37. According to William Michael Rossetti's notes (1904), this poem was accompanied by "two coloured designs . . . No. 1 shows the blanched form of the ghost in a sky lit with cresset flames. On one side the sky is bright blue, the flames golden; on the other side, dark twilight gray, and the flames red. No. 2 is the globe of the earth, rudely lined for latitude and longitude. The equator divides it into a green northern and a grey-purple southern hemisphere. Over the former flare sunbeams in a blue sky; below the latter the firmament is dimly dark, and the pallid moon grey towards extinction." Quoted in Flowers and Crump, *Complete Poems of Christina Rossetti*, 889.

38. Elbert Hubbard, *Little Journeys to the Homes of Famous Women* (London: Putnam, 1897), 158. All further references to this book are cited parenthetically by page number in the text.

39. Edmund Gosse, "Christina Rossetti," *Century Magazine* 46 (June 1893): 212.

40. Brigden lists four sites associated with Elizabeth Barrett Browning's life in London: 74 Gloucester Place, 50 Wimpole Street, St. Marylebone Church, and Devonshire Street. Thomas Brigden, *Eminent Men and Women of Marylebone and Their Homes* (London: J. Bumpus, 1891).

41. Barrett Browning reinforced this notion through her own self-characterizations. She wrote to a fellow poet, "I live in London to be sure, and, except for the glory of it, I might live in a desert—so profound is my solitude, and so complete my isolation from things and persons without." Quoted in Brigden, *Eminent Men and Women of Marylebone,* 6. For a discussion of the ways Barrett Browning addressed notions of "spectacle and withdrawl" in her poetry, see Shires, "Author as Spectacle and Commodity," 202.

42. Hubbard, *Little Journeys,* 29.

43. Baildon, *Homes and Haunts,* 37 (his italics). See also Hubbard, who writes in *Little Journeys to the Homes of Famous Women,* "Much of the time Miss Barrett lived in a darkened room, seeing no one but her nurse, the physician, and her father" (27). Hubbard notes that after Robert came into her life, "Elizabeth Barrett ran up the shades and flung open the shutters. The sunlight came dancing through the apartment, flooding each dark corner and driving out all the shadows that lurked therein. It was no longer a darkened room" (36). Fawcett similarly reinforces Barrett's isolation: "She now lived in London with her father, and was confined to one large darkened room, and saw no one but her own family, and a few intimate friends, the chief of whom were Miss Mitford, Mrs. Jameson, and Mr. John Kenyon." Mrs. Henry Fawcett [Millicent Garrett Fawcett], *Some Eminent Women of Our Times* (London: Macmillan, 1889), 113–14.

44. Fawcett, *Some Eminent Women of Our Times,* 112.

45. Hubbard, *Little Journeys,* 6.

46. [Anne Thackeray Ritchie], "Elizabeth Barrett Browning," in the *Dictionary of National Biography*, ed. Leslie Stephen (London: Smith, Elder, 1886), 7:78–82.

47. John H. Ingram, *Elizabeth Barrett Browning* (Boston: Roberts, 1888), 263.

48. Quoted in Ingram, *Elizabeth Barrett Browning*, 263.

49. Ingram, *Elizabeth Barrett Browning*, 263.

50. Hubbard, *Little Journeys*, 20–21.

51. Baildon, *Homes and Haunts*, 46–47.

52. Samantha Matthews, "Entombing the Woman Poet: Tributes to Elizabeth Barrett Browning," *Studies in Browning and His Circle* 24 (June 2001): 47.

53. Matthews, "Entombing the Woman Poet," 49.

54. Quoted in Arthur Adcock, *Famous Houses and Literary Shrines of London* (London: Dent, 1912), 253–54.

55. Wolfe, *Literary Pilgrimage*; Adcock, *Famous Houses*; Alan Eyre, *St. John's Wood: Its History, Its Houses, Its Haunts, and Its Celebrities* (London: Chapman, 1913); Gordon Home, *What to See in England* (London: Black, 1903); Thomas Barratt, *The Annals of Hampstead*, 3 vols. (London: Black, 1912).

56. Barratt, *Annals of Hampstead*, 3:11.

57. Wolfe, *Literary Pilgrimage*, 23.

58. Stephen, *George Eliot*, 4.

59. Charles Olcott, *George Eliot: Scenes and People in Her Novels* (New York: Crowell, 1910), 5. All further references to this book are cited parenthetically by page number in the text.

60. Sidney Lanier, *The English Novel: A Study in the Development of Personality* (New York: Scribner's, 1908), 164.

61. Olcott, *George Eliot*, 6.

62. W. Robertson Nicoll, preface to *A Mill on the Floss*, by George Eliot (London: Dent, 1908), viii.

63. MacCannell, *The Tourist*, 13.

64. William Archer, "An Academy of the Dead," *Monthly Review* 1 (December 1900): 118–27. All further references to this article are cited parenthetically by page number in the text.

65. A memorial stone honoring George Eliot was placed in Poets' Corner in 1980, and a stained-glass window honoring Elizabeth Gaskell will be erected in September of 2010. However, Christina Rossetti has not yet been memorialized in Westminster Abbey.

66. MacCannell, *The Tourist*, 13.

CHAPTER 3. THE WOMAN OF LETTERS AT HOME

I would like to express my gratitude to Barbara Todd and Pamela Corpron Parker for their invaluable feedback on drafts of this chapter. An earlier version of this chapter appeared in *Victorian Literature and Culture* 34, no. 1 (2006): 291–310.

1. Martineau's publications before moving to the Lake District in 1846 include *Illustrations of Political Economy*, 9 vols. (London: Charles Fox, 1832–34); *Society in America* (1837; repr., London: Transaction, 1981); *Retrospect of Western*

Travel, 2 vols. (London: Saunders and Otley, 1838); *Deerbook*, 3 vols. (London: Edward Moxon, 1839); *The Hour and the Man*, 3 vols. (London: Edward Moxon, 1841); *Life in the Sickroom* (London: Edward Moxon, 1844); and *Letters on Mesmerism*, 2nd ed. (London: Edward Moxon, 1845).

2. For a partial listing of Martineau's early essays, see Francis Mineka, *The Dissidence of Dissent: The Monthly Repository, 1806–38* (Chapel Hill: University of North Carolina Press, 1944); and Walter Houghton, ed., *The Wellesley Index to Victorian Periodicals, 1824–1900*, 5 vols. (Toronto: University of Toronto Press, 1966–89).

3. Ernest de Selincourt, introduction to *Wordsworth's Guide to the Lakes*, by William Wordsworth (1835; repr., Oxford: Oxford University Press, 1970), ix.

4. See James Buzard, *The Beaten Track: European Tourism, Literature, and the Ways to Culture, 1800–1918* (Oxford: Clarendon, 1993), 20–21; W. M. Merchant, introduction to *A Guide through the District of the Lakes in the North of England*, by William Wordsworth (London: Hart-Davis, 1951), 9–15; and Peter Bicknell, introduction to *The Illustrated Wordsworth's Guide to the Lakes* (New York: Congdon and Weed, 1984), 11–15.

5. See Ann Radcliffe, *Observations during a Tour to the Lakes of Lancashire, Westmoreland and Cumberland* (London: Robinson, 1795); and Thomas Gray, *Sketch of a Tour from Lancaster round the Principal Lakes in Lancashire, Cumberland, and Westmoreland: to which is Added, Mr. Gray's Journal* (Carlisle, UK: F. Jolie, 1803).

6. Buzard, *Beaten Track*, 6.

7. Ibid.

8. Harriet Martineau, *Autobiography*, 2 vols. (1877; repr., London: Virago, 1983), 2:212, 225.

9. Ibid., 2:213.

10. Deborah Logan, ed., *The Collected Letters of Harriet Martineau* (London: Pickering and Chatto, 2007), 3:18–19.

11. Martineau, *Autobiography*, 2:225.

12. James Payn, *Some Literary Recollections* (London: Smith, Elder, 1884), 103.

13. Martineau, *Autobiography*, 2:411.

14. Ibid., 2:414. All further references to this book are cited parenthetically by page number in the text.

15. In addition to the articles cited below, see "Lake and Mountain Holidays," published in *The People's Journal* 2 (July 1846): 1–3, 72–74, 149–50.

16. Harriet Martineau, "A Year at Ambleside," in *Harriet Martineau at Ambleside*, ed. Barbara Todd (Carlisle: Bookcase, 2002), 69–70. All further references to this book are cited parenthetically by page number in the text.

17. In her *Autobiography*, Martineau also uses a seasonal metaphor to discuss her own life stages. She remarks that after her years in Tynemouth, she did not realize that the "spring, summer, and autumn of life were yet to come. . . . At past forty years of age, I began to relish life, without drawback." Martineau, *Autobiography*, 2:205.

18. She completed only thirteen.

19. For discussion of the reception of Martineau's public persona before moving to the Lake District, see Patricia Marks, "Harriet Martineau: *Fraser's* 'Maid of (Dis)Honor,'" *Victorian Periodicals Review* 19, no. 1 (1986): 28–34; and Alexis

Easley, "Victorian Women Writers and the Periodical Press: The Case of Harriet Martineau," *Nineteenth-Century Prose* 24, no. 1 (1997): 39–50.

20. See also Harriet Martineau, "Lights of the English Lake District," *Atlantic Monthly* 7 (1861): 556.

21. Other visitors and friends planted trees on Martineau's property. See William Charles Macready, *The Diaries of William Charles Macready*, ed. William Toynbee (New York: Benjamin Blom, 1969), 2:331; and R. K. Webb, *Harriet Martineau: A Radical Victorian* (London: Heinemann, 1960), 255. This makes it especially interesting that Martineau chooses to focus on the "Wordsworth tree."

22. "Literary Relics," *Chambers's Edinburgh Journal* 6 (December 1846): 382. For a fascinating discussion of the so-called Wellington tree on the battlefield at Waterloo, see Stuart Semmel, "Reading the Tangible Past: British Tourism, Collecting, and Memory after Waterloo," *Representations* 69 (2000): 9–37.

23. For an analysis of the positive aspects of Martineau's relationship with Wordsworth, see Kenneth Fielding, *Harriet Martineau and William Wordsworth* (Rydal, UK: Rydal Church Trust, 2002).

24. For a discussion of Martineau's representations of Wordsworth in her *Autobiography*, see David Amigoni, "Gendered Authorship, Literary Lionism and the Virtues of Domesticity: Contesting Wordsworth's Fame in the Writings of Harriet Martineau and Thomas Carlyle," *Critical Survey* 13, no. 2 (2001): 26–41. Amigoni argues that Martineau contests Wordsworth's masculine model of solitary authorship by depicting "domesticity and the feminine . . . [as] sources of positive value" (37). Of course, I am arguing that Martineau has a much more complex relationship with Wordsworth than Amigoni allows. In her *Autobiography* and elsewhere in her writings on the Lake District, Martineau at once emulates and revises the narrative of Wordsworth's literary career.

25. Martineau, *Autobiography*, 2:238.

26. Martineau, "Lights of the English Lake District," 545 (my emphasis). All further references to this article are cited parenthetically by page number in the text.

27. Harriet Martineau, *Guide to Windermere* (Windermere, UK: J. Garnett, 1854); Harriet Martineau, *Guide to Keswick and Its Environs* (Windermere, UK: J. Garnett, 1857). The title of the *Complete Guide* varies somewhat through various editions. For example, in 1876 it is titled *The English Lake District*. The *Complete Guide* was designed as a portable guide for travelers, and in 1858 it was also published in large-scale format as a gift book with hand-colored plates.

28. Logan, *Collected Letters of Harriet Martineau*, 3:325.

29. Payn, *Some Literary Recollections*, 128–29. After Martineau's health declined in the late 1850s, her niece Maria took over the research and editing of the guidebooks. See Todd, *Harriet Martineau at Ambleside*, 191.

30. Payn, *Some Literary Recollections*, 128.

31. The first of these guides was published as an anonymous introduction to John Wilkinson's *Select Views of Cumberland, Westmoreland, and Lancashire*. In 1822, the essay was republished under Wordsworth's name as *A Description of the Scenery of the Lakes in the North of England*. And in 1835, it appeared as *A Guide through the District of the Lakes in the North of England*. See Merchant, introduction to *A Guide through the District*, 30–31.

32. For additional information about the publication history of Wordsworth's *Guide,* see Selincourt, introduction to *Wordsworth's Guide to the Lakes*; Merchant, introduction to *A Guide through the District*; and Peter Newby, "Literature and the Fashioning of Tourist Taste," in *Humanistic Geography and Literature: Essays on the Experience of Place,* ed. Douglas C. D. Pocock (London: Croom Helm, 1981), 130–41.

33. There were other competitors as well, including *Adams's Illustrated Guide to the Lakes* (London: W. J. Adams, 1855); *The English Lakes* (London: Nelson, 1859); and *Black's Picturesque Guide to the English Lakes* (Edinburgh: A. and C. Black, 1851). For a review of various guides to the Lake District, see Clement Shorter, "A Literary Causerie," *Bookman* 15 (October 1898): 6–8.

34. As Peter Newby points out, the number of tourists grew steadily after 1847, reaching almost half a million by 1907. Newby, "Literature and the Fashioning of Tourist Taste," 134. See Buzard for extensive discussion of railway travel and its effect on tourist practices. Buzard, *Beaten Track,* 35–44.

35. Shorter, "Literary Causerie," 7.

36. Harriet Martineau, *Complete Guide to the English Lakes,* 1st ed. (Windermere, UK: J. Garnett, 1855). All further references to this book are cited parenthetically by page number in the text.

37. Newby, "Literature and the Fashioning of Tourist Taste," 134.

38. Martineau, *Autobiography,* 2:266.

39. The intrusiveness of literary tourists only increased. After Martineau became ill in the late 1850s, her doctor wrote to the newspapers declaring the "absolute necessity" of literary tourists "not harassing her by the intrusion of visits of mere idle curiosity" (quoted in Webb, *Harriet Martineau,* 311).

40. Buzard, *Beaten Track,* 6.

41. Newby, "Literature and the Fashioning of Tourist Taste," 131.

42. It is important to note that Wordsworth's critiques of "false taste" in the Lake District are primarily directed at new residents of the region, not tourists. See William Wordsworth, *A Guide through the District of the Lakes in the North of England,* ed. W. M. Merchant (1835; repr., London: Hart-Davis, 1951), 104–8.

43. Semmel, "Reading the Tangible Past," 10 (his emphasis).

44. Some recent reprints include Peter Bicknell, ed., *The Illustrated Wordsworth's Guide to the Lakes* (New York: Congdon and Weed, 1984); Martineau's *Guide to Windermere* (1854; repr., Giggleswick, UK: Castleberg, 1995); and Martineau's *Directory of the Lake District,* ed. R. Grigg (Warrington, UK: Beewood Coldell, 1989).

45. For a discussion of the development of cultural anxieties regarding the commodification of culture during the nineteenth century, see Buzard, *Beaten Track,* 11.

46. Shorter, "A Literary Causerie," 7. All further references to this article are cited parenthetically by page number in the text.

47. See also Payn's description of his visits to the Knoll in *Some Literary Recollections.*

48. Maria Weston Chapman, "Memorials," in *Autobiography,* by Harriet Martineau (London: Smith, Elder, 1877), 3:379, 380, 382. All further references to these memorials are cited parenthetically by page number in the text.

49. Quoted in Chapman, "Memorials,"401.

50. See Henry Jenkinson's *Practical Guide to the English Lake District,* 6th ed. (London: E. Stanford, 1879), 5, 58; Herman Prior's *Guide to the Lake District of England,* 5th ed. (Windermere: J. Garnett, 1885), 146; and *English Lakes* (London: Nelson, 1859), xxxix, 13.

51. For example, the Knoll is not mentioned in Eliza Lynn Linton's *The Lake Country* (London: Smith, Elder, 1864) or Edwin Waugh's *In the Lake Country* (Manchester, UK: John Heywood, 1880).

52. Martineau is mentioned in *Ward and Lock's Pictorial and Descriptive Guide to the English Lake District* (London: Ward and Lock, 1915); Frederick Sessions's *Literary Celebrities of the English Lake-District* (London: E. Stock, 1905); and A. G. Bradley's *Highways and Byways in the Lake District* (London: Macmillan, 1901); but not in Daniel Scott's *Cumberland and Westmoreland* (London: Metheun, 1920) or Ashley Abraham's *Beautiful Lakeland* (Keswick, UK: Abraham, 1912).

53. It is difficult to find references to the Knoll in mid- to late-twentieth century guidebooks to the Lake District. For example, the Knoll was omitted from Ian Ousby's popular *Blue Guide to Literary Britain and Ireland,* 2nd ed. (London: A. and C. Black, 1990).

54. David Lowenthal, *The Past Is a Foreign Country* (Cambridge: Cambridge University Press, 1985), 240.

CHAPTER 4. HARRIET MARTINEAU

This chapter is also scheduled to appear in *Women's History Review* (forthcoming).

1. Harriet Martineau, *The History of England from the Commencement of the Nineteenth Century to the Crimean War,* 4 vols. (Philadelphia: Porter and Coates, 1864–66).

2. "Miss Martineau's *The History of the Peace,*" *National Quarterly Review* 9 (September 1864): 387.

3. Rosemary Jann, *The Art and Science of Victorian History* (Columbus: Ohio State University Press, 1985), 212.

4. For an overview of the Whig historical tradition, see J. W. Burrow, *A Liberal Descent: Victorian Historians and the English Past* (Cambridge: Cambridge University Press, 1981); Neil McCaw, *George Eliot and Victorian Historiography: Imagining the National Past* (London: Palgrave, 2000); Bonnie Smith, "The Contribution of Women to Modern Historiography in Great Britain, France, and the United States, 1750–1940," *American Historical Review* 89, no. 3 (1984): 709–32; Rosemary Mitchell, *Picturing the Past: English History in Text and Image, 1830–70* (Oxford: Clarendon, 2000); Jann, *Art and Science of Victorian History.*

5. In the *History,* Martineau writes, "We have, what the old Tories have not, and cannot conceive of,—the deepest satisfaction in every proof that the national soul is alive and awake, that the national mind is up and stirring." Martineau, *History of England,* 3:164. Martineau thus expressed a basic tenet of Whig history, as identified by Neil McCaw, the idea that the "present therein resides at the summit of human (historical) experience, within a totalized

national history and experience." McCaw, *George Eliot and Victorian Historiography*, 36.

6. The use of the term *English* rather than *British* is conventional in most Whig histories of the period, including Martineau's. Even though the *History* is focused on the Empire, with a particular focus on Anglo-Irish relations, it nevertheless reflects what Rosemary Mitchell has called the "hegemony of the English historical vision." Mitchell, *Picturing the Past*, 10.

7. See Rohan Maitzen, *Gender, Genre, and Victorian Historical Writing* (New York: Garland, 1998); Mitchell, *Picturing the Past*. Other examples of Victorian near-contemporary history include Archibald Alison's *History of Europe during the French Revolution* (Edinburgh: Blackwood, 1833–42); Thomas Carlyle's *The French Revolution* (London: Chapman and Hall, 1837); John Roebuck's *History of the Whig Ministry of 1830 to the Passing of the Reform Bill* (London: J. W. Parker, 1852); Albany Fonblanque's *England under Seven Administrations* (London: Bentley, 1837); and George Porter's *The Progress of the Nation in Its Various Social and Economical Relations from the Beginning of the Nineteenth Century to the Present Time* (London: Knight, 1836–43). Writing contemporary history seems to have been a somewhat unusual enterprise at the time, however. A critic for the *Christian Examiner* notes that "of this nineteenth century, Miss Martineau is now the most complete English historian." "Miss Martineau's History of England," *Christian Examiner and Religious Miscellany* 81, no. 2 (1866): 83.

8. Harriet Martineau, *Autobiography*, 2 vols. (1877; repr. London: Virago, 1983). The autobiography was published posthumously in 1877.

9. As many critics have noted, women's work as historians is best understood by working across genre. Mary Spongberg writes, "'Women's history' in the past took multiple forms, and evolved both in relation to and in reaction to masculinist conceptions of history and the prevailing prescriptions of gender." Mary Spongberg, *Writing Women's History since the Renaissance* (Basingstoke: Palgrave, 2002), 6. Such an approach is especially appropriate for investigating the work of Harriet Martineau. As Deborah Logan has pointed out, "It is revealing to consider the intersections in her [Martineau's] writing between what we have come to regard as sharply distinct genres—biography, autobiography, journalism, sociology, history, literature, and fiction—but which are in fact quite intimately linked and ultimately resistant to the sorts of arbitrary distinctions imposed on them by individual disciplines." Deborah Logan, introduction to *Harriet Martineau's Writing on British History and Military Reform* (London: Pickering and Chatto, 2005), 1:xvii–xviii.

10. There are a wide variety of critical and historical studies on this topic. See, for example, Jann, *Art and Science of Victorian History*; and Mitchell, *Picturing the Past*.

11. For an overview of the variety of histories written by women during the early nineteenth century, see Spongberg, *Writing Women's History*, 109–29; Maitzen, *Gender, Genre, and Victorian Historical Writing*, 3–26; Mitchell, *Picturing the Past*, 140–69; and Rosemary Mitchell, "'The Busy Daughters of Clio': Women Writers of History from 1820–1880," *Women's History Review* 7, no. 1 (1998): 107–34. Curiously, it is also possible that women writers viewed women's history writing as a lesser genre. Elizabeth Barrett Browning, when hearing of Martineau's

decision to write the *History*, remarked, "I regret her fine imagination being so wasted." Philip Kelley, Scott Lewis, and Edward Hagan, eds., *The Brownings' Correspondence* (Winfield, KS: Wedgestone Press, 1984–), 15:143. It is important to note that Barrett Browning wrote this comment in 1848, one year before the publication of the *History*; thus, she was clearly commenting on Martineau's choice of genre, not the quality of her writing.

12. The *History of England during the Thirty Years' Peace* was one of a series of works of popular history published by Knight. His other publications in this vein include Porter's *Progress of the Nation; The Penny Cyclopaedia of the Society for the Diffusion of Useful Knowledge* (London: Knight, 1833–43); and George Craik's *The Pictorial History of England: Being a History of the People, as well as a History of the Kingdom* (London: Knight, 1849).

13. *Illustrations of Political Economy*, 9 vols. (London: Charles Fox, 1832–34); *Society in America* (1837; repr., London: Transaction, 1981); and *Retrospect of Western Travel*, 2 vols. (London: Saunders and Otley, 1838).

14. Charles Knight, *Passages of a Working Life during Half a Century*, 3 vols. (London: Bradbury, 1865), 3:74.

15. Martineau, *History of England*, 1:1.

16. In this regard, Martineau perhaps differs from many other women historians of the period. As Maitzen points out, most Victorian women historians tended to "emphasize their difference, their separation, from the history men." Maitzen, *Gender, Genre, and Victorian Historical Writing*, 55. See also Mitchell, "Busy Daughters of Clio," 119–23.

17. Martineau, *History of England*, 1:1.

18. In her *Autobiography*, Martineau was more specific, noting that she began the project in August of 1848 and concluded in November of 1849. Martineau, *Autobiography*, 318, 320. R. K. Webb notes that the "book [Martineau's *History*] was published in thirty monthly numbers, for which she received forty pounds each." R. K. Webb, *Harriet Martineau: A Radical Victorian* (London: Heinemann, 1960), 277.

19. Martineau, *Autobiography*, 2:318. All further references to this book are cited parenthetically by page number in the text.

20. See Martineau's *Autobiography*, 2:301. See also Deborah Logan's bibliography of Martineau's sources. Logan, introduction, 1:xxxiii–lvi.

21. "I was indebted to him for every kind of encouragement," Martineau writes in her *Autobiography*, 2:319. This included an extended visit at Knight's home in the autumn of 1849. The friendship became strained after the publication of Martineau's atheistic *Atkinson Letters*, which may have led Knight to abandon a projected continuation of the *History*, 1846 to the present. Martineau later wrote this projected volume for the 1864 American edition. See Mitchell's "Busy Daughters of Clio" for a discussion of the important yet contradictory role of male mentors in Victorian women's development as historians.

22. Deborah Logan, ed., *The Collected Letters of Harriet Martineau* (London: Pickering and Chatto, 2007), 3:148.

23. Maria Weston Chapman, "Memorials," in *Autobiography*, by Harriet Martineau (London: Smith, Elder, 1877), 3:334. All further references to these memorials are cited parenthetically by page number in the text.

24. Charles MacFarlane, *Reminiscences of a Literary Life* (New York: Scribner's, 1917), 93, 95. This memoir was written in 1855 and published posthumously. It is likely that Knight's decision to exclude MacFarlane was based partly on doubts about his friend's abilities as a historian. See Knight, *Passages of a Working Life*, 2:260.

25. Chapman, "Memorials," 3:334 (Chapman's emphasis).

26. MacFarlane, *Reminiscences*, 95.

27. Elisabeth Sanders Arbuckle, ed., *Harriet Martineau's Letters to Fanny Wedgwood* (Stanford, CA: Stanford University Press, 1983), 108. Webb notes that "by summer, 1849, the sale had doubled and was still increasing." Webb, *Harriet Martineau*, 277–78.

28. In addition to the *Christian Examiner* and *National Quarterly Review* articles cited above, see "Review of *The History of England during the Thirty Years' Peace*," *Bentley's Miscellany* 27 (March 1850): 310–11; "Miss Martineau's Introduction to the *History of the Peace*," *Littell's Living Age* 30 (1851): 136–38; "Contemporary England," *New Englander* 25 (1866): 618–52. Even the usually hostile *Quarterly Review* found Martineau's *History* a "book likely to survive the fleeting publications of the day." "Mr. Roebuck and Miss Martineau," *Quarterly Review* 91 (1852): 169.

29. [George Henry Lewes], "Review of *The History of England during the Thirty Years' Peace, 1815–1845*," *British Quarterly Review* 11 (May 1850): 356. All further references to this article are cited parenthetically by page number in the text. See Maitzen for an overview of the Victorian debate over women's suitability as historians in *Gender, Genre, and Victorian Historical Writing*, 3–26.

30. See Maitzen, *Gender, Genre, and Victorian Historical Writing*; Smith, "Contribution of Women to Modern Historiography"; and Mitchell, "Busy Daughters of Clio," for discussion of the rise of social history during the nineteenth century.

31. Logan, *Collected Letters of Harriet Martineau*, 3:144.

32. Martineau, *Autobiography*, 2:309.

33. See Webb for a discussion of Martineau's early development as a national instructor. Webb, *Harriet Martineau*, 99–133.

34. "Miss Martineau's *The History of the Peace*," 388.

35. Linda Colley, *Britons: Forging the Nation, 1707–1837* (New Haven, CT: Yale University Press, 1992), 272.

36. Ibid.

37. Martineau, *History of England*, 2:283. All further references to this book are cited parenthetically by page number in the text.

38. Colley, *Britons*, 273.

39. Martineau, *Autobiography*, 1:81.

40. Martineau, *History of England*, 4:184.

41. Martineau, *Society in America*, 291.

42. Martineau, *History of England*, 4:185.

43. In this regard, Martineau is an important forerunner to the explicitly feminist historians of the second half of the nineteenth century. As Mary Spongberg has pointed out, "Women historians influenced by first-wave feminism used history not only to highlight women's oppression, but to challenge the idea that

women were only domestic beings; to force the lives of 'great women' into the popular imagination and to record their own struggles to gain greater political equality." *Writing Women's History,* 131.

44. Martineau, *History of England,* 3:181.

45. [Harriet Martineau], "Female Industry," *Edinburgh Review* 109 (April 1859): 293–336. For background on the Langham Place group, see Candida Lacey, ed., *Barbara Leigh Smith Bodichon and the Langham Place Group* (1986; repr., London: Routledge, 2001); Solveig Robinson, "'Amazed at Our Success': The Langham Place Editors and the Emergence of a Feminist Critical Tradition," *Victorian Periodicals Review* 29, no. 2 (1996): 159–72; and Sheila Herstein, "*The English Woman's Journal* and the Langham Place Circle: A Feminist Forum and Its Women Editors," in *Innovators and Preachers: The Role of the Editor in Victorian England,* ed. Joel Weiner (Westport, CT: Greenwood, 1985), 61–76.

46. For an overview of Martineau's contributions to the Woman Question, see Valerie Sanders, *Reason over Passion: Harriet Martineau and the Victorian Novel* (Sussex, UK: Harvester Press, 1986), 168–85; Valerie Pichanick, "An Abominable Submission: Harriet Martineau's Views on the Role and Place of Woman," *Women's Studies* 5 (1977): 13–32; Alexis Easley "Gendered Observations: Harriet Martineau and the Woman Question," in *Victorian Women Writers and the "Woman Question,"* ed. Nicola Thompson (Cambridge: Cambridge University Press, 1999), 80–98; and Caroline Roberts, *The Woman and the Hour: Harriet Martineau and Victorian Ideologies* (Toronto: University of Toronto Press, 2002).

47. Martineau would later perfect the art of obituary writing as a contributor to the *Daily News.* Selected memoirs of the "distinguished dead" were republished in Harriet Martineau, *Biographical Sketches* (London: Macmillan, 1869).

48. Martineau, *History of England,* 2:499.

49. Lewes, "Review," 371.

50. Martineau, *History of England,* 4:605. Martineau likewise refers to Ann Radcliffe as the "mother of modern English romance," 2:497.

51. Arbuckle, *Harriet Martineau's Letters to Fanny Wedgwood,* 108 (Martineau's emphasis). Martineau was motivated to rewrite the chapters because in her view the book's success had ensured that it would "now certainly be a standard" history of the period. Thus, she felt that it "should be all my own." Logan, *Collected Letters of Harriet Martineau,* 3:224. Martineau's proposal to rewrite the Craik and Mac-Farlane chapters was rejected by her publisher, and the "dreary" chapters were republished verbatim. Logan, *Collected Letters of Harriet Martineau,* 4:70–71.

52. Martineau, *Society in America,* 53.

53. Martineau, *History of England,* 4:214.

54. [Harriet Martineau], "Literary Lionism," *London and Westminster Review* 32 o.s. (April 1839): 275.

55. Martineau, *History of England,* 4:215.

56. Martineau, "Literary Lionism," 281.

57. "Miss Martineau's History of England," 83.

58. "Contemporary England," 620.

59. The only exception is a footnote where she draws attention to her firsthand experience as source material for her chapter on Lord Durham. Martineau, *History of England,* 4:145.

60. See chapter 3.

61. Logan, *Collected Letters of Harriet Martineau*, 3:148 (Martineau's emphasis).

62. Arbuckle, *Harriet Martineau's Letters to Fanny Wedgwood*, 275. All further references to this book are cited parenthetically by page number in the text.

63. Martineau, *Autobiography*, 1:349.

64. This is not to say that Martineau objected to vivid narration or other novelistic techniques in her history writing. As Deborah Logan has pointed out, there are decided affinities between Martineau's fiction and history writing. Logan, *Harriet Martineau's Writing on British History*, 1:xvii. Interestingly, George Eliot privately objected to Martineau's "sentimental, rhetorical style." George Eliot, *The Journals of George Eliot*, ed. Margaret Harris and Judith Johnston (Cambridge: Cambridge University Press, 1998), 73.

65. Martineau, *Autobiography*, 1:400.

66. Interestingly, though, Martineau privately expressed pleasure that the publication of the *History* had changed public perception of her character. In a letter to Helen Martineau, she writes that she was "rather amused . . . at the astonishment of people (strangers) who had before fancied me a violent politician." Logan, *Collected Letters of Harriet Martineau*, 3:145–46.

67. Martineau, *Autobiography*, 2:447.

68. Martineau, *History of England*, 4:610.

69. Martineau, *Autobiography*, 2:304.

70. Martineau, *History of England*, 4:209.

71. Martineau, *Autobiography*, 2:124.

72. Martineau, *History of England*, 4:210.

73. Martineau, *Autobiography*, 2:127.

74. In addition to the examples cited below, see Martineau's cross-references to the *History* in the *Autobiography*, 1:433 and 2:246.

75. Jann, *Art and Science of Victorian History*, xiv–xv.

76. Martineau, *History of England*, 4:606.

77. Carlyle's *Past and Present* had been published by Chapman and Hall in 1843, the first two volumes of Macaulay's *History* had been published by J. M. Dent in 1848, and Hallam's *Constitutional History* had been published by John Murray in 1827.

78. Martineau, *History of England*, 4:607.

79. The biographies of the great Victorian historians are followed by tributes to Dickens and Bulwer, who are, in Martineau's view, the two great novelists of her age. In the 1864 edition, Martineau lists no women among the great novelists of the present day. Interestingly, in the original 1849–50 edition of the *History*, two women were included: Joanna Baillie and Maria Edgeworth. However, by 1864, both had died, so Martineau converted their biographies to obituaries and moved them into the necrology section of the chapter. It is interesting that by 1865 Martineau did not find replacements for the women writers she had once included in the pantheon of contemporary literary greats. Granted, she did not add any new male biographies either, so the omission is perhaps simply a failure of effort rather than a marker of her disappointment with latter-day claimants to literary fame.

80. Martineau, *Autobiography*, 1:349.

81. Martineau, *History of England*, 2:497. Martineau is most likely referring to Thrale's *Anecdotes of the Late Samuel Johnson* (London: T. Cadell, 1786).

82. Jameson was an influential art historian who published *Memoirs of Celebrated Female Sovereigns* (London: Colburn and Bentley, 1831) and *Legends of the Madonna* (London: Brown, Green, and Longmans, 1852); Penrose, pseud. "Mrs. Markham," was the author of the best-selling *History of England* (Edinburgh: Constable, 1823). Agnes Strickland, working with her sister Elizabeth, wrote *The Lives of the Queens of England* (London: Colburn, 1840–48), and Hannah Lawrance was the author of *The Historical Memoirs of the Queens of England* (London: Edward Moxon, 1838).

83. As Linda Peterson has pointed out, Martineau's also distanced herself from female literary tradition in her *Autobiography*. Linda Peterson, *Traditions of Victorian Women's Autobiography: The Poetics and Politics of Life Writing* (Charlottesville: University Press of Virginia, 1999), 67.

84. Mitzi Myers, "*Harriet Martineau's Autobiography*: The Making of a Female Philosopher," in *Women's Autobiography: Essays in Criticism*, ed. Estelle Jelinek (Bloomington: Indiana University Press, 1980), 67.

CHAPTER 5. ROOMS OF THE PAST

This chapter was previously published in *Clio's Daughters: Victorian Women Making History*, ed. Lynette Felber (Newark: Delaware Universty Press, 2007).

1. Of course, women's involvement in the field of domestic architecture as managers, designers, and writers begins much earlier than the nineteenth century. In this chapter, I focus on the nineteenth century because it was during this era that periodical journalism and historic preservation, as interconnected fields of literary and professional activity, provided women with unprecedented opportunities to engage in public discourse focused on the reconstruction of domestic spaces. For a brief overview of women's involvement in the field of architecture before the nineteenth century, see Lynne Walker, "Women and Architecture," in *A View from the Interior: Feminism, Women and Design*, ed. Judy Attfield and Pat Kirkham (London: The Women's Press, 1989), 92–93. For a discussion of the gendering of domestic space in the eighteenth-century novel, see Cynthia Wall, "Gendering Rooms: Domestic Architecture and Literary Acts," *Eighteenth-Century Fiction* 5, no. 4 (1993): 349–72.

2. See Mary Spongberg, *Writing Women's History since the Renaissance* (Basingstoke, UK: Palgrave, 2002), 1–11.

3. Spongberg, for example, discusses biography as one such alternative form of historical writing. Spongberg, *Writing Women's History*, 109–29. See also Heather Huyck, who explores a variety of ways that "tangible history," including "human-created, or at least human-influenced, landscapes, structures, and artifacts," can supplement more conventional methods of accessing women's history. Heather Huyck, "Proceeding from Here," in *Restoring Women's History through Historic Preservation*, ed. Gail L. Dubrow and Jennifer B. Goodman (Baltimore: Johns Hopkins University Press, 2003), 355.

4. As Mary Spongberg has pointed out, during the late nineteenth century, women's historical writing shifted from celebrating their achievements in the domestic realm to marking their contributions to a feminist political history. Spongberg, *Writing Women's History*, 131.

5. Lynne Walker provides a useful overview of the history of British women in the field of architecture. She notes that most women architects operated within an "amateur tradition" during the nineteenth century. The 1891 census lists only nineteen women in the profession. It was not until the 1920s that women were admitted to professional schools and organizations in significant numbers. The paucity of Victorian women architects has led feminist scholars to redefine the field in interesting ways. Walker, "Women and Architecture," 92, 99–101. In her overview of recent theoretical approaches to the study of women and architecture, Penny Sparke highlights recent scholarship that explores women's roles as "amateur producers and consumers" of architectural arts in addition to their roles as designers and domestic artisans. Penny Sparke, introduction to *Women's Places: Architecture and Design, 1860–1960*, ed. Brenda Martin and Penny Sparke (London: Routledge, 2003), xiii. For an historical overview of women and architecture in America during the nineteenth century, see Barbara Howe, "Women and Architecture," in *Reclaiming the Past: Landmarks of Women's History*, ed. Page Putnam Miller (Bloomington: Indiana University Press, 1992), 27–62. For a contemporary account, see Joseph Dana Miller, "Women as Architects," *Frank Leslie's Popular Monthly* 50 (June 1900): 199–204.

6. For background on the reformist periodical press, see Brian Maidment, "Magazines of Popular Progress and the Artisans," *Victorian Periodicals Review* 17, no. 3 (1984): 83–94.

7. Gaston Bachelard, *The Poetics of Space*, trans. Maria Jolas (Boston: Beacon, 1994), xxxvii.

8. Quoted in David Lowenthal, *The Past Is a Foreign Country* (Cambridge: Cambridge University Press, 1985), 14.

9. Elizabeth Langland, *Nobody's Angels: Middle-Class Women and Domestic Ideology in Victorian Culture* (Ithaca, NY: Cornell University Press, 1995), 8.

10. Ibid., 9.

11. Mark Girouard, *The Victorian Country House* (New Haven, CT: Yale University Press, 1979), 31.

12. [W. H. Leeds], "Modern Architecture and Architectural Study," *Foreign Quarterly Review* 7 (April 1831): 440. His emphasis. All further references to this article are cited parenthetically by page number in the text.

13. J. C. Loudon, *The Encyclopaedia of Cottage, Farm, and Villa Architecture* (London: Longman, 1836), 1. All further references to this book are cited parenthetically by page number in the text.

14. Spongberg provides a useful overview of the ways women's historiography was shaped by middle-class philanthropic activism during the Victorian era. Spongberg, *Writing Women's History*, 142–45. See also Walker for a discussion of women and philanthropic architecture during the early years of the nineteenth century. Walker, "Women and Architecture," 92–95.

15. Loudon, *Encyclopaedia of Cottage, Farm, and Villa Architecture*, 2.

16. See Alexis Easley, *First-Person Anonymous: Women Writers and Victorian Print Media, 1830–70* (Aldershot, UK: Ashgate, 2004), 81–115.

17. Gillies was author of *The Voyage of the* Constance (London: Sampson Low, 1860); *The Carewes: A Tale of the Civil Wars* (London: W. Kent, 1861); *Great Fun for Our Little Friends* (London: Sampson Low, 1862); and *More Fun with Our Little Friends* (London: Sampson Low, 1864).

18. Mary Gillies, "Associated Homes for the Middle Class," Pts. 1–3, *Howitt's Journal* 1 (March 27, 1847): 171–74; 1 (May 15, 1847): 270–73; 2 (July 17, 1847): 38–41. All further references to this series are cited parenthetically by page number in the text.

19. The concept of communal housing was well established within socialist communities during the early years of the nineteenth century. See Barbara Taylor, *Eve and the New Jerusalem: Socialism and Feminism in the Nineteenth Century* (New York: Pantheon, 1983), 238–60.

20. Harriet Martineau, *Household Education* (London: Edward Moxon, 1849); *Health, Husbandry and Handicraft* (London: Bradbury and Evans, 1861); and *Autobiography* (1877; repr., London: Virago, 1983).

21. Harriet Martineau, "A Year at Ambleside," in *Harriet Martineau at Ambleside*, ed. Barbara Todd (Carlisle, UK: Bookcase, 2002), 41–157. All further references to this book are cited parenthetically by page number in the text.

22. F. W. Fitzpatrick, "Woman and Domestic Architecture," *Midland Monthly* 7 (1897): 558–65. All further references to this article are cited parenthetically by page number in the text.

23. Walker, "Women and Architecture," 102.

24. See David Lowenthal for an overview of late-nineteenth-century historic preservation movements. Lowenthal, *Past Is a Foreign Country*, 395–96.

25. Matthew Campbell, Jacqueline Labbe, and Sally Shuttleworth, introduction to *Memory and Memorials, 1789–1914*, ed. Matthew Campbell, Jacqueline Labbe, and Sally Shuttleworth (London: Routledge, 2000), 1. As Rosemary Jann has pointed out, Victorian historians were "literary" in the sense that they "plundered the past for the raw stuff of imagination and shaped what they found to their own political, social, and aesthetic ends." "The assertion of narrative order," she argues, "was an assertion of moral order as well." *The Art and Science of Victorian History* (Columbus: Ohio State University Press, 1985), xi, xiii.

26. Campbell, Labbe, and Shuttleworth, *Memory and Memorials,* 1. For a contemporary view, see Robert Hunter's article published in the *Nineteenth Century* in 1898. In this article, Hunter develops the idea of a "collective national life" by reviewing legislative efforts to preserve natural and historic landmarks in Britain and around the world. Robert Hunter, "Places and Things of Interest and Beauty," *Nineteenth Century* 43 (April 1898): 570–89.

27. This impulse to preserve the homes of great women is connected to the biographical tendency in Victorian women's historiography. See Spongberg, *Writing Women's History*, 122–23.

28. George Lumsden, "How the House Came to Be Purchased," in *Illustrated Memorial Volume of the Carlyle's House Purchase Fund Committee* (London: The Car-

lyle's House Memorial Trust, 1896), 20, 24. All further references to this book are cited parenthetically by page number in the text.

29. Mary C. Aitken Carlyle co-edited with Charles Norton *The Letters of Thomas Carlyle, 1826–1836,* 2 vols. (London: Macmillan, 1888). Helen Allingham, in addition to editing her husband's (poet William Allingham's) letters and papers, also illustrated *The Homes of Tennyson* (London: A. and C. Black, 1905) and *The Cottage Homes of England* (London: E. Arnold, 1909).

30. James Froude's *Reminiscences,* 2 vols. (London: Longmans, Green 1881); *The Letters and Memorials of Jane Welsh Carlyle,* 2 vols. (New York: Scribner's Sons, 1893); and *Life of Thomas Carlyle,* 4 vols. (London: Longmans, Green, 1882–84).

31. Reginald Blunt, *The Carlyles' Chelsea Home* (London: Bell, 1895), 45.

32. In the *Letters and Memorials of Jane Carlyle,* edited by James Froude, Thomas Carlyle is depicted as a temperamental, neglectful, and sometimes tyrannical husband who is unaware of his wife's illnesses, talents, and jealousies. For example, in one journal entry, Jane refers to the "demoralisation, the desecration, of the institution of marriage." Froude, *Letters and Memorials,* 2:48. Even more controversial than Froude's representation of domestic discord in the Carlyle marriage was his suggestion that their relationship was sexless. For an overview of this controversy, see chapter 7. See also Waldo Dunn, *Froude and Carlyle: A Study of the Froude-Carlyle Controversy* (London: Longmans, Green, 1930), 204–17.

33. Bill Bell, "Empty Spaces: A Visit to Cheyne Row," *The Carlyle Society Occasional Papers* 5 (1992): 27.

34. Stephen, Leslie, "Carlyle's House at Chelsea," *The Academy* 47 (January 5, 1895): 12.

35. Lumsden, "How the House Came to Be Purchased," 2. All further references to this essay are cited parenthetically by page number in the text.

36. Marion Harland, *Where Ghosts Walk: The Haunts of Familiar Characters in History and Literature* (1895; repr., New York: Putnam, 1898).

37. "The Carlyle House in Chelsea," *The Nation* 62 (April 9, 1896): 286. All further references to this article are cited parenthetically by page number in the text.

38. Judith Walkowitz, *City of Dreadful Delight: Narratives of Sexual Danger in Late-Victorian London* (Chicago: University of Chicago Press, 1992), 85–102.

39. Ibid., 87.

40. Anne Skabarnicki, "Marriage as Myth: The Carlyles at Home," in *Portraits of Marriage in Literature,* ed. Anne Hargrove and Maurine Magliocco (Macomb: Western Illinois University Press, 1984), 47.

41. Jane MacNeil, "The Homes of Carlyle," *Munsey's Magazine* 25 (1901): 639. All further references to this article are cited parenthetically by page number in the text.

42. Mary Krout, *A Looker-on in London* (London: B. F. Stevens and Brown, 1899), 52.

43. Virginia Woolf, "Great Men's Houses," in *The London Scene: Five Essays by Virginia Woolf* (New York: Random House, 1982), 25. All further references to this essay are cited parenthetically by page number in the text.

44. The Brontë Society, for example, was formed in 1893, the Dickens Fellowship was founded in 1902, and the George Eliot Fellowship was founded in 1930.

45. Today the Brontë Society estimates that 71 percent of its membership is female (e-mail communication with Hedley Hickling, August 21, 2006).

46. Ward (1851–1920) served as president of the society until 1917.

47. As Amanda Collins has shown, part of the reason for the selection of Mary Ward as president of the Brontë Society might have been due to her managerial work for the Passmore Edwards Settlement, which provided education to the working classes of North London. Amanda Collins, "Forging an Afterlife: Mrs. Humphry Ward and the Relics of the Brontës," *Australasian Victorian Studies Journal* 7 (December 2001): 15.

48. [Mary Augusta Ward], "Charlotte and Emily Brontë," *Cornhill Magazine* 8 (March 1900): 289; Mary Augusta Ward, "Some Thoughts on Charlotte Brontë," in *Charlotte Brontë, 1816–1916: A Centenary Memorial,* ed. Butler Wood (New York: E. P. Dutton, 1918).

49. See Collins for an in-depth analysis of the ways Ward attempted to "position herself as an historical and literary successor to Charlotte Brontë" and her sisters. Collins, "Forging an Afterlife," 15. Collins's discussion of Ward's fictional treatment of the proposed demolition of Haworth Parsonage in *David Grieve* is especially illuminating. See also Beth Sutton-Ramspeck, "The Personal Is Poetical: Feminist Criticism and Mary Ward's Readings of the Brontës," *Victorian Studies* 34, no.1 (1990): 55–75.

50. Ward, "Some Thoughts on Charlotte Brontë," 32.

51. In this respect, she follows in the footsteps of Elizabeth Gaskell, whose *Life of Charlotte Brontë* prompted an intense interest in Brontëana in the second half of the nineteenth century. See Sutton Ramspeck's "Personal Is Poetical" for a discussion of Ward's proto-feminist literary criticism focused on the works of the Brontë sisters.

52. Ward, "Some Thoughts on Charlotte Brontë," 21.

53. See Easley, *First-Person Anonymous*, 183.

54. Ward, "Some Thoughts on Charlotte Brontë," 24.

55. Lucasta Miller, *The Brontë Myth* (New York: Knopf, 2004), 246. Peter Collister also provides insightful analysis of the "restraint and tact" of Ward's literary criticism on the Brontës. Peter Collister, "After 'Half a Century': Mrs. Humphry Ward on Charlotte and Emily Brontë," *English Studies* 66, no. 5 (1985): 414.

56. Ward, "Some Thoughts on Charlotte Brontë," 30.

57. See Sutton-Ramspeck's discussion of Ward's complex position on the Woman Question. "Shot Out of the Canon: Mary Ward and the Claims of Conflicting Feminism," in *Victorian Women Writers and the Woman Question,* ed. Nicola Thompson (Cambridge: Cambridge University Press, 1999), 204–22.

58. Mary Augusta Ward, introduction to *Villette,* by Charlotte Brontë (London: Smith, Elder, 1899), xxiv.

59. This is mentioned in the Brontë Society *Annual Report* (Haworth, UK: Brontë Society, 1912).

60. See (the Brontë Society) *Annual Report* for 1912. Esther Chadwick, *Mrs. Gaskell: Haunts, Homes, and Stories* (London: Pitman, 1910); and *In the Footsteps of the Brontës* (London: Pitman, 1914).

61. Charles Lemon, *A Centenary History of the Brontë Society, 1893–1993* (Haworth, UK: Brontë Society, 1993), 21.

62. Jocelyn Kellett and Donald Hopewell, "The Brontë Parsonage," in *Haworth Parsonage* (Haworth, UK: Brontë Society, 1978), 40.

63. Donald Hopewell, "Catherine Mabel Edgerley: An Appreciation," *Transactions of the Brontë Society* 11, no. 2 (1947): 104.

64. Mabel Edgerley, "The Structure of Haworth Parsonage," *Transactions of the Brontë Society* 9, no. 1 (1936): 27–31.

65. Mabel Edgerley, *Brontë Papers* (Shipley, UK: Outhwaite, 1951).

66. Virginia Woolf, "Haworth, November, 1904," in *The Essays of Virginia Woolf*, ed. Andrew McNeillie (New York: Harcourt, 1986), 1:5. All further references to this essay are cited parenthetically by page number in the text.

67. Gail L. Dubrow, "Restoring Women's History through Historic Preservation: Recent Developments in Scholarship and Public Historical Practice," in *Restoring Women's History through Historic Preservation*, ed. Gail L. Dubrow and Jennifer B. Goodman (Baltimore: Johns Hopkins University Press, 2003), 7.

68. Lowenthal, *Past Is a Foreign Country*, 26.

69. Gail Dubrow provides a useful overview of recent scholarship in the complementary fields of women's history and historic preservation. Dubrow, "Restoring Women's History."

70. Huyck, "Proceeding from Here," 355.

71. Ibid.

Chapter 6. Women Writers and Celbrity News

A version of this chapter is scheduled to appear in *Women Writers and the Artifacts of Celebrity in the Nineteenth Century* (forthcoming, Ashgate).

1. *Oxford English Dictionary Online*, s.v. "celebrity," http://www.dictionary.oed.com.

2. During the Victorian period, these newspapers and periodicals were loosely categorized as "society journalism" or "personal journalism." "Mr. Edmund Yates," *Athenaeum*, May 26, 1894, 679–80; and H. R. Bourne, *English Newspapers: Chapters in the History of Journalism* (New York: Russell and Russell, 1966), 2:294–325.

3. "Journals and Journalists of To-day: Dr. R. Nicoll and the *British Weekly*," *Sketch* 4 (January 24, 1894): 697.

4. For the early history of gossip columns in the British press, including Yates's early experiments in the genre, see Bourne, *English Newspapers*, 2:299–304; Joel Weiner, "Edmund Yates: Gossip as Editor," in *Innovators and Preachers: The Role of the Editor in Victorian England*, ed. Joel Wiener (Westport, CT: Greenwood, 1985), 260–69; and P. D. Edwards, *Dickens's Young Men: George Augustus Sala, Edmund Yates and the World of Victorian Journalism* (Aldershot, UK: Ashgate, 1997), 41–43.

5. Edmund Yates, *Recollections and Experiences* (Leipzig: Tauchnitz, 1885), 2:297.

6. Ibid., 2:310.

7. Margaret Beetham, *A Magazine of Her Own?: Domesticity and Desire in the Woman's Magazine, 1800–1914* (London: Routledge, 1996), 89.

8. Weiner, "Edmund Yates: Gossip as Editor," 268.

9. Quoted in Beetham, *Magazine of Her Own,* 92.

10. Yates, *Recollections and Experiences,* 2:307.

11. For discussion of the role of the interview in celebrity culture at the fin de siècle, see Richard Salmon, "Signs of Intimacy: The Literary Celebrity in the 'Age of Interviewing,'" *Victorian Literature and Culture* 25, no. 1 (1997): 166–67. In the *Weekly Gallery of Celebrities,* Yates's own home is referred to in vaguest outlines: "In the April of 1853, he [Yates] married Miss Louisa Wilkinson, a lady famous alike for her charm of manner and beauty; and only those who know somewhat of the interior of the *maison* Yates can possibly know how very happy the marriage has been." "Mr. Edmund Hodgson Yates," *Weekly Gallery of Celebrities* 1, no. 4 (1891): 46.

12. Yates, *Recollections and Experiences,* 2:307. Selected "Celebrities at Home" features were republished in Edmund Yates, *Celebrities at Home,* 3 vols. (London: Office of "The World," 1877–79).

13. Yates, *Recollections and Experiences,* 2:307–8.

14. Weiner, "Edmund Yates: Gossip as Editor," 269.

15. Salmon, "Signs of Intimacy," 166–67.

16. Beetham, *Magazine of Her Own,* 96.

17. Chris Rojek, *Celebrity* (London: Reaktion Books, 2001), 14.

18. For more background on Robinson, see *Manchester Faces and Places* (Manchester, UK: Hammond, 1892), 119–20; and James Stone, *Emily Faithfull: Victorian Champion of Women's Rights* (Toronto: P. D. Meany, 1994).

19. Arlene Young, "Ladies and Professionalism: The Evolution and the Idea of Work in the *Queen,* 1861–1900," *Victorian Periodicals Review* 40, no. 3 (2007): 189–215. As a contributor to the *Queen,* Robinson was a strong supporter of women's employment in the artistic professions. In one column, for example, she writes, "I am quite prepared to urge the application of feminine skill in the direction of such useful handicrafts as wood carving and fret sawing, for I believe that women possess a fertility of invention and an expertness of hand which will enable them to excel in this art." Charlotte Robinson, "Woodcarving and Fretwork," *Queen,* December 1, 1888, 728.

20. [Edmund Yates], "Celebrities at Home: Miss Charlotte Robinson," *World,* May 14, 1890, 12. All further references to this article are cited parenthetically by page number in the text.

21. Martha Vicinus, "Lesbian Perversity and Victorian Marriage: The 1864 Codrington Divorce Trial," *Journal of British Studies* 36, no. 1 (1997): 70–98.

22. Maria Frawley, "The Editor as Advocate: Emily Faithfull and the *Victoria Magazine,*" *Victorian Periodicals Review* 31, no. 1 (1998): 97.

23. Vicinus, "Lesbian Perversity and Victorian Marriage," 94.

24. Yates, "Celebrities at Home: Miss Charlotte Robinson," 12. In fact, Robinson and Faithfull were life partners. When Faithfull died in 1895, she left all her assets to Robinson. Vicinus, "Lesbian Perversity," 85.

25. [Edmund Yates], "Miss M. E. Braddon (Mrs. Maxwell) at Richmond," in *Celebrities at Home,* 1:317. All further references to this article are cited parenthetically by page number in the text.

26. See Richard Salmon for a discussion of the "topos of the secret" in the Braddon interview, which seems to serve as a "sign of resistance to the journalist's intrusion, whilst, in fact, merely deferring and intensifying the voyeuristic impulse of the narrative." Salmon, "Signs of Intimacy," 167.

27. Mary Elizabeth Braddon, *Lady Audley's Secret* (Peterborough, Ontario: Broadview Press, 2003), 347.

28. Margaret Oliphant, "Novels," *Blackwood's Edinburgh Magazine* 102 (September 1867): 263.

29. For more background on the Yates-Braddon friendship, see Yates, *Recollections and Experiences*; and Robert Lee Wolff, *Sensational Victorian: The Life and Fiction of Mary Elizabeth Braddon* (New York: Garland, 1979).

30. See Beegan for extensive discussion of the techniques and effects of photomechanical production in popular periodicals and newspapers at the fin de siècle. Gerry Beegan, *The Mass Image: A Social History of Photomechanical Reproduction in Victorian London* (Basingstoke, UK: Palgrave, 2008).

31. Geraldine Beare, *Index to the* Strand Magazine, *1891–1950* (Westport, CT: Greenwood Press, 1982).

32. For extensive discussion of Corelli's self-marketing strategies, see Annette Federico, *Idol of Suburbia: Marie Corelli and Late-Victorian Literary Culture* (Charlottesville: University Press of Virginia, 2000), 14–52.

33. Arthur Lawrence, "Illustrated Interviews: Miss Marie Corelli," *Strand Magazine* 16 (July 1898): 17. All further references to this article are cited parenthetically by page number in the text.

34. As Richard Salmon points out, interview articles during this period show a marked "self-reflexivity" as journalists attempted to justify their own intrusions into the private lives and spaces of celebrities. Salmon, "Signs of Intimacy," 160.

35. For extended discussion of Braddon's war with the press, see Federico, *Idol of Suburbia*, 14–52.

36. Lawrence, "Illustrated Interviews: Miss Marie Corelli," 22.

37. Quoted in Federico, *Idol of Suburbia*, 35.

38. Grant Richards, "Notes: Literary and Dramatic," *Weekly Gallery of Celebrities* 1, no. 6 (1891): 72.

39. Raymond Blathwayt, "How Celebrities Have Been Photographed," *Windsor Magazine* 2 (December 1895): 640.

40. For more background on this development, see Tuchman and Fortin, who write, "What we can safely infer is that during the nineteenth century, sometimes subtly and sometimes blatantly, elite men defined the high-culture novel and made it their own." Gaye Tuchman and Nina Fortin, *Edging Women Out: Victorian Novelists, Publishers, and Social Change* (New Haven, CT: Yale University Press, 1989), 218.

41. Lawrence, "Illustrated Interviews: Marie Corelli," 22.

42. See, for example, "The Latest: New Photos and Where to Get Them," *Weekly Gallery of Celebrities* 1, no. 4 (1891): 48. In this installment of the weekly feature, photos of Emily Faithfull, Lady Ridgeway, and Rudyard Kipling are listed, among others.

43. See Beegan for an analysis of the use of illustration in the *Sketch*. "Pictures of women," he notes, "were one of the *Sketch's* major selling points." Beegan, *Mass Image*, 122.

44. "Our Own Trumpet," *Sketch* 5 (January 31, 1894): 1. All further references to this article are cited parenthetically by page number in the text.

45. Ellen Velvin, "Illustrated Interview with Edna Lyall," *Windsor Magazine* 1 (January 1895): 18. All further references to this article are cited parenthetically by page number in the text.

46. According to Reginald Pound, the series "conferred on *The Strand* much of its early prestige." Reginald Pound, *Mirror of the Century:* The Strand Magazine, *1891–1950* (New York: A. S. Barnes, 1966), 34.

47. "Portraits of Celebrities: Miss Charlotte M. Yonge," *Strand Magazine* 2 (November 1891): 479.

48. Federico, *Idol of Suburbia*, 22.

49. For a complete list, see Beare, *Index to the* Strand Magazine.

50. Frances Low, "Distinguished Women and Their Dolls," *Strand Magazine* 8 (September 1894): 250. All further references to this article are cited parenthetically by page number in the text.

51. This is a particularly interesting statement from Ritchie considering that her mother, Isabella Thackeray, had almost drowned her elder sister in a fit of madness in the summer of 1840. *Oxford Dictionary of National Biography Online*, s.v. "Anne Isabella Ritchie" (by D. J. Taylor), http://www.oxforddnb.com.

52. Beegan, *Mass Image*, 7.

53. "Celebrities at Play," *Strand Magazine* 2 (August 1891): 145. All further references to this article are cited parenthetically by page number in the text.

CHAPTER 7. REPRESENTATIONS OF THE AUTHORIAL BODY

I would like to acknowledge the valuable assistance of Jim Curley of the Wangensteen Historical Library, University of Minnesota, as I prepared this chapter.

1. W. F. Bynum and Janice Wilson, "Periodical Knowledge: Medical Journals and Their Editors in Nineteenth-Century Britain," in *Medical Journals and Medical Knowledge: Historical Essays*, ed. W. F. Bynum, Stephen Lock, and Roy Porter (London: Routledge, 1992), 30.

2. Lisa Kochanek, "Reframing the Freak: From Sideshow to Science," *Victorian Periodicals Review* 30, no. 3 (1997): 227.

3. Jane Wood, *Passion and Pathology in Victorian Fiction* (Oxford: Oxford University Press, 2001), 1–2.

4. In addition to Wood's *Passion and Pathology*, see Kristine Swenson, *Medical Women and Victorian Fiction* (Columbia: University of Missouri Press, 2005); Athena Vrettos, *Somatic Fictions: Imagining Illness in Victorian Culture* (Stanford, CA: Stanford University Press, 1995); and Helen Small, *Love's Madness: Medicine, the Novel, and Female Insanity, 1800–1865* (Oxford: Clarendon, 1996).

5. For useful overviews of late-nineteenth-century celebrity culture, see Jeffrey Richards, *Sir Henry Irving: A Victorian Actor and His World* (London: Hamble-

don and London, 2005), 259–81; Margaret Stetz, "Life's 'Half Profits': Writers and Their Readers in Fiction of the 1890s," in *Nineteenth-Century Lives: Essays Presented to Jerome Hamilton Buckley*, ed. Laurence Lockridge, John Maynard, and Donald Stone (Cambridge: Cambridge University Press, 1989), 169–87; Richard Salmon, "Signs of Intimacy: The Literary Celebrity in the 'Age of Interviewing,'" *Victorian Literature and Culture* 25, no. 1 (1997): 159–77; and Annette Federico, *Idol of Suburbia: Marie Corelli and Late-Victorian Literary Culture* (Charlottesville: University Press of Virginia, 2000), 14–52.

6. Robert Green, "Dickens's Doctors," *Boston Medical and Surgical Journal* 166, no. 25 (June 20, 1912): 926–28. See also W. H. Maidlow, "A Note on Charles Dickens and the Doctors," *St. Bartholomew's Hospital Journal* 24 (February 1917): 52.

7. "Occasional Notes of the Quarter: Tennyson as a Psychologist," *Journal of Mental Science* 39 (1893): 66.

8. Warren Babcock, "On the Morbid Heredity and Predisposition to Insanity of the Man of Genius," *Journal of Nervous and Mental Disease* 20, no. 12 (1895): 747–69; John F. Nisbet, *The Insanity of Genius* (1891; repr., London: S. Paul, 1912); and Cesare Lombroso, *The Man of Genius* (1888; repr., London: Walter Scott, 1908).

9. See Amariah Brigham, *Remarks on the Influence of Mental Cultivation and Mental Excitement upon Health* (1832; repr., New York: Scholars' Facsimiles, 1973); R. R. Madden, *The Infirmities of Genius* (London: Saunders and Otley, 1833); and W. Newnham, *Essay on the Disorders Incident to Literary Men* (London: Hatchard, 1836). For background on the debates over madness and genius, see the essays collected in Penelope Murray, ed., *Genius: The History of an Idea* (Oxford: Basil Blackwell, 1989).

10. *The Provincial Medical and Surgical Journal* became the *British Medical Journal* in 1857. For a detailed history of the *British Medical Journal*, see Peter Bartrip, *Mirror of Medicine: A History of the* British Medical Journal (Oxford: Clarendon, 1990).

11. Bartrip, *Mirror of Medicine*, 71.

12. Ernest Hart, "Medical Journalism," *Medical News* 62 (June 17, 1893): 653.

13. Ibid., 655; and John Burnham, "The Evolution of Editorial Peer Review," *JAMA* 263, no.10 (1990): 1323–29.

14. "Introductory Address," *Provincial Medical and Surgical Journal* 1, no. 1 (October 3, 1840): 3.

15. In interpreting the woman doctor as a challenge to a masculinized medical gaze, I rely on recent studies of Victorian medical women, including Swenson's *Medical Women and Victorian Fiction* and Vrettos's *Somatic Fictions*.

16. See, for example, Barbara Ehrenreich and Deirdre English, *Complaints and Disorders: The Sexual Politics of Sickness* (Old Westbury, NY: Feminist Press, 1973); and Sara Delamont and Lorna Duffin, eds., *The Nineteenth-Century Woman: Her Cultural and Physical World* (London: Croom Helm, 1978).

17. I build on recent studies that examine the complex workings of gender within the Victorian medical profession and investigate constructions and counterconstructions of women's bodies within literary and medical discourses. See, for example, Wood, *Passion and Pathology*; Swenson, *Medical Women and Victorian Fiction*; Vrettos, *Somatic Fictions*; Small, *Love's Madness*; Judith Walkowitz, *City of*

Dreadful Delight: Narratives of Sexual Danger in Late-Victorian London (Chicago: Chicago University Press, 1992); Mary Jacobus, Evelyn Fox Keller, and Sally Shuttleworth, eds., *Body/Politics: Women and the Discourses of Science* (London: Routledge 1989); Ludmilla Jordanova, *Sexual Visions: Images of Gender in Science and Medicine between the Eighteenth and Twentieth Centuries* (New York: Harvester 1993); and Elaine Showalter, *The Female Malady: Women, Madness, and English Culture, 1830–1980* (New York: Pantheon, 1985).

18. In the years prior to the publication of *Letters on Mesmerism*, Harriet Martineau had published a number of influential works of fiction and nonfiction, including *Illustrations of Political Economy*, 9 vols. (London: Charles Fox, 1832–34), *Society in America* (1837; repr., London: Transaction, 1981), and *Deerbrook*, 3 vols. (London: Edward Moxon, 1839).

19. Harriet Martineau, *Letters on Mesmerism*, 2nd ed. (London: Edward Moxon, 1845).

20. Thomas Greenhow, *Medical Report of the Case of Miss H—M—* (London: Highley, 1845). For details on this earlier controversy, see Alison Winter, *Mesmerized: Powers of Mind in Victorian Britain* (Chicago: University of Chicago Press, 1998); and Roger Cooter, "Dichotomy and Denial: Mesmerism, Medicine and Harriet Martineau," in *Science and Sensibility: Gender and Scientific Enquiry, 1780–1945*, ed. Marina Benjamin (Oxford: Basil Blackwell, 1991), 144–73.

21. For example, he describes a "uterine discharge" and a protruding tumor "resembling the end of a bullock's tongue." Greenhow, *Medical Report*, 9–10.

22. "Editorial," *Provincial Medical and Surgical Journal* 1, no. 2 (June 12, 1844): 159–60.

23. "Editorial," *Provincial Medical and Surgical Journal* 2, no. 5 (January 29, 1845): 70. All further references to this editorial are cited parenthetically by page number in the text.

24. As the author of *How to Observe Morals and Manners* (1838; repr., London: Transaction, 1988), Martineau was a pioneer in the field of social scientific method, particularly the use of rational observation as a means of deducing general sociological principles. Later, she would become a champion of positivism when she translated Auguste Comte's *Positive Philosophy*. Harriet Martineau, ed., *The Positive Philosophy of Auguste Comte*, 2 vols. (London: Chapman, 1853). See Winter, *Mesmerized*, 224, and Cooter, "Dichotomy and Denial,"160–64, for a discussion of the relationship between Martineau's reputation as a rational thinker and her notoriety as a champion of mesmerism.

25. "Sir James Graham's Unregistered Practitioners," *Provincial Medical and Surgical Journal* 2, no. 5 (January 29, 1845): 72. All further references to this article are cited parenthetically by page number in the text. For more information on the provisions of this bill, see Arvel Erickson, "An Early Attempt at Medical Reform in England, 1844–1845," *Journal of the History of Medicine and Allied Sciences* 5, no. 2 (Spring 1950): 144–55.

26. "The Late Harriet Martineau," *British Medical Journal* 2 (July 1, 1876): 20–21. All further references to this article are cited parenthetically by page number in the text.

27. In her self-written obituary, published in the *Daily News* on June 29, 1876, Martineau remarked that the "commotion [over her cure] was just what might

have been anticipated from the usual reception of new truths in science and the medical art. That she recovered when she ought to have died was an unpardonable offence." "An Autobiographic Memoir," in *Harriet Martineau on Women*, ed. Gayle Graham Yates (New Brunswick, NJ: Rutgers, 1985), 43–44.

28. Thomas Watson, "The Late Miss Martineau," *British Medical Journal* 2 (July 8, 1876): 64; James Martin, "The Case of Miss Martineau," *British Medical Journal* 2 (July 15, 1876): 99. All further references to Martin's letter are cited parenthetically by page number in the text.

29. Thomas Greenhow, "Termination of the Case of Miss Harriet Martineau," *British Medical Journal* 1 (April 14, 1877): 449–50. All further references to this article are cited parenthetically by page number in the text.

30. His emphasis. W. O. Markham took issue with this statement in his defense of Martineau published in the *BMJ*. He writes, "A transposition of the words—many facts and little imagination—would, in my opinion, be a much truer expression of the nature of its [the autobiography's] contents." W. O. Markham, "The Case of Miss Martineau," *British Medical Journal* 2 (November 17, 1877): 712.

31. T. Spencer Wells, "Remarks on the Case of Miss Martineau," *British Medical Journal* 1 (May 5, 1877): 543. All further references to this article are cited parenthetically by page number in the text.

32. See Winter, *Mesmerized*; and Cooter, "Dichotomy and Denial," for discussion of mesmerism and the politics of women's health during the nineteenth century.

33. Hart's arguments and experiments disproving mesmerism were published in the *British Medical Journal* and the *Nineteenth Century* during the 1890s. These articles were reprinted and expanded in his book *Hypnotism, Mesmerism and the New Witchcraft* (1893; repr., New York: Da Cappo Press, 1982).

34. Interestingly, Hart was reprimanded by hospital officials after they learned of his experiments hypnotizing a female acquaintance (Hart, *Hypnotism, Mesmerism, and the New Witchcraft*, 5–6). Nevertheless, he undertook a series of experiments intended to illuminate the physiological causes of hypnotism.

35. Harriet Martineau, *Autobiography* (1877; repr., London: Virago, 1983), 2:193.

36. Martineau, *Letters on Mesmerism*, v–xii.

37. James Froude, *Reminiscences*, 2 vols. (London: Longmans, Green, 1881); *Letters and Memorials of Jane Welsh Carlyle*, 2 vols. (New York: Scribner's Sons, 1883); *Life of Thomas Carlyle*, 4 vols. (London: Longmans, Green, 1882–84); and *My Relations with Carlyle* (London: Longmans, Green, 1903).

38. James Crichton-Browne, "Froude and Carlyle: The Imputation Considered Medically," *British Medical Journal* 2 (June 27, 1903): 1498–1502.

39. Michael Neve and Trevor Turner, "What the Doctor Thought and Did: Sir James Crichton-Browne (1840–1938)," *Medical History* 39 (1995): 399–432.

40. James Crichton-Browne and Alexander Carlyle, eds., *The New Letters and Memorials of Jane Welsh Carlyle*, 2 vols. (London: John Lane, 1903); James Crichton-Browne and Alexander Carlyle, eds., *The Nemesis of Froude: A Rejoinder to James Anthony Froude's "My Relations with Carlyle"* (London: John Lane, 1903).

41. Crichton-Browne, "Froude and Carlyle," 1498–99. All further references to this article are cited parenthetically by page number in the text.

42. This point reinforces Crichton-Browne's widely publicized theory relating to the over-education of children, particularly girls, who were susceptible to neuroses as a result of intellectual strain. Neve and Turner, "What the Doctor Thought," 412–13.

43. James Crichton-Browne, "Carlyle—His Wife and Critics," *Journal of Mental Science* 44 (1898): 79, 81.

44. See also, for example, his extensive medical footnote on Jane Carlyle's opium addiction in the *New Letters*. Crichton-Browne, *New Letters and Memorials of Jane Welsh Carlyle*, 2:265.

45. Crichton-Browne, *Nemesis of Froude*, 59.

46. For example, see Frank Harris, "Talks with Carlyle," *English Review* 7 (February 1911): 419–34; and David Alec Wilson, *The Truth About Carlyle: An Exposure of the Fundamental Fiction Still Current* (London: Alston Rivers, 1913).

47. George Gould, "The Role of Eyestrain in Civilization," *British Medical Journal* 2 (September 19, 1903): 663–66; (September 26, 1903): 757–60. All further references to these articles are cited parenthetically by page number in the text. Gould subsequently expanded and republished the articles as a six-volume set of books. George Gould, *Biographic Clinics*, 6 vols. (Philadelphia: Blakiston, 1903–9). In the expanded book version, Gould includes extensive quotations from letters, journals, novels, and other literary sources.

48. Gould, "Role of Eyestrain in Civilization," 663.

49. See Bartrip, *Mirror of Medicine*, 64–65.

50. "Obituary: Mr. Ernest Hart," *The Practitioner* 60 (February 1898): 117–18.

51. R. S. Stevenson, quoted in Bartrip, *Mirror of Medicine*, 64.

52. "Obituary: Ernest Hart," *British Medical Journal* 2 (January 15, 1898): 185.

53. Babcock, "On the Morbid Heredity and Predisposition to Insanity of the Man of Genius," 753.

54. "Obituary: Ernest Hart," 175.

55. For example, in 1883, the *BMJ* gave an account of a ceremony honoring Ernest Hart during which his wife was presented with a portrait that had been commissioned by special subscription. In his acceptance speech, Hart made particular mention of the importance of his wife as a collaborator: "It is intimately true that I have always been able to turn to my wife for solace, support, and encouragement in all that is best in my daily work, and in that which has met with your especial approval. She has always placed public objects high above private aims; and, in her enthusiasm for humanity, and her loving devotion, I have been able to find that encouragement and support, which we all of us need in the anxieties and toils of active life" (735–36). "Proceedings at the Presentation of a Portrait of Mr. Ernest Hart," *British Medical Journal* 1 (April 14, 1883): 735–36.

56. "Obituary: Ernest Hart," 182. All further references to this article are cited parenthetically by page number in the text.

57. The unsubstantiated allegation that Hart had murdered his wife provided the plot of Julia Frankau's novel *Dr. Phillips: A Maida Vale Idyll* (London: Vizetelly, 1887). See also the brief editorial notice of the events surrounding the death of Hart's wife published in the *Medical Times and Gazette*, November 16, 1861, 509.

58. "Obituary: Ernest Hart," 184 (her emphasis).

59. Mrs. Ernest Hart [Alice M. Hart], *Diet in Sickness and in Health* (London: Scientific Press, 1895).

60. Her signature on the book's title page reads, "Mrs. Ernest Hart, formerly student of the Faculty of Medicine of Paris, and of the London School of Medicine for Women." This is followed by a list of her publications. Hart, *Diet in Sickness and in Health.*

61. Henry Thompson, introduction to *Diet in Sickness and in Health*, xii.

62. "Obituary: Ernest Hart," 185.

63. "Death of Mr. Ernest Hart," *The Jewish Chronicle*, January 14, 1898, 12.

CHAPTER 8. THE CELEBRITY CAUSE

1. Octavia Hill, "The Homes of the London Poor," *Macmillan's Magazine* 30 (June 1874): 131–38.

2. C. Edmund Maurice, ed., *The Life of Octavia Hill as Told in Her Letters* (London: Macmillan, 1913), 322.

3. In 1873, she also worked with Lord Shuttleworth on a committee of the Charity Organization Society on the dwellings of the working classes in London. Out of these conversations came the Artisan's Dwelling Act, which Shuttleworth presented at the House of Commons in 1874. The ADA was passed in 1875. Maurice, *Life of Octavia Hill*, 323.

4. For background on *Macmillan's* as a venue for women writers, see George Worth, Macmillan's Magazine, *1859–1907: "No Flippancy or Abuse Allowed"* (Aldershot, UK: Ashgate, 2003), 74–79.

5. The correspondent in this case is Sir Sydney Carlyle Cockerell (1867–1962), son of Hill's friend and early supporter Sydney John Cockerell (1842–77). In this essay, I include middle initials so as to distinguish the two men from each other.

6. Sydney C. Cockerell, "Octavia Hill: Enthusiast and Pioneer," *London Times*, February 28, 1935, 13F.

7. Quoted in Cockerell, "Octavia Hill: Enthusiast and Pioneer," 14A.

8. Emily Maurice, ed., *Octavia Hill: Early Ideals* (London: Allen and Unwin, 1928), 170.

9. Hill's sister Gertrude was married to Lewes's son Charles.

10. See, for example, Octavia Hill, "A Few Words to Fresh Workers," *Nineteenth Century* 26 (September 1889): 455.

11. Maurice, *Life of Octavia Hill*, 348.

12. Diana Maltz, *British Aestheticism and the Urban Working Classes, 1870–1900* (London: Palgrave, 2005), 43.

13. The efforts of the Kyrle Society were preceded by those of the Commons Preservation Society (CPS), founded in 1865. Octavia Hill became involved in the CPS from about 1875 and remained active in the organization after the Kyrle Society was formed in 1876. For a full history of the open space movement, including legislative developments, see Anne Hoole Anderson, "Bringing Beauty Home to the People: The Kyrle Society, 1877–1917," in *Octavia Hill's Letters to Fellow-Workers, 1872–1911*, ed. Robert Whelan, et al. (London: Kyrle Books, 2005), 703–33; and H. L. Malchow, "Public Gardens and Social Action in Late

Victorian London," *Victorian Studies* 29, no. 1 (1985): 97–124.

14. Barbara Gates, *Kindred Nature: Victorian and Edwardian Women Embrace the Living World* (Chicago: University of Chicago Press, 1998), 135.

15. Maurice, *Life of Octavia Hill*, 333.

16. Octavia Hill, "Space for the People," *Macmillan's Magazine* 32 (August 1875): 328–30. All further references to this article are cited parenthetically by page number in the text.

17. Octavia Hill to Sydney J. Cockerell, July 16, 1875. Westminster City Archives, D. Misc 84/3, 19. Her emphasis.

18. Octavia Hill, "The Northern Heights of London," *London Times,* July 20, 1875, 4F.

19. Maurice, *Life of Octavia Hill*, 332.

20. Edward Bond, "The Northern Heights of London," *London Times,* August 23, 1875, 10B; "Hampstead," *London Times,* October 5, 1875, 8E. In October 1875, the open space was developed into the neighborhood currently bisected by Fitzjohn's Avenue.

21. For detailed histories of the Kyrle Society, see Anderson, "Bringing Beauty Home to the People," and Maltz, *British Aestheticism and the Urban Working Classes.*

22. Octavia Hill, "Public Garden and Hall for Southwark," *London Times,* March 14, 1887, 7A.

23. Sydney C. Cockerell, "Notation on 'Public Garden and Hall for Southwark,'" March 14, 1887. Westminster City Archives, D. Misc 84/2, 1.

24. Octavia Hill to Sydney C. Cockerell, May 1888. Sydney Cockerell Letters, British Library, Mss. 52722, fol., 45.

25. "Redcross Hall and Garden," *London Times,* June 4, 1888, 13D.

26. Octavia Hill, "More Air for London," *Nineteenth Century* 23 (February 1888), 181. All further references to this article are cited parenthetically by page number in the text.

27. "An Open Space for Deptford," reprinted from the *Daily Graphic,* February 1, 1892 (London, British Library), 2.

28. Whelan, *Letters to Fellow-Workers,* 342.

29. Hill, "A Few Words to Fresh Workers," 452.

30. Octavia Hill, "A More Excellent Way of Charity," *Macmillan's Magazine* 35 (December 1876): 126.

31. Octavia Hill, *Our Common Land* (London: Macmillan, 1877).

32. In her privately published *Letters to Fellow-Workers*, Hill also made frequent references to her publications. See, for example, her 1887 letter, where she refers readers to the "February number of the *Nineteenth Century*" in case they would like to know more about her recent efforts to preserve open spaces. Hill, *Letters to Fellow-Workers,* 227.

33. Hill, "A More Excellent Way of Charity," 127.

34. Octavia Hill, *Homes of the London Poor* (London: Macmillan, 1875).

35. Ann Parry, "The Grove Years 1868-1883: A 'New Look' for *Macmillan's Magazine?" Victorian Periodicals Review* 19, no. 4 (1986): 152.

36. Quoted in Gillian Darley, *Octavia Hill: A Life* (London: Constable, 1990), 153. Her second book, *Our Common Land* (1877), was apparently less successful. Hill, *Letters to Fellow-Workers,* 104.

37. Maurice, *Life of Octavia Hill*, 348.

38. Hill, "More Air for London," 187.

39. Quoted in Darley, *Octavia Hill*, 168. Hill's emphasis.

40. The *Letters* were only recently published in a complete edition by Kyrle Books, 2005. Editor Robert Whelan notes that the *Letters* constitute an extensive record of Hill's work, which "exceed in length all of her other printed writings put together." Robert Whelan, introduction to *Octavia Hill's Letters to Fellow-Workers*, xxxi. The circulation of the letters, he notes, was approximately 500.

41. Quoted in Darley, *Octavia Hill*, 167.

42. Octavia Hill to Sydney C. Cockerell, March 31, 1892. Westminster City Archives, D. Misc 84/2, 173. Hill was particularly sensitive about the publication of her private correspondence due to her conflict with John Ruskin, who accused her of attempting to derail his plans for a utopian venture, St. George's Guild, in Sheffield. In 1877, he published a letter denouncing her in his periodical for working men, *Fors Clavigera*, and subsequently published his correspondence with her on the controversy. See Darley, *Octavia Hill*, 192–96.

43. Florence Nightingale, "A 'Note' of Interrogation," *Fraser's Magazine* 7 n.s. (May 1873): 567.

44. "The Charge of the Five Hundred," *Punch* 88 (March 21, 1885): 141.

45. For discussion of other *Punch* satires of the Kyrle Society, see Maltz, *British Aestheticism and the Urban Working Classes*, 54.

46. Octavia Hill to Sydney C. Cockerell, August 22, 1899. Westminster City Archives, D. Misc 84/2, 221.

47. I draw this conclusion based on my own survey of the press.

48. Linley Sambourne, "Our Plea for Open Spaces," *Punch* 84 (June 9, 1883): 266. All further references to this image are cited parenthetically by page number in the text. The opening inscription reads, "The Rhymester, musing in City Slums, indulges in Elegiacs concerning possible Elysia for the City Children." The rejoinder at the bottom of the page continues, "Recognized! Ay, but by whom? The wise of heart and the kindly! / Scarce by the Kings of Gold, the Lords of the Rail and Mart / Little by *Bumble* the bumptious, blundering coldly, blindly, / On in the olden ways, stolid and tough of heart. / Then, whilst the Springtide burst of rejuvenescent beauty / Breaks upon holt and hedgerow, quickens the pulse like wine, / Where are the souls will list to the bidding of citizen duty / To claims of the City children considerate ear incline?"

49. Freshwater Place, John Ruskin's freehold property in Marylebone, came under Hill's management in 1866. According to Darley, the inscription was inspired by the *Seven Lamps of Architecture*, wherein Ruskin expressed admiration for the way a German or Swiss builder would inscribe stones "with a summary of his life and of its experience, raising thus the habitation into a kind of monument." Darley, *Octavia Hill*, 144. For more information on the creation of the inscription, see Maurice, *Life of Octavia Hill*, 292–97.

50. Maurice, *Life of Octavia Hill*, 293–94. All further references to this book are cited parenthetically by page number in the text.

51. Regrettably, the tiles eventually disintegrated, and the building was demolished in the mid-twentieth century. Another inscription on the Church of St. John's, Waterloo, remains intact.

52. See Diana Maltz for discussion of the ways that these inscriptions may also have expressed Hill's "haughtiness towards her tenants." Maltz, *British Aestheticism and the Urban Working Classes*, 61.

53. For background on legislation relating to the reclamation of urban churchyards during this period see Whelan, introduction to *Letters to Fellow-Workers*, xlvi–xlvii. Whelan notes that the efforts of the Kyrle Society were "almost immediately successful, getting the churchyards in Drury Lane and Waterloo opened, soon to be followed by Bloomsbury and Bethnal Green" (xlvii).

54. Hill, *Our Common Land*, 111. All further references to this book are cited parenthetically by page number in the text.

55. Interestingly, the grave of George Fox was untouched. Hill lamented that they could "draw so marked a distinction between the unknown, who had surely been loved, and the known, who had been famous (126–27).

56. H. D. Rawnsley, "The National Trust," *Cornhill Magazine* 2 n.s. (February 1897): 249.

57. Octavia Hill, "Memorial to John Ruskin," *London Times*, August 23, 1900, 6F.

58. Arthur Severn, "The Memorial to John Ruskin," *London Times*, September 4, 1900, 6B.

59. In addition, a bronze medallion memorializing Ruskin was erected in Westminster Abbey in 1902.

60. "Memorial to John Ruskin," *London Times*, October 8, 1900, 7F.

61. Friar's Crag became part of the National Trust's Borrowdale land holdings, which today comprise 29,173 acres in the Lake District.

62. Rawnsley, "National Trust," 249.

63. Octavia Hill, "Natural Beauty as a National Asset." *Nineteenth Century* 58 (December 1905): 938. All further references to this article are cited parenthetically by page number in the text.

64. Darley, *Octavia Hill*, 311, 317.

65. The Hill family purchases in Kent were even more extensive than alluded to here. See Darley, *Octavia Hill*, 311–13; and Hill, *Letters to Fellow Workers*, 660–64.

66. Darley, *Octavia Hill*, 336.

67. William Thompson Hill, *Octavia Hill: Pioneer of the National Trust and Housing Reformer* (London: Hutchinson, 1956), 76–77.

68. Hill, *Letters to Fellow Workers*, 510. All further references to this book are cited parenthetically by page number in the text.

69. See also her essay "Natural Beauty as a National Asset," where she imagines these properties as a retreat for the "Londoner who takes a Saturday afternoon from gas-lighted city office or many-storied London street" (940).

70. Hill, "A Few Words to Fresh Workers," 454. All further references to this article are cited parenthetically by page number in the text.

71. Octavia Hill, "Trained Workers for the Poor," *Nineteenth Century* 33 (January 1893): 40. All further references to this article are cited parenthetically by page number in the text.

72. Octavia Hill, "Women and the Suffrage," *London Times*, July 15, 1910, 9A. All further references to this letter are cited parenthetically by page number in the text.

73. See also her letter of 1882, where she remarks, "I would rather work in the unsought-after, out-of-sight places, side by side with my fellow workers, face to face with tenants, than in the conspicuous forefront of any great movement." Hill, *Letters to Fellow Workers*, 156.

Coda

1. Stephen Greenblatt, *Shakespearean Negotiations: The Circulation of Social Energy in Renaissance England* (Berkeley: University of California Press, 1989), 1.

2. Ibid.

3. Ibid., 6.

4. Ibid., 19.

5. Ibid., 6.

6. Ibid., 20.

7. Terry Eagleton, *Literary Theory: An Introduction* (Minneapolis: University of Minnesota Press, 1983). See also D. J. Palmer, *The Rise of English Studies* (London: Oxford University Press, 1965); and Brian Doyle, "The Hidden History of English Studies," in *Re-Reading English*, ed. Peter Widdowson (London: Methuen, 1982), 17–31.

8. Charles Kingsley, *Introductory Lectures Delivered at Queen's College, London* (London: John Parker, 1849), 57. All further references to this book are cited parenthetically by page number in the text.

9. Robert Chambers, *Chambers's Cyclopaedia of English Literature* (Boston: Gould and Lincoln, 1853), i. All further references to this book are cited parenthetically by page number in the text. The first edition of *Chambers's Cylcopaedia* appeared in 1844.

10. For extended discussion of the gradual acceptance of English literature as a valid field of study at Oxford and Cambridge, see Palmer, *Rise of English Studies*.

11. Doyle, "Hidden History of English Studies," 25.

12. Robert Chambers, *Chambers's Cyclopaedia of English Literature*, 3rd ed. (New York: John Alden, 1885).

13. Henry Morley, *A First Sketch of English Literature* (London: Cassell, 1892).

14. Palmer, *Rise of English Studies*, 50.

15. H. A. Dobson, *The Civil Service Series: A Handbook of English Literature* (London: Crosby Lockwood, 1880), 193. The Indian Civil Service Exams were instituted in 1855.

16. George Craik, *A Compendious History of English Literature and of the English Language*, 2 vols. (London: Griffin, Bohn, 1861). All further references to this book are cited parenthetically by page number in the text.

17. [Henry Craik], "The Study of English Literature," *Quarterly Review* 156 (July 1883): 189.

18. John Churton Collins, "Can English Literature Be Taught?" *Nineteenth Century* 129 (November 1887): 642. Even with his qualms about the state of English pedagogy, Collins was a major supporter of the effort to create English literature as a rigorous, systematic field of study. For extended discussion of Collins's campaign to establish a school of English literature at Oxford, see Palmer, *Rise of English Studies*, 78–103.

19. Craik, "Study of English Literature," 192.

20. Collins, "Can English Literature Be Taught?," 649.

21. Craik, *Compendious History of English Literature*, 540. All further references to this book are cited parenthetically by page number in the text.

22. Leslie Stephen, in *English Literature and Society*, uses the same analogy, asking, "Are changes in literary fashions enveloped in the same inscrutable mystery as changes in ladies' dresses?" Leslie Stephen, *English Literature and Society in the Eighteenth Century* (London: Putnam, 1907), 17.

23. Alfred Ainger, "The Teaching of English Literature," *Macmillan's Magazine* 61 (December 1889), 107.

24. G. E. Hadow and W. H. Hadow, eds., *The Oxford Treasury of English Literature*, 3 vols. (Oxford: Clarendon, 1906–8).

25. Hadow was a tutor at Lady Margaret Hall from 1906 to 1911. For more background on Hadow's tenure at Oxford, see Vera Brittain, *The Women at Oxford: A Fragment of History* (New York: Macmillan, 1960).

26. Palmer, *Rise of English Studies*, 116. Of course, although women were permitted to stand for examinations during this period, they were not eligible to receive degrees from Oxford until 1920. See Brittain's *Women at Oxford* for further discussion of the extended campaign for women's education at Oxford.

27. Ainger, "Teaching of English Literature," 112.

28. Doyle, "Hidden History of English Studies," 25.

29. Stephen, *English Literature and Society*, 13.

30. Ainger, "Teaching of English Literature," 113 (his emphasis).

31. Collins, "Can English Literature Be Taught?," 651.

32. Craik, "Study of English Literature," 210.

33. Matthew Arnold, "The Function of Criticism at the Present Time," in *Lectures and Essays in Criticism*, ed. R. H. Super (Ann Arbor: University of Michigan Press, 1962), 282. All further references to this essay are cited parenthetically by page number in the text.

34. Matthew Arnold, "A Guide to English Literature," *Nineteenth Century* 2 (December 1877): 843–53. All further references to this article are cited parenthetically by page number in the text.

35. Stopford Brooke, *English Literature* (London: Macmillan, 1897).

36. Stopford Brooke, *English Literature* (London: Macmillan, 1919). All further references to this book are cited parenthetically by page number in the text.

37. F. R. Leavis, "What's Wrong with Criticism?," *Scrutiny* 1, no. 2 (1932): 138.

Bibliography

Abraham, Ashley. *Beautiful Lakeland*. Keswick, UK: Abraham, 1912.

Adams's Illustrated Guide to the Lakes. London: W. J. Adams, 1855.

Adcock, Arthur. *Famous Houses and Literary Shrines of London*. London: Dent, 1912.

Ainger, Alfred. "The Teaching of English Literature." *Macmillan's Magazine* 61 (December 1889): 101–13.

Alison, Archibald. *History of Europe during the French Revolution*. Edinburgh: Blackwood, 1833–42.

Allbut, Robert. *Rambles in Dickens' Land*. 1886. Reprint, New York: Truslove, Hanson and Comba, 1899.

Allingham, Helen. *The Cottage Homes of England*. London: E. Arnold, 1909.

———. *The Homes of Tennyson*. London: A. and C. Black, 1905.

Amigoni, David. "Gendered Authorship, Literary Lionism and the Virtues of Domesticity: Contesting Wordsworth's Fame in the Writings of Harriet Martineau and Thomas Carlyle." *Critical Survey* 13, no. 2 (2001): 26–41.

Andersen, Hans Christian. "A Visit to Charles Dickens." *Temple Bar* 31 (December 1870): 27–46.

Anderson, Anne Hoole. "Bringing Beauty Home to the People: The Kyrle Society, 1877–1917." In *Octavia Hill's Letters to Fellow-Workers, 1872–1911*, edited by Robert Whelan et al., 703–33. London: Kyrle Books, 2005.

Arbuckle, Elisabeth Sanders, ed. *Harriet Martineau's Letters to Fanny Wedgwood*. Stanford, CA: Stanford University Press, 1983.

Archer, William. "An Academy of the Dead." *Monthly Review* 1 (December 1900): 118–27.

Arnold, Matthew. "The Function of Criticism at the Present Time." In *Lectures and Essays in Criticism*, edited by R. H. Super. Ann Arbor: University of Michigan Press, 1962.

———. "A Guide to English Literature." *Nineteenth Century* 2 (December 1877): 843–53.

Ashby-Sterry, J. "Charles Dickens and Southwark." *English Illustrated Magazine* 62 (November 1888): 105–15.

Aspland, Lindsey. Frontispiece to *Guide to the English Lakes, by Harriet Martineau*. Windermere, UK: J. Garnett, 1876.

Babcock, Warren. "On the Morbid Heredity and Predisposition to Insanity of the Man of Genius." *Journal of Nervous and Mental Disease* 20, no.12 (1895): 747–69.

Bachelard, Gaston. *The Poetics of Space.* Translated by Maria Jolas. Boston: Beacon, 1994.

[Bagehot, Walter]. "Charles Dickens." *National Review* 14 (October 1858): 458–86.

Baildon, H. B. *Homes and Haunts of Famous Authors.* London: Wells Gardner, Darton, 1906.

Barloon, Jim. "The Black Hole of London: Rescuing Oliver Twist." *Dickens Studies Annual* 28 (1999): 1–12.

Barratt, Thomas. *The Annals of Hampstead.* 3 vols. London: Black, 1912.

Bartrip, Peter. *Mirror of Medicine: A History of the* British Medical Journal. Oxford: Clarendon, 1990.

Baudrillard, Jean. "Symbolic Exchange and Death." In *Selected Writings,* edited by Mark Poster, 122–51. Translated by Charles Levin. 2nd ed. Stanford, CA: Stanford University Press, 2001.

Baxendale, Kenneth. *Charles Dickens' London, 1812–70.* West Wickham, Kent, UK: Alteridem, 1984.

Beare, Geraldine. *Index to the* Strand Magazine, *1891–1950.* Westport, CT: Greenwood Press, 1982.

Beegan, Gerry. *The Mass Image: A Social History of Photomechanical Reproduction in Victorian London.* Basingstoke, UK: Palgrave, 2008.

Beetham, Margaret, *A Magazine of Her Own?: Domesticity and Desire in the Woman's Magazine, 1800–1914.* London: Routledge, 1996.

Bell, Bill. "Empty Spaces: A Visit to Cheyne Row." *The Carlyle Society Occasional Papers* 5 (1992): 21–34.

Bicknell, Peter. Introduction to *The Illustrated Wordsworth's Guide to the Lakes.* New York: Congdon and Weed, 1984.

Birkett, Dea. "Fake Snow and Faux Fun." *New Statesman* 136, nos. 4875–4877 (December 17–January 3, 2008): 25.

Black's Picturesque Guide to the English Lakes. Edinburgh: A. and C. Black, 1851.

Blathwayt, Raymond. "How Celebrities Have Been Photographed." *Windsor Magazine* 2 (December 1895): 639–48.

Blunt, Reginald. *The Carlyles' Chelsea Home.* London: Bell, 1895.

Bond, Edward. "The Northern Heights of London." *London Times,* August 23, 1875, 10B.

Bourne, H. R. *English Newspapers: Chapters in the History of Journalism.* 2 vols. New York: Russell and Russell, 1966.

Bowker, R. R. "London as a Literary Centre." *Harper's New Monthly Magazine* 76 (May 1888): 815–44.

Braddon, Mary Elizabeth. *Lady Audley's Secret.* Peterborough, Ontario: Broadview Press, 2003.

Bradley, A. G. *Highways and Byways in the Lake District.* London: Macmillan, 1901.

Brenan, Gerald. Introduction to *Rambles in Dickens' Land,* by Robert Allbut. 1886. Reprint, New York: Truslove, Hanson and Comba, 1899.

Brigden, Thomas. *Eminent Men and Women of Marylebone and Their Homes.* London: J. Bumpus, 1891.

Brigham, Amariah. *Remarks on the Influence of Mental Cultivation and Mental Excitement upon Health*. 1832. Reprint, New York: Scholars' Facsimiles, 1973.

Brittain, Vera. *The Women at Oxford: A Fragment of History*. New York: Macmillan, 1960.

Brocklebank, Lisa. "Psychic Reading." *Victorian Studies* 48, no. 2 (2005): 233–39.

Brontë Society. *Annual Report*. Haworth, UK: Brontë Society, 1912.

Brooke, Stopford. *English Literature*. London: Macmillan, 1897.

———. *English Literature*. London: Macmillan, 1919.

Burnham, John. "The Evolution of Editorial Peer Review." *JAMA* 263, no.10 (1990): 1323–29.

Burrow, J. W. *A Liberal Descent: Victorian Historians and the English Past*. Cambridge: Cambridge University Press, 1981.

Buzard, James. *The Beaten Track: European Tourism, Literature, and the Ways to Culture, 1800–1918*. Oxford: Clarendon, 1993.

Bynum, W. F., and Janice Wilson. "Periodical Knowledge: Medical Journals and Their Editors in Nineteenth-Century Britain." In *Medical Journals and Medical Knowledge: Historical Essays*, edited by W. F. Bynum, Stephen Lock, and Roy Porter, 29–48. London: Routledge, 1992.

Campbell, Matthew, Jacqueline Labbe, and Sally Shuttleworth. Introduction to *Memory and Memorials: 1789–1914,* edited by Matthew Campbell, Jacqueline Labbe, and Sally Shuttleworth, 1–11. London: Routledge, 2000.

"The Carlyle House in Chelsea." *The Nation* 62 (April 9, 1896): 286–87.

Carlyle, Mary Aitken C., and Charles Norton, eds. *The Letters of Thomas Carlyle, 1826–1836*. 2 vols. London: Macmillan, 1888.

Carlyle, Thomas. *The French Revolution*. London: Chapman and Hall, 1837.

———. *Past and Present*. London: Chapman and Hall, 1843.

"Celebrities at Play." *Strand Magazine* 2 (August 1891): 145–49.

Chadwick, Esther. *In the Footsteps of the Brontës*. London: Pitman, 1914.

———. *Mrs. Gaskell: Haunts, Homes, and Stories*. London: Pitman, 1910.

Chambers, Robert. *Chambers's Cyclopaedia of English Literature*. Boston: Gould and Lincoln, 1853.

———. *Chambers's Cyclopaedia of English Literature*. 3rd ed. New York: John Alden, 1885.

Chancellor, E. Beresford. *The Literary Ghosts of London: Homes and Footprints of Famous Men and Women*. London: Richards, 1933.

Chapman, Maria Weston. "Memorials." In *Autobiography*, by Harriet Martineau. Vol. 3. London: Smith, Elder, 1877.

"The Charge of the Five Hundred." *Punch* 88 (March 21, 1885): 141.

"Charles Dickens and London." *Bookman* 41 (February 1912): 238–46.

Cockerell, Sydney C. "Notation on 'Public Garden and Hall for Southwark.'" March 14, 1887. Westminster City Archives, D. Misc 84/2, 1.

———. "Octavia Hill: Enthusiast and Pioneer." *London Times*, February 2, 1935.

Colley, Linda. *Britons: Forging the Nation, 1707–1837*. New Haven, CT: Yale University Press, 1992.

Collins, Amanda. "Forging an Afterlife: Mrs. Humphry Ward and the Relics of the Brontës." *Australasian Victorian Studies Journal* 7 (December 2001): 12–25.

Collins, John Churton. "Can English Literature Be Taught?" *Nineteenth Century* 129 (November 1887): 642–58.

Collins, Philip. "Dickens and the City." In *Visions of the Modern City: Essays in History, Art, and Literature,* edited by William Sharpe and Leonard Wallock, 97–117. New York: Columbia University Press, 1983.

Collister, Peter. "After 'Half a Century': Mrs. Humphry Ward on Charlotte and Emily Brontë." *English Studies* 66, no. 5 (1985): 410–31.

"Contemporary England." *New Englander* 25 (1866): 618–52.

Conway, Moncure Daniel. *Autobiography: Memories and Experiences.* 2 vols. Boston: Houghton Mifflin, 1905.

———. "Footprints of Charles Dickens." *Harper's New Monthly Magazine* 41 (September 1870): 610–16.

Cooter, Roger. "Dichotomy and Denial: Mesmerism, Medicine and Harriet Martineau." In *Science and Sensibility: Gender and Scientific Enquiry, 1780–1945,* edited by Marina Benjamin, 144–73. Oxford: Basil Blackwell, 1991.

Corkran, Alice. *The Poet's Corner, or, Haunts and Homes of the Poets.* London: Ernest Nister, 1892.

Craik, George. *A Compendious History of English Literature.* 2 vols. London: Griffin, Bohn, 1861.

———. *The Pictorial History of England: Being a History of the People, as well as a History of the Kingdom.* London: Knight, 1849.

[Craik, Henry]. "The Study of English Literature." *Quarterly Review* 156 (July 1883): 187–215.

Crary, Jonathan. *Techniques of the Observer: On Vision and Modernity in the Nineteenth Century.* Cambridge, MA: MIT Press, 1990.

Crichton-Browne, James. "Carlyle—His Wife and Critics." *Journal of Mental Science* 44 (1898): 76–95.

———. "Froude and Carlyle: The Imputation Considered Medically." *British Medical Journal* 2 (June 27, 1903): 1498–1502.

Crichton-Browne, James, and Alexander Carlyle, eds. *The Nemesis of Froude: A Rejoinder to James Anthony Froude's "My Relations with Carlyle."* London: John Lane, 1903.

———. *The New Letters and Memorials of Jane Welsh Carlyle.* 2 vols. London: John Lane, 1903.

Darley, Gillian. *Octavia Hill: A Life.* London: Constable, 1990.

"Death of Mr. Ernest Hart." *The Jewish Chronicle,* January 14, 1898, 12–13.

Delamont, Sara, and Lorna Duffin, eds. *The Nineteenth-Century Woman: Her Cultural and Physical World.* London: Croom Helm, 1978.

Demoor, Marysa, ed. *Marketing the Author: Author Personae, Narrative Selves, and Self-Fashioning, 1880–1930.* Basingstoke, UK: Palgrave, 2004.

Dexter, Walter. "Charles Dickens's London." *English Illustrated Magazine* 25 (September 1901): 547–53.

Dickens, Charles. *The Letters of Charles Dickens*. Edited by Graham Storey and Kathleen Tillotson. 12 vols. Oxford: Clarendon, 1995.

Dickens, Charles, Jr. *Dickens's Dictionary of London, 1879: An Unconventional Handbook*. 1879. Reprint, London: Howard Baker, 1972.

———. "Disappearing Dickensland." *North American Review* 156 (June 1893): 670–84.

———. "Notes on Some Dickens Places and People." *Pall Mall Magazine* 9 (July 1896): 342–55.

———. "Pickwickian Topography." *English Illustrated Magazine* 111 (December 1892): 186–98.

Dickens, Charles, III. "Relics of Dickens' London." *Munsey's Magazine* 27, no. 6 (September 1902): 833–42.

The Dickens Fellowship. "Charles Dickens Museum." http://www.dickensmuseum.com.

———. *The Dickens House*. London: The Dickens Fellowship, n.d., ca. 1926.

A Dickens Pilgrimage. New York: Dutton, 1914.

Dickens World [visitor attraction]. http://www.dickensworld.co.uk.

Dickerson, Vanessa. *Victorian Ghosts in the Noontide: Women Writers and the Supernatural*. Columbia: University of Missouri Press, 1996.

Dobson, H. A. *The Civil Service Series: A Handbook of English Literature*. London: Crosby Lockwood, 1880.

Doyle, Brian. "The Hidden History of English Studies." In *Re-Reading English*, edited by Peter Widdowson, 17–31. London: Methuen, 1982.

Dubrow, Gail L. "Restoring Women's History through Historic Preservation: Recent Developments in Scholarship and Public Historical Practice." In *Restoring Women's History through Historic Preservation*, edited by Gail L. Dubrow and Jennifer B. Goodman, 1–14. Baltimore: Johns Hopkins University Press, 2003.

Dunn, Waldo. *Froude and Carlyle: A Study of the Froude-Carlyle Controversy*. London: Longmans, Green, 1930.

Eagleton, Terry. *Literary Theory: An Introduction*. Minneapolis: University of Minnesota Press, 1983.

Easley, Alexis. *First-Person Anonymous: Women Writers and Victorian Print Media, 1830–70*. Aldershot, UK: Ashgate, 2004.

———. "Gendered Observations: Harriet Martineau and the Woman Question." In *Victorian Women Writers and the 'Woman Question,'* edited by Nicola Thompson, 80–98. Cambridge: Cambridge University Press, 1999.

———. "Victorian Women Writers and the Periodical Press: The Case of Harriet Martineau." *Nineteenth-Century Prose* 24, no. 1 (1997): 39–50.

Edgerley, Mabel. *Brontë Papers*. Shipley, UK: Outhwaite, 1951.

———. "The Structure of Haworth Parsonage." *Transactions of the Brontë Society* 9, no. 1 (1936): 27–31.

"Editorial." *Medical Times and Gazette*, November 16, 1861, 509.

"Editorial." *Provincial Medical and Surgical Journal* 1, no. 2 (June 12, 1844): 159–61.

"Editorial." *Provincial Medical and Surgical Journal* 2, no. 5 (January 29, 1845): 70–72.

Edwards, P. D. *Dickens's Young Men: George Augustus Sala, Edmund Yates and the World of Victorian Journalism.* Aldershot, UK: Ashgate, 1997.

Ehrenreich, Barbara, and Deirdre English. *Complaints and Disorders: The Sexual Politics of Sickness.* Old Westbury, NY: Feminist Press, 1973.

Eliot, George. *The Journals of George Eliot.* Edited by Margaret Harris and Judith Johnston. Cambridge: Cambridge University Press, 1998.

The English Lakes. London: Nelson, 1859.

Erickson, Arvel. "An Early Attempt at Medical Reform in England, 1844–1845." *Journal of the History of Medicine and Allied Sciences* 5, no. 2 (Spring 1950): 144–55.

Eyre, Alan. *St. John's Wood: Its History, Its Houses, Its Haunts, and Its Celebrities.* London: Chapman, 1913.

Fawcett, Mrs. Henry [Millicent Garrett Fawcett]. *Some Eminent Women of Our Times.* London: Macmillan, 1889.

Federico, Annette. *Idol of Suburbia: Marie Corelli and Late-Victorian Literary Culture.* Charlottesville: University Press of Virginia, 2000.

Fielding, Kenneth. *Harriet Martineau and William Wordsworth.* Rydal, UK: Rydal Church Trust, 2002.

Fitzpatrick, F. W. "Woman and Domestic Architecture." *Midland Monthly* 7 (1897): 558–65.

Flanders, Judith. "Great Forebodings about Dickens World." *The Guardian,* April 17, 2007. http://www. guardian.co.uk (accessed April 26, 2009).

Flowers, Betty, and R. W. Crump, eds. *The Complete Poems of Christina Rossetti.* London: Penguin, 2001.

Fonblanque, Albany. *England under Seven Administrations.* London: Bentley, 1837.

Frankau, Julia. *Dr. Phillips: A Maida Vale Idyll.* London: Vizetelly, 1887.

Frawley, Maria. "The Editor as Advocate: Emily Faithfull and the *Victoria Magazine.*" *Victorian Periodicals Review* 31, no. 1 (1998): 87–104.

———, ed. *Life in the Sickroom,* by Harriet Martineau. Peterborough, Ontario: Broadview, 2003.

Freeman, Nicholas. *Conceiving the City: London, Literature and Art, 1870–1914.* Oxford: Oxford University Press, 2007.

Freud, Sigmund. *The Uncanny.* Translated by David McLintock. New York: Penguin, 2003.

Froude, James. *The Letters and Memorials of Jane Welsh Carlyle.* 2 vols. New York: Scribner's, 1883.

———. *Life of Thomas Carlyle.* 4 vols. London: Longmans, Green, 1882–84.

———. *My Relations with Carlyle.* London: Longmans, Green, 1903.

———. *Reminiscences.* 2 vols. London: Longmans, Green, 1881.

Gates, Barbara. *Kindred Nature: Victorian and Edwardian Women Embrace the Living World.* Chicago: University of Chicago Press, 1998.

"George Eliot's Country." In *George Eliot: Scenes and People in Her Novels,* by Charles Olcott, 6–7. New York: Crowell, 1910.

Gillies, Mary. "Associated Homes for the Middle Class." Pts. 1–3. *Howitt's Journal* 1 (March 27, 1847): 171–74; 1 (May 15, 1847): 270–73; 2 (July 17, 1847): 38–41.

———. *The Carewes: A Tale of the Civil Wars.* London: W. Kent, 1861.

———. *Great Fun for Our Little Friends.* London: Sampson Low, 1862.

———. *More Fun with Our Little Friends.* London: Sampson Low, 1864.

———. *The Voyage of the* Constance. London: Sampson Low, 1860.

Girouard, Mark. *The Victorian Country House.* New Haven, CT: Yale University Press, 1979.

Glendening, John. *The High Road: Romantic Tourism, Scotland, and Literature, 1720–1820.* New York: St. Martin's Press, 1997.

Gomel, Elana. "'Spirits in the Material World': Spiritualism and Identity in the *Fin de Siècle.*" *Victorian Literature and Culture* 35 (2007): 189–213.

Gould, George. *Biographic Clinics.* 6 vols. Philadelphia: Blakiston, 1903–9.

———. "The Role of Eyestrain in Civilization." Pts. 1 and 2. *British Medical Journal* 2 (September 19, 1903): 663–66; (September 26, 1903): 757–60.

Gosse, Edmund. "Christina Rossetti." *Century Magazine* 46 (June 1893): 211–17.

Gray, Thomas. *Sketch of a Tour from Lancaster round the Principal Lakes in Lancashire, Cumberland, and Westmoreland: to which is Added, Mr. Gray's Journal.* Carlisle, UK: F. Jolie, 1803.

Green, Frank. *London Homes of Dickens.* 1928. Reprint, London: Folcroft, 1970.

Green, Robert. "Dickens's Doctors." *Boston Medical and Surgical Journal* 166, no. 25 (June 20, 1912): 926–28.

Greenblatt, Stephen. *Shakespearean Negotiations: The Circulation of Social Energy in Renaissance England.* Berkeley: University of California Press, 1989.

Greenhow, Thomas. *Medical Report of the Case of Miss H—M—.* London: Highley 1845.

———. "Termination of the Case of Miss Harriet Martineau." *British Medical Journal* 1 (April 14, 1877): 449–50.

Hadow, G. E., and W. H. Hadow, eds. *The Oxford Treasury of English Literature.* 3 vols. Oxford: Clarendon, 1906–8.

Hallam, Henry. *The Constitutional History of England from the Accession of Henry VII to the Death of George II.* London: John Murray, 1827.

"Hampstead." *London Times,* October 5, 1875, 8E.

Harland, Marion. *Where Ghosts Walk: The Haunts of Familiar Characters in History and Literature.* 1895. Reprint, New York: Putnam, 1898.

"Harriet Martineau's Architectural Plans for the Knoll." University of Birmingham Library, Harriet Martineau Papers, HM 1302.

Harris, Frank. "Talks with Carlyle." *English Review* 7 (February 1911): 419–34.

Harrison, Frederic. "London Improvements." *New Review* 7 (October 1892): 414–21.

Hart, Ernest. *Hypnotism, Mesmerism and the New Witchcraft.* 1893. Reprint, New York: Da Cappo Press, 1982.

————. "Medical Journalism." *Medical News* 62 (June 17, 1893): 653–58.

Hart, Mrs. Ernest [Alice M. Hart]. *Diet in Sickness and in Health.* London: Scientific Press, 1895.

Hawkins, Ann, and Maura Ives, eds. *Women Writers and the Artifacts of Celebrity in the Long Nineteenth Century.* Aldershot, UK: Ashgate, forthcoming.

Herstein, Sheila. *"The English Woman's Journal* and the Langham Place Circle: A Feminist Forum and Its Women Editors." In *Innovators and Preachers: The Role of the Editor in Victorian England,* edited by Joel Wiener, 61–76. Westport, CT: Greenwood, 1985.

Hill, Octavia. "A Few Words to Fresh Workers." *Nineteenth Century* 26 (September 1889): 452–61.

————. "The Homes of the London Poor." *Macmillan's Magazine* 30 (June 1874): 131–38.

————. *Homes of the London Poor.* London, Macmillan, 1875.

————. Letter to Sydney Cockerell. July 16, 1875. Westminster City Archives, D. Misc 84/3, 19.

————. Letter to Sydney Cockerell. May 1888. Sydney Cockerell Letters, British Library. Mss. 52722, fol., 45.

————. Letter to Sydney Cockerell. March 31, 1892. Westminster City Archives, D. Misc 84/2, 173.

————. Letter to Sydney Cockerell. August 22, 1899. Westminster City Archives, D. Misc 84/2, 221.

————. *Letters to Fellow-Workers, 1872–1911,* edited by Robert Whelan, et al. London: Kyrle Books, 2005.

————. "Memorial to John Ruskin." *London Times,* August 23, 1900, 6F.

————. "More Air for London." *Nineteenth Century* 23 (February 1888): 181–88.

————. "A More Excellent Way of Charity." *Macmillan's Magazine* 35 (December 1876): 126–31.

————. "Natural Beauty as a National Asset." *Nineteenth Century* 58 (December 1905): 935–41.

————. "The Northern Heights of London." *London Times,* July 20, 1875, 4F.

————. "An Open Space for Deptford." Reprinted from the *Daily Graphic,* February 1, 1892. London, British Library.

————. *Our Common Land.* London: Macmillan, 1877.

————. "Public Garden and Hall for Southwark." *London Times,* March 14, 1887, 7A.

————. "Space for the People." *Macmillan's Magazine* 32 (August 1875): 328–32.

————. "Trained Workers for the Poor." *Nineteenth Century* 33 (January 1893): 36–43.

————. "Women and the Suffrage." *London Times,* July 15, 1910, 9A.

Hill, William Thompson. *Octavia Hill: Pioneer of the National Trust and Housing Reformer.* London: Hutchinson, 1956.

Hills and Saunders. "Miss Lily Hanbury." *Sketch* 5 (March 7, 1894).

Hinkson, Katharine Tynan. "Some Reminiscences of Christina Rossetti." *Bookman* 1, no. 1 (1895): 28–29.

Home, Gordon. *What to See in England.* London: Black, 1903.

Hopewell, Donald. "Catherine Mabel Edgerley: An Appreciation." *Transactions of the Brontë Society* 11, no. 2 (1947): 101–5.

Houghton, Walter, ed. *The Wellesley Index to Victorian Periodicals: 1824–1900.* 5 vols. Toronto: University of Toronto Press, 1966–89.

Howe, Barbara. "Women and Architecture." In *Reclaiming the Past: Landmarks of Women's History,* edited by Page Putnam Miller, 27–62. Bloomington: Indiana University Press, 1992.

Howitt, William. *Homes and Haunts of the Most Eminent British Poets.* London: Bentley, 1847.

Hubbard, Elbert. *Little Journeys to the Homes of Famous Women.* London: Putnam, 1897.

Hueffer, Ford Madox [Ford Madox Ford]. *The Soul of London: A Survey of a Modern City.* London: Alston Rivers, 1905.

Hughes, William. *A Week's Tramp in Dickens-land; Together with Personal Reminiscences of the "Inimitable Boz" Therein Collected.* London: Chapman and Hall, 1893.

Hunter, Robert. "Places and Things of Interest and Beauty." *Nineteenth Century* 43 (April 1898): 570–89.

Huntley, Dana. "Visiting in Dickens World." *British Heritage* (September 2008): 42–45.

Huyck, Heather. "Proceeding from Here." In *Restoring Women's History through Historic Preservation,* edited by Gail L. Dubrow and Jennifer Goodman, 355–64. Baltimore: Johns Hopkins University Press, 2003.

Ingram, John H. *Elizabeth Barrett Browning.* Boston: Roberts, 1888.

"In the Footsteps of Dickens." *Bookworm* (January 1892): 77–81.

"Introductory Address." *Provincial Medical and Surgical Journal* 1, no. 1 (October 3, 1840): 1–4.

Irving, Washington. *The Sketch Book of Geoffrey Crayon, Gent.* 1819–20. Reprint, London: Dent, 1963.

Jacobus, Mary, Evelyn Fox Keller, and Sally Shuttleworth, eds. *Body/Politics: Women and the Discourses of Science.* London: Routledge, 1989.

James, Henry. *Autobiography.* New York: Criterion, 1956.

Jameson, Anna. *Legends of the Madonna.* London: Brown, Green, and Longmans, 1852.

———. *Memoirs of Celebrated Female Sovereigns.* London: Colburn and Bentley, 1831.

Jann, Rosemary. *The Art and Science of Victorian History.* Columbus: Ohio State University Press, 1985.

Jenkinson, Henry. *Practical Guide to the English Lake District.* 6th ed. London: E. Stanford, 1879.

Jordanova, Ludmilla. *Sexual Visions: Images of Gender in Science and Medicine between the Eighteenth and Twentieth Centuries.* New York: Harvester, 1993.

"Journals and Journalists of To-day: Dr. R. Nicoll and the *British Weekly*." *Sketch* 4 (January 24, 1894): 696–97.

Kellett, Jocelyn, and Donald Hopewell. "The Brontë Parsonage." In *Haworth Parsonage*, 27–41. Haworth, UK: Brontë Society, 1978.

Kelley, Philip, Scott Lewis, and Edward Hagan, eds. *The Brownings' Correspondence*. 16 vols. Winfield, KS: Wedgestone Press, 1984–.

Kent, W. "The Blind Side of Dickens." *Bookman* 58 (June 1920): 107–10.

Kingsley, Charles. *Introductory Lectures Delivered at Queen's College, London*. London: John Parker, 1849.

Kitton, Frederic. *Charles Dickens: His Life, Writings, and Personality*. London: Jack, 1902.

Knight, Charles. *Passages of a Working Life during Half a Century*. 3 vols. London: Bradbury, 1865.

Kochanek, Lisa. "Reframing the Freak: From Sideshow to Science." *Victorian Periodicals Review* 30, no. 3 (1997): 227–43.

Krout, Mary. *A Looker-on in London*. London: B. F. Stevens and Brown, 1899.

Lacey, Candida, ed. *Barbara Leigh Smith Bodichon and the Langham Place Group*. 1986. Reprint, London: Routledge, 2001.

Langland, Elizabeth. *Nobody's Angels: Middle-Class Women and Domestic Ideology in Victorian Culture*. Ithaca, NY: Cornell University Press, 1995.

Lanier, Sidney. *The English Novel: A Study in the Development of Personality*. New York: Scribner's, 1908.

"The Late Charles Dickens." *London Journal* 52 (August 1870): 28–29.

"The Late Harriet Martineau." *British Medical Journal* 2 (July 1, 1876): 20–21.

"The Latest: New Photos and Where to Get Them." *Weekly Gallery of Celebrities* 1, no. 4 (1891): 48.

Lawrance, Hannah. *The Historical Memoirs of the Queens of England*. London: Edward Moxon, 1838.

Lawrence, Arthur. "Illustrated Interviews: Miss Marie Corelli." *Strand Magazine* 16 (July 1898): 17–26.

Leavis, F. R. "What's Wrong with Criticism?" *Scrutiny* 1, no. 2 (1932): 132–46.

[Leeds, W. H.]. "Modern Architecture and Architectural Study." *Foreign Quarterly Review* 7 (April 1831): 432–61.

Leighton, Angela, and Margaret Reynolds, eds. *Victorian Women Poets: An Anthology*. Oxford: Blackwell, 1995.

Lemon, Charles. *A Centenary History of the Brontë Society, 1893–1993*. Haworth, UK: Brontë Society, 1993.

[Lewes, George Henry.] "Review of *The History of England during the Thirty Years' Peace, 1815–1845*." *British Quarterly Review* 11 (May 1850): 355–71.

Linton, Eliza Lynn. *The Lake Country*. London: Smith, Elder, 1864.

"Literary Relics." *Chambers's Edinburgh Journal* 6 (December 1846): 382–83.

Logan, Deborah, ed. *The Collected Letters of Harriet Martineau*. 5 vols. London: Pickering and Chatto, 2007.

————, ed. *Illustrations of Political Economy: Selected Tales,* by Harriet Martineau. Peterborough, Ontario: Broadview, 2004.

————. Introduction to *Harriet Martineau's Writing on British History and Military Reform.* 6 vols. London: Pickering and Chatto, 2005.

Lombroso, Cesare. *The Man of Genius.* 1888. Reprint, London: Walter Scott, 1908.

Lootens, Tricia. *Lost Saints: Silence, Gender, and Victorian Literary Canonization.* Charlottesville: University Press of Virginia, 1996.

Loudon, J. C. *The Encyclopaedia of Cottage, Farm, and Villa Architecture.* London: Longman, 1836.

Low, Frances. "Distinguished Women and Their Dolls." *Strand Magazine* 8 (September 1894): 250–57.

Lowenthal, David. *The Past Is a Foreign Country.* Cambridge: Cambridge University Press, 1985.

Lumsden, George. "How the House Came to Be Purchased." In *Illustrated Memorial Volume of the Carlyle's House Purchase Fund Committee,* 1–26. London: The Carlyle's House Memorial Trust, 1896.

Macaulay, Thomas Babington. *History of England.* London: J. M. Dent, 1848.

MacCannell, Dean. *The Tourist: A New Theory of the Leisure Class.* New York: Schocken, 1976.

MacFarlane, Charles. *Reminiscences of a Literary Life.* New York: Scribner's, 1917.

Macfarlane, Harold. "The Value of a Dead Celebrity." *Cornhill Magazine* 8 (March 1900): 367–71.

MacNeil, Jane. "The Homes of Carlyle." *Munsey's Magazine* 25 (1901): 633–39.

Macready, William Charles. *The Diaries of William Charles Macready.* Edited by William Toynbee. 2 vols. New York: Benjamin Blom, 1969.

Madden, R. R. *The Infirmities of Genius.* London: Saunders and Otley, 1833.

Maidlow, W. H. "A Note on Charles Dickens and the Doctors." *St. Bartholomew's Hospital Journal* 24 (February 1917): 52.

Maidment, Brian. "Magazines of Popular Progress and the Artisans." *Victorian Periodicals Review* 17, no. 3 (1984): 82–94.

Maitzen, Rohan. *Gender, Genre, and Victorian Historical Writing.* New York: Garland, 1998.

Malchow, H. L. "Public Gardens and Social Action in Late Victorian London." *Victorian Studies* 29, no. 1 (1985): 97–124.

Maltz, Diana. *British Aestheticism and the Urban Working Classes, 1870–1900.* London: Palgrave, 2005.

Manchester Faces and Places. Manchester, UK: Hammond, 1892.

Mandler, Peter. "'The Wand of Fancy': The Historical Imagination of the Victorian Tourist." In *Material Memories,* edited by Marius Kwint, Christopher Breward, and Jeremy Aynsley, 125–41. Oxford: Berg, 1999.

Markham, W. O. "The Case of Miss Martineau." *British Medical Journal* 2 (November 17, 1877): 711–12.

Marks, Patricia. "Harriet Martineau: *Fraser's* 'Maid of (Dis)Honor.'" *Victorian Periodicals Review* 19, no. 1 (1986): 28–34.

Marsh, Joss Lutz. "Imagining Victorian London, an Entertainment and Itinerary (Chas. Dickens' Guide)." *Stanford Humanities Review* 3, no. 1 (1993): 67–97.

Martin, James. "The Case of Miss Martineau." *British Medical Journal* 2 (July 15, 1876): 99.

Martineau, Harriet. "An Autobiographic Memoir." In *Harriet Martineau on Women*, edited by Gayle Graham Yates, 35–49. New Brunswick, NJ: Rutgers University Press, 1985.

———. *Autobiography*. 2 vols. 1877. Reprint, London: Virago, 1983.

———. *Biographical Sketches*. London: Macmillan, 1869.

———. *Complete Guide to the English Lakes*. 1st ed. Windermere, UK: J. Garnett, 1855.

———. *Deerbrook*. 3 vols. London: Edward Moxon, 1839.

———. *Directory of the Lake District*. Edited by R. Grigg. Warrington, UK: Beewood Coldell, 1989.

———. *The English Lake District*. Windermere, UK: J. Garnett, 1876.

———. "Female Industry." *Edinburgh Review* 109 (April 1859): 293–336.

———. *Guide to Keswick and Its Environs*. Windermere, UK: John Garnett, 1857.

———. *Guide to Windermere*. 1854. Reprint, Giggleswick, UK: Castleberg, 1995.

———. *Guide to Windermere*. Windermere, UK: J. Garnett, 1854.

———. *Health, Husbandry and Handicraft*. London: Bradbury and Evans, 1861.

———. *The History of England from the Commencement of the Nineteenth Century to the Crimean War*. 4 vols. Philadelphia: Porter and Coates, 1864–66.

———. *The Hour and the Man*. 3 vols. London: Edward Moxon, 1841.

———. *Household Education*. London: Edward Moxon, 1849.

———. *How to Observe Morals and Manners*. 1838. Reprint, London: Transaction, 1988.

———. *Illustrations of Political Economy*. 9 vols. London: Charles Fox, 1832–34.

———. "Lake and Mountain Holidays." *The People's Journal* 2 (July 1846): 1–3, 72–74, 149–50.

———. *Letters on Mesmerism*. 2nd ed. London: Edward Moxon, 1845.

———. *Life in the Sickroom*. London: Edward Moxon, 1844.

———. "Lights of the English Lake District." *Atlantic Monthly* 7 (May 1861): 541–58.

———. "Literary Lionism." *London and Westminster Review* 32 o.s. (April 1839): 261–81.

———, ed. *The Positive Philosophy of Auguste Comte*. 2 vols. London: Chapman, 1853.

———. *Retrospect of Western Travel*. 2 vols. London: Saunders and Otley, 1838.

———. *Society in America*. 1837. Reprint, London: Transaction, 1981.

———. "A Year at Ambleside." In *Harriet Martineau at Ambleside*, edited by Barbara Todd, 41–157. Carlisle, UK: Bookcase, 2002.

Matthews, Brander. "The Future Literary Centre of the English Language." *Bookman* 12, no. 3 (1900): 238–42.

Matthews, Samantha. "Entombing the Woman Poet: Tributes to Elizabeth Barrett Browning." *Studies in Browning and His Circle* 24 (June 2001): 31–53.

Maurice, C. Edmund, ed. *The Life of Octavia Hill as Told in Her Letters.* London: Macmillan, 1913.

Maurice, Emily, ed. *Octavia Hill: Early Ideals.* London: Allen and Unwin, 1928.

Mazzeno, Laurence. *The Dickens Industry: Critical Perspectives, 1836–2005.* Rochester, NY: Camden House, 2008.

McCaw, Neil. *George Eliot and Victorian Historiography: Imagining the National Past.* London: Palgrave, 2000.

McCormick, A. D. "London Bridge Steps." In "Charles Dickens and Southwark," by J. Ashby-Sterry. *English Illustrated Magazine* 62 (November 1888): 106.

"Memorial to John Ruskin." *London Times,* October 8, 1900: 7F.

Merchant, W. M. Introduction to *A Guide through the District of the Lakes in the North of England,* by William Wordsworth, 9–32. London: Hart-Davis, 1951.

Miller, Joseph Dana. "Women as Architects." *Frank Leslie's Popular Monthly* 50 (June 1900): 199–204.

Miller, Lucasta. *The Brontë Myth.* New York: Knopf, 2004.

Miltoun, Francis. *Dickens' London.* Boston: Page, 1903.

Mineka, Francis. *The Dissidence of Dissent:* The Monthly Repository, *1806–38.* Chapel Hill: University of North Carolina Press, 1944.

"Miss Martineau's History of England." *Christian Examiner and Religious Miscellany* 81, no. 2 (1866): 78–89.

"Miss Martineau's *The History of the Peace.*" *National Quarterly Review* 9 (September 1864): 387–90.

"Miss Martineau's Introduction to the *History of the Peace.*" *Littell's Living Age* 30 (1851): 136–38.

Mitchell, Rosemary. "'The Busy Daughters of Clio': Women Writers of History from 1820–1880." *Women's History Review* 7, no. 1 (1998): 107–34.

———. *Picturing the Past: English History in Text and Image, 1830–70.* Oxford: Clarendon, 2000.

Morley, Henry. *A First Sketch of English Literature.* London: Cassell, 1892.

"Mr. Edmund Hodgson Yates." *Weekly Gallery of Celebrities* 1, no. 4 (1891): 46–47.

"Mr. Edmund Yates." *Athenaeum* (May 26, 1894): 679–80.

"Mr. Roebuck and Miss Martineau." *Quarterly Review* 91 (1852): 160–95.

Murray, Penelope, ed. *Genius: The History of an Idea.* Oxford: Basil Blackwell, 1989.

Myers, Mitzi. "*Harriet Martineau's Autobiography*: The Making of a Female Philosopher." In *Women's Autobiography: Essays in Criticism,* edited by Estelle Jelinek, 53–70. Bloomington: Indiana University Press, 1980.

Nead, Lynda. "Mapping the Self: Gender, Space and Modernity in Mid-Victorian London." In *Rewriting the Self: Histories from the Renaissance to the Present,* edited by Roy Porter, 167–85. New York: Routledge, 1997.

Neve, Michael, and Trevor Turner. "What the Doctor Thought and Did: Sir James Crichton-Browne (1840–1938)." *Medical History* 39 (1995): 399–432.

Newby, Peter. "Literature and the Fashioning of Tourist Taste." In *Humanistic Geography and Literature: Essays on the Experience of Place,* edited by Douglas C. D. Pocock, 130–41. London: Croom Helm, 1981.

Newnham, W. *Essay on the Disorders Incident to Literary Men.* London: Hatchard, 1836.

Nicoll, W. Robertson. Preface to *A History of English Literature,* edited by William Francis Collier. London: Nelson, 1910.

———. Preface to *A Mill on the Floss,* by George Eliot. London: Dent, 1908.

Nightingale, Florence. "A 'Note' of Interrogation." *Fraser's Magazine* 7 n.s. (May 1873): 567–77.

Nisbet, John F. *The Insanity of Genius.* 1891. Reprint, London: S. Paul, 1912.

Nord, Deborah Epstein. "The Urban Peripatetic: Spectator, Streetwalker, Woman Writer." *Nineteenth-Century Literature* 46, no. 3 (1991): 351–75.

"Obituary: Ernest Hart." *British Medical Journal* 2 (January 15, 1898): 175–86.

"Obituary: Mr. Ernest Hart." *The Practitioner* 60 (February 1898): 117–18.

"Occasional Notes of the Quarter: Tennyson as a Psychologist." *Journal of Mental Science* 39 (1893): 65–71.

Olcott, Charles. *George Eliot: Scenes and People in Her Novels.* New York: Crowell, 1910.

Oliphant, Margaret. "Novels." *Blackwood's Edinburgh Magazine* 102 (September 1867): 257–75.

Oppenheimer, Janet. *The Other World: Spiritualism and Psychical Research in England, 1850–1914.* Cambridge: Cambridge University Press, 1985.

"Our Gallery of Borderlanders: Tennyson." *Borderland* 4, no. 4 (1897): 349–59.

"Our '100-Picture' Gallery: Through Dickens-Land." *Strand Magazine* 33 (April 1907): 411–18.

"Our Own Trumpet." *Sketch* 5 (January 31, 1894): 1.

Ousby, Ian. *Blue Guide to Literary Britain and Ireland.* 2nd ed. London: A. and C. Black, 1990.

Owen, Alex. *The Darkened Room: Women, Power and Spiritualism in Late Victorian England.* 1989. Reprint, Chicago: University of Chicago Press, 2004.

Palmer, D. J. *The Rise of English Studies.* London: Oxford University Press, 1965.

Parry, Ann. "The Grove Years 1868–1883: A 'New Look' for *Macmillan's Magazine?*" *Victorian Periodicals Review* 19, no. 4 (1986): 149–57.

Payn, James. *Some Literary Recollections.* London: Smith, Elder, 1884.

Pemberton, T. Edgar. *Dickens's London: or, London in the Works of Charles Dickens.* London: Tinsley, 1876.

The Penny Cyclopaedia of the Society for the Diffusion of Useful Knowledge. London: Knight, 1833–43.

Penrose, Elizabeth. *History of England.* Edinburgh: Constable, 1823.

Peterson, Linda. *Becoming a Woman of Letters: Myths of Authorship and Facts of the Victorian Market.* Princeton, NJ: Princeton University Press, 2009.

———. *Traditions of Victorian Women's Autobiography: The Poetics and Politics of Life Writing.* Charlottesville: University Press of Virginia, 1999.

Pichanick, Valerie. "An Abominable Submission: Harriet Martineau's Views on the Role and Place of Woman." *Women's Studies* 5 (1977): 13–32.

Poovey, Mary. *Uneven Developments: The Ideological Work of Gender in Mid-Victorian England.* Chicago: University of Chicago Press, 1988.

Porter, George. *The Progress of the Nation, in Its Various Social and Economical Relations, from the Beginning of the Nineteenth Century to the Present Time.* London: Knight, 1836–43.

"Portraits of Celebrities: Miss Charlotte M. Yonge." *Strand Magazine* 2 (November 1891): 479.

Pound, Reginald. *Mirror of the Century:* The Strand Magazine, *1891–1950.* New York: A. S. Barnes, 1966.

Prior, Herman. *Guide to the Lake District of England.* 5th ed. Windermere, UK: J. Garnett, 1885.

"Proceedings at the Presentation of a Portrait of Mr. Ernest Hart." *British Medical Journal* 1 (April 14, 1883): 734–36.

Radcliffe, Ann. *A Journey Made in the Summer of 1794: Through Holland and the Western Frontier of Germany with a Return down the Rhine; to Which are Added Observations during a Tour to the Lakes of Lancashire, Westmoreland and Cumberland.* London: Robinson, 1795.

Ragan, Harger. "In the Footsteps of Dickens." *Cosmopolitan* 15 (May 1893): 3–14.

Rawnsley, H. D. "The National Trust." *Cornhill Magazine* 2 n.s. (February 1897): 245–49.

"Redcross Hall and Garden." *London Times,* June 4, 1888, 13D.

"The (Reputed) 'Old Curiousity Shop.'" In *Dickens' London,* by Francis Miltoun, 126. Boston: Page, 1903.

"Review of *The History of England during the Thirty Years' Peace.*" *Bentley's Miscellany* 27 (March 1850): 310–11.

Richards, Grant. "Notes: Literary and Dramatic." *Weekly Gallery of Celebrities* 1, no. 6 (1891): 72.

Richards, Jeffrey. *Sir Henry Irving: A Victorian Actor and His World.* London: Hambledon and London, 2005.

[Ritchie, Anne Thackeray]. "Elizabeth Barrett Browning." In *The Dictionary of National Biography,* edited by Leslie Stephen. Vol. 7. London: Smith, Elder, 1886.

Roberts, Caroline. *The Woman and the Hour: Harriet Martineau and Victorian Ideologies.* Toronto: University of Toronto Press, 2002.

Robinson, Charlotte. "Woodcarving and Fretwork." *Queen* (December 1, 1888): 728.

Robinson, Solveig. "'Amazed at Our Success': The Langham Place Editors and the Emergence of a Feminist Critical Tradition." *Victorian Periodicals Review* 29, no. 2 (1996): 159–72.

Roebuck, John. *History of the Whig Ministry of 1830 to the Passing of the Reform Bill.* London: J. W. Parker, 1852.

Rojek, Chris. *Celebrity.* London: Reaktion Books, 2001.

Rossetti, Christina. "At Home." In *The Complete Poems of Christina Rossetti,* edited by Betty Flowers and R. W. Crump, 22. London: Penguin, 2001.

Royle, Nicholas. *The Uncanny.* New York: Routledge, 2003.

Salmon, Richard. "Signs of Intimacy: The Literary Celebrity in the 'Age of Interviewing.'" *Victorian Literature and Culture* 25, no. 1 (1997): 159–77.

Sambourne, Linley. "Our Plea for Open Spaces." *Punch* 84 (June 9, 1883): 266.

Sanders, Valerie. *Reason over Passion: Harriet Martineau and the Victorian Novel.* Sussex, UK: Harvester Press, 1986.

Schwarzbach, F. S. *Dickens and the City.* London: Athlone, 1979.

Scott, Daniel. *Cumberland and Westmoreland.* London: Metheun, 1920.

Selincourt, Ernest de. Introduction to *Wordsworth's Guide to the Lakes,* by William Wordsworth, iii–xxviii. 1835. Reprint, Oxford: Oxford University Press, 1970.

Semmel, Stuart. "Reading the Tangible Past: British Tourism, Collecting, and Memory after Waterloo." *Representations* 69 (2000): 9–37.

Sessions, Frederick. *Literary Celebrities of the English Lake-District.* London: E. Stock, 1905.

Severn, Arthur. "The Memorial to John Ruskin." *London Times,* September 4, 1900, 6B.

Sharp, William. "Literary Geography: The Country of Dickens." *Pall Mall Magazine* 29 (February 1903): 237–47.

Shattock, Joanne, ed. *Women and Literature in Britain, 1800–1900.* Cambridge: Cambridge University Press, 2001.

Shires, Linda. "The Author as Spectacle and Commodity: Elizabeth Barrett Browning and Thomas Hardy." In *Victorian Literature and the Victorian Visual Imagination,* edited by Carol Christ and John Jordan, 198–212. Berkeley: University of California Press, 1995.

Shorter, Clement. "A Literary Causerie." *Bookman* 15 (October 1898): 6–8.

Showalter, Elaine. *The Female Malady: Women, Madness, and English Culture, 1830–1980.* New York: Pantheon, 1985.

"Sir James Graham's Unregistered Practitioners." *Provincial Medical and Surgical Journal* 2, no. 5 (January 29, 1845): 72.

Skabarnicki, Anne. "Marriage as Myth: The Carlyles at Home." In *Portraits of Marriage in Literature,* edited by Anne Hargrove and Maurine Magliocco, 39–54. Macomb: Western Illinois University Press, 1984.

Small, Helen. *Love's Madness: Medicine, the Novel, and Female Insanity.* Oxford: Oxford University Press, 1996.

Smith, Bonnie. "The Contribution of Women to Modern Historiography in Great Britain, France, and the United States, 1750–1940." *American Historical Review* 89, no. 3 (1984): 709–32.

Smith, Grahame. *Dickens and the Dream of Cinema.* Manchester, UK: Manchester University Press, 2003.

Sparke, Penny. Introduction to *Women's Places: Architecture and Design, 1860–1960,* edited by Brenda Martin and Penny Sparke, ix–xx. London: Routledge, 2003.

Spongberg, Mary. *Writing Women's History since the Renaissance.* Basingstoke, UK: Palgrave, 2002.

Stanford's Maps. "The Parks and Open Spaces within a Radius of 6 Miles from Charing Cross." In "More Air for London," by Octavia Hill. *Nineteenth Century* 23 (February 1888): 184–85.

Stephen, Leslie. "Carlyle's House at Chelsea." *The Academy* 47 (January 5, 1895): 12.

———. *English Literature and Society in the Eighteenth Century.* London: Putnam, 1907.

———. *George Eliot.* New York: Macmillan, 1902.

Stetz, Margaret. "Life's 'Half Profits': Writers and Their Readers in Fiction of the 1890s." In *Nineteenth-Century Lives: Essays Presented to Jerome Hamilton Buckley,* edited by Laurence Lockridge, John Maynard, and Donald Stone, 169–87. Cambridge: Cambridge University Press, 1989.

Stone, James. *Emily Faithfull: Victorian Champion of Women's Rights.* Toronto: P. D. Meany, 1994.

Strickland, Agnes, and Elizabeth Strickland. *The Lives of the Queens of England.* London: Colburn, 1840–48.

Sutton-Ramspeck, Beth. "The Personal Is Poetical: Feminist Criticism and Mary Ward's Readings of the Brontës." *Victorian Studies* 34, no. 1 (1990): 55–75.

———. "Shot Out of the Canon: Mary Ward and the Claims of Conflicting Feminism." In *Victorian Women Writers and the Woman Question,* edited by Nicola Thompson, 204–22. Cambridge: Cambridge University Press, 1999.

Swenson, Kristine. *Medical Women and Victorian Fiction.* Columbia: University of Missouri Press, 2005.

Tambling, Jeremy. *Going Astray: Dickens and London.* Harlow, UK: Pearson, 2009.

Taylor, Barbara. *Eve and the New Jerusalem: Socialism and Feminism in the Nineteenth Century.* New York: Pantheon, 1983.

Thompson, Henry. Introduction to *Diet in Sickness and in Health,* by Mrs. Ernest Hart, xi–xii. London: Scientific Press, 1895.

Thornbury, Walter. *Haunted London.* London: Hurst and Blackett, 1865.

Thrale, Hester. *Anecdotes of the Late Samuel Johnson.* London: T. Cadell, 1786.

Ticknor, Caroline. "London and Charles Dickens." *The Lamp* 29 (August 1904): 34–36.

Todd, Barbara. *Harriet Martineau at Ambleside.* Carlisle, UK: Bookcase, 2002.

Tosh, John. *A Man's Place: Masculinity and the Middle-Class Home in Victorian England.* New Haven, CT: Yale University Press, 1999.

Tuchman, Gaye, and Nina Fortin. *Edging Women Out: Victorian Novelists, Publishers, and Social Change.* New Haven, CT: Yale University Press, 1989.

Underwood, Sara. "Our Gallery of Borderlanders: Elizabeth Barrett Browning." *Borderland* 4, no. 4 (1897): 363–66.

Velvin, Ellen. "Illustrated Interview with Edna Lyall." *Windsor Magazine* 1 (January 1895): 18–25.

Vicinus, Martha. "Lesbian Perversity and Victorian Marriage: The 1864 Codrington Divorce Trial." *Journal of British Studies* 36, no. 1 (1997): 70–98.

Vrettos, Athena. *Somatic Fictions: Imagining Illness in Victorian Culture.* Stanford, CA: Stanford University Press, 1995.

Walker, Lynne. "Women and Architecture." In *A View from the Interior: Feminism, Women and Design,* edited by Judy Attfield and Pat Kirkham, 90–105. London: The Women's Press, 1989.

Walkowitz, Judith. *City of Dreadful Delight: Narratives of Sexual Danger in Late-Victorian London.* Chicago: University of Chicago Press, 1992.

Wall, Cynthia. "Gendering Rooms: Domestic Architecture and Literary Acts." *Eighteenth-Century Fiction* 5, no. 4 (1993): 349–72.

Ward and Lock's Pictorial and Descriptive Guide to the English Lake District. London: Ward and Lock, 1915.

Ward, H. Snowden, and Catherine Ward. *The Real Dickens Land with an Outline of Dickens's Life.* London: Chapman and Hall, 1904.

[Ward, Mary Augusta]. "Charlotte and Emily Brontë." *Cornhill Magazine* 8 (March 1900): 289.

Ward, Mary Augusta. Introduction to *Villette,* by Charlotte Brontë, xi–xxxiv. London: Smith, Elder, 1899.

———. "Some Thoughts on Charlotte Brontë." In *Charlotte Brontë, 1816–1916: A Centenary Memorial,* edited by Butler Wood, 15–38. New York: E. P. Dutton, 1918.

Watson, Nicola, ed. *Literary Tourism and Nineteenth-Century Culture.* Basingstoke, UK: Palgrave, 2009.

———. *The Literary Tourist: Readers and Places in Romantic and Victorian Britain.* Basingstoke, UK: Palgrave, 2008.

Watson, Thomas. "The Late Miss Martineau." *British Medical Journal* 2 (July 8, 1876): 64.

Waugh. Edwin. *In the Lake Country.* Manchester, UK: John Heywood, 1880.

Webb, R. K. *Harriet Martineau: A Radical Victorian.* London: Heinemann, 1960.

Weiner, Joel. "Edmund Yates: Gossip as Editor." In *Innovators and Preachers: The Role of the Editor in Victorian England,* edited by Joel Wiener, 260–69. Westport, CT: Greenwood, 1985.

Wells, T. Spencer. "Remarks on the Case of Miss Martineau." *British Medical Journal* 1 (May 5, 1877): 543.

Welsh, Alexander. *The City of Dickens.* Oxford: Clarendon, 1971.

Whelan, Robert. Introduction to *Octavia Hill's Letters to Fellow-Workers, 1872–1911,* edited by Robert Whelan, et al., xxvii–lviii. London: Kyrle Books, 2005.

Williams, Raymond. *The Country and the City.* New York: Oxford University Press, 1973.

Wilson, David Alec. *The Truth about Carlyle: An Exposure of the Fundamental Fiction Still Current.* London: Alston Rivers, 1913.

Winter, Alison. *Mesmerized: Powers of Mind in Victorian Britain.* Chicago: University of Chicago Press, 1998.

"With Dickens in Hatton Garden." *Chambers's Journal* 5 (1902): 381–84.

Wolfe, Theodore. *A Literary Pilgrimage among the Haunts of Famous British Authors.* Philadelphia: Lippincott, 1895.

Wolff, Robert Lee. *Sensational Victorian: The Life and Fiction of Mary Elizabeth Braddon.* New York: Garland, 1979.

Wolfreys, Julian. *Victorian Hauntings: Spectrality, Gothic, the Uncanny and Literature.* London: Palgrave, 2002.

Wood, Jane. *Passion and Pathology in Victorian Fiction.* Oxford: Oxford University Press, 2001.

Woolf, Virginia. "Great Men's Houses." In *The London Scene: Five Essays by Virginia Woolf,* 23–29. New York: Random House, 1982.

———. "Haworth, November, 1904." In *The Essays of Virginia Woolf,* edited by Andrew McNeillie, 1:5–9. 3 vols. New York: Harcourt, 1986.

Wordsworth, William. *A Guide through the District of the Lakes in the North of England.* Edited by W. M. Merchant. 1835. Reprint, London: Hart-Davis, 1951.

———. *Illustrated Wordsworth's Guide to the Lakes.* Edited by Peter Bicknell. New York: Congdon and Weed, 1984.

Worth, George. Macmillan's Magazine, *1859–1907: "No Flippancy or Abuse Allowed."* Aldershot, UK: Ashgate, 2003.

Yates, Edmund. *Celebrities at Home.* 3 vols. London: Office of "The World," 1877–79.

[———]. "Celebrities at Home: Miss Charlotte Robinson." *World,* May 14, 1890, 12– 13.

———. "Miss M. E. Braddon (Mrs. Maxwell) at Richmond." In *Celebrities at Home,* 1:317–24.

———. *Recollections and Experiences.* 2 vols. Leipzig: Tauchnitz, 1885.

Young, Arlene. "Ladies and Professionalism: The Evolution and the Idea of Work in the *Queen,* 1861–1900." *Victorian Periodicals Review* 40, no. 3 (2007): 189–215.

Index